MOMMY MAN

MOMMY MAN

HOW I WENT FROM MILD-MANNERED GEEK TO GAY SUPERDAD

JERRY MAHONEY

TAYLOR TRADE PUBLISHING
Lanham • Boulder • New York • Toronto • Plymouth, UK

Published by Taylor Trade Publishing
An imprint of Rowman & Littlefield
4501 Forbes Boulevard, Suite 200, Lanham, Maryland 20706
www.rowman.com

10 Thornbury Road, Plymouth PL6 7PP, United Kingdom

Distributed by NATIONAL BOOK NETWORK

British Library Cataloguing in Publication Information Available

Library of Congress Cataloging-in-Publication Data

Mahoney, Jerry, 1971–
    Mommy man : how I went from mild-mannered geek to gay superdad / Jerry Mahoney.
        p. cm.
    Includes bibliographical references and index.
    ISBN 978-1-58979-922-6 (cloth : alk. paper) — ISBN 978-1-58979-923-3 (electronic)
    1. Gay fathers. 2. Gay parents. 3. Child rearing. I. Title.
    HQ76.13.M34 2014
    306.874'208664—dc23

                                                                    2013038246

Printed in the United States of America

For Susie

CONTENTS

Contents

PROLOGUE

DEAR FUTURE BABY,

Someday, when you're in fourth grade or so, the school nurse will come to your classroom. She'll send one or two of the super-conservative kids off to do word puzzles in the library, and then, for the rest of you, she'll reveal one of life's big mysteries: where babies come from.

When most kids get the news, they're shocked, incredulous, and just a bit queasy. And then, suddenly, it hits them. "Wait a second. That means that my parents did . . . *that?!*"

Well, for you, my future baby, I have some good news. Your parents didn't do "that." Well, not exactly. But "that" isn't how you were made. The story of where you came from is much more complex, and it's not something the school nurse is likely to cover—or possibly even understand.

See, because Daddy and I are both, well, *daddies*, we had to find a different way to make a baby, and it's not something a lot of people have done before. In fact, someone even told us we were "pioneers." Can you believe that? Your dad, who can't hold a baseball bat or kill a bug, has something in common with ol' Davy Crockett besides neither of us being all that fond of bears.

So consider this an adventure story, if you will, a firsthand account from the wild frontier. Learn this story well, kid, because I guarantee you'll be recounting it to a lot of confused people for most of your life.

While we're on the subject of those people, I'd like to say one more thing. Some of them aren't going to like this story. They'll think it's weird or unnatural, that the school nurse's way should be the only way. A lot of people don't believe two daddies should be having babies at all.

But I hope when you're done reading this, one thing is clear to you: your daddies went through a *lot* to have you. Plenty of babies are created because of carelessness, boredom, self-destruction, social status, fear, jealousy, prom night, Pabst Blue Ribbon, emotional blackmail, the need for cheap labor or to round out a family singing group. But you're here because of sacrifice, perseverance, and most of all, love. Along the way, there were plenty of happy moments and sad moments, nervous moments and extremely nervous moments, and tons and tons of bills the likes of which I hope you will never know. (I'm not trying to make you feel guilty about the cost, but I do hope this explains your somewhat flimsy college fund.)

So let the negative people think what they want. But when you see a boy or girl with two daddies or two mommies, it's a safe bet that those parents love that kid with all their hearts. It's certainly true in our case.

Buckle up for this crazy tale, kid, because I suspect at times, you'll be shocked, incredulous and just a bit queasy.

Trust me, though. It's a great story.

Love,
Dad
(you know, the shorter one)

1

BEFORE IT GETS BETTER

I'M PRETTY SURE THAT, by the time any child of mine is old enough to read this book, the entire world will be gay. It's practically happened already. There are gays on every TV network, gays on the radio, and gays all over the news. As I write this, closeted Republicans are being outed at the rate of roughly six thousand per news cycle. Larry Craig, Roy Ashburn, Ken Mehlman, Ted Haggard. Before long, all the gays across the land, whether they're a catcher for the Mets or a former governor of Florida, will feel free to live openly with their buff Latin boyfriends hand in hand.

By then, every respectable preschool will have its own gay-straight alliance, you'll be able to get gay married at any Walmart in the country by a lesbian Catholic priest, and President Neil Patrick Harris will declare national holidays on the anniversary of the Stonewall riots and on Academy Awards night. Teenagers will co-opt gay culture and lingo the way they did with hip-hop. All the cool kids will wear rainbow flag T-shirts and rave about how "fierce" yesterday's pep rally was. High school history classes will show Martin Luther King Jr.'s "I Have a Dream" speech alongside

YouTube clips of Dan Savage tongue-lashing homophobes on *Larry King Live*. Maybe they'll even change the stars on Old Glory to pink triangles. So of course, gay families will be a Grade-A nonissue. There'll be one on every block, and that'll be the cool house to go to on Halloween. We'll have earned some hip slang nickname that doesn't even refer to sexuality. "You know the Smiths down the street?" kids will say. "It's a Papa-palooza in that house!" No one will protest if there's a gay dad running their PTA or a lesbimom coaching their kid's Little League team. It won't even merit a human interest story on the local news, which is most likely hosted by a pair of drag queens. The idea that anyone would want to prevent same-sex couples from adopting or fostering children will be as absurd as suggestions to make the cat the national bird. It's the kind of thing a homeless person might rant about on a street corner, not a view that would be seriously espoused on the op-ed page of whatever newspapers still remain in print.

At least, I hope that's the world my kid will grow up in. But when I was young, things were different. To use the parlance of the day, being a gay teen, like totally sucked, dude.

It's not quite that there were no gays back in the 1980s. In fact, if you had polled the average school yard, estimates of the prevalence of homosexuality would have run close to 100 percent. If people didn't like the way you dressed, you were gay. If they didn't like the bands whose pictures hung in your locker, you were gay. If they didn't like your Swatch (and, surprisingly, there were some perfectly heterosexual Swatches), then, oh boy, were you gay. Back then, there was no such thing as "homophobia." Nobody was *afraid* of gay people. We were *terrified* of them and proud of it. They were pervs and weirdos and dirty old men who hung out in the bushes behind the middle school after the late bus left. If somebody had thought to invent the word "homophobic" back then, it would have been the highest of compliments.

"Dude, that guy is so cool. He's totally homophobic." "Yo, what's up, my homophobe?" Or "Hey, cool Swatch. You must be a raging homophobe!"

So as a gay kid, all I could do was suck it up, play straight, and play along. I never knew when my homophobia might be tested. I would go to see a perfectly fun movie like *Bill & Ted's Excellent Adventure*, only to find out one of the running jokes was the two lovable protagonists calling each other "fag." No one warned the public about it, no critics condemned it as hateful, no one even thought it was worth commenting on. It was just a joke and, judging by the reaction of the audience around me, a hilarious one. So I was forced to bust a gut, too—unless I wanted someone to think I was some kind of fag myself.

Everyone raved about the movie *Lucas*, in which Corey Haim played a sad, scrawny outcast who tried to win over the girl of his dreams by joining the high school football team. Sad, scrawny outcast? Sign me up! The reviews said it was sweet and heart-warming—and it was—but smack in the middle is a scene where Lucas accuses the bad guy of being a "fag" in the locker room showers, supposedly a moment of stand-up-and-cheer comeup-pance for a character we despise. Watching that scene with my friends, I died a little inside. (On the plus side, though, there were naked jocks.)

For years, I hoped I would start liking girls, the same way I was hoping that a belated growth spurt might someday push me past five feet five inches. But with each passing day, it became clearer that the cheerleaders just weren't doing it for me, and the football players were looking hunkier and hunkier. Luckily, both groups were way out of my league anyway, so I fell pretty easily into the role of the sensitive, shy kid who didn't date. If the fish weren't biting, nobody expected me to cast my rod.

Let's be honest. I was a geek. I aced my SATs. I ruled the math team and dominated the calculus club. (Yes, those were two separate groups, and boy, was I grateful.) There was no word problem too wordy, no square root too square. When other kids whined about algebra, I laughed. Science was my sport. I even quit band when I got to high school and it became marching band because I didn't want to have to go to football games or stand up.

And when I was alone, I wrote. Sitting down with a blank notebook and a pen was a safe way for me to explore anything that interested me. I wrote a book on how to beat Q*Bert, which I never finished because I never beat Q*Bert. I wrote a children's book about an obnoxious teddy bear who cheats at Monopoly and spoils the ends of movies but can do no wrong in the eyes of the boy who loves him. And, when I was fourteen, I wrote two-thirds of a novel. It was an adventure story about a teenager named Jason who gets stranded on an island that's booby-trapped for some reason. The story made no sense, but the descriptions of Jason were very vivid. His neatly cropped blond hair, his charming smile, his firm, manly shoulders. A crucial plot point required Jason to take his shirt off. I rewrote that scene many times.

Of course, I never told anyone about my novel because I wasn't just the only gay kid in my school. I was the only gay person in the *entire world*. This was long before Ellen DeGeneres came out, before there were sitcoms about quippy queens who live in oversized Manhattan apartments and movies about cowboys cozying up to each other by the Colorado River. It would be years before anyone uttered the phrase, "It gets better." No one in my family was gay. Certainly none of my friends were gay. All my favorite singers, like George Michael and Freddie Mercury, were totally unimpeachably straight. Even Boy George, well, that was just a gimmick. We all knew he was up to his earrings in babes.

I wish I could say I had some scandalously fulfilling secret life, like I was quietly hooking up with the dreamy and equally closeted class president or that I spent my summers at an all-boys camp where the activities slate included baseball, basket weaving, and blow jobs in the top bunk. But there was only room for one in my closet, and it got pretty lonely in there.

I wanted an adolescence like the horny teenagers in *Porky's*, where all that mattered was getting laid. I'd be the short, wise-cracking Casanova who somehow always bagged the hottest chicks. They'd call me Sweet Talk, and dudes would gather in the locker room every Monday morning to hear tales of my weekend conquests. "Hey Sweet Talk, tell us again about the Swedish exchange student!" they'd implore.

Instead, I found the next best thing—a group of friends with pretty much no hope of getting laid. We were the dweebs, the chubs, the chubby dweebs, the dweeby chubs—and all of us were hopelessly shy. The price I paid for membership in this pariah posse was an occasional afternoon of Dungeons & Dragons. The reward? An unspoken agreement that we wouldn't talk about girls at all, no way, never, not in a million years. Since intercourse wasn't in the cards for any of us, we built a bubble around ourselves and pretended that sex didn't exist. The best things in life were Friendly's ice cream, *Family Ties,* and heated rounds of Pictionary.

Greg always seemed like he fell into this group by mistake. He was six feet tall, thin, good-looking, and borderline cool. He watched basketball games, and he actually understood what was going on. If the rest of us were the guys who got picked last in gym, Greg probably got picked somewhere toward the middle of the bottom half—which was awesome. He even subscribed to *Playboy*. Well, to be fair, his dad subscribed to *Playboy*, but when he was done reading the articles, he let his son do as he wished with the rest of the publication. This was the one way women would occasionally enter our bubble. When we were hanging out at Greg's house, someone might come across the latest issue and flip through. There'd be nervous giggles about abnormally large nipples and speculation as to which models shaved their clam, and then we'd get back to playing Nintendo.

Of course, like all of us, Greg had his quirks, and those were the things that made the two of us best friends. Our common interests ran the geeky gamut from watching game shows to religiously quoting *The Goonies* to memorizing *Billboard* magazine. Casey Kasem's *American Top 40* countdown on the radio wasn't enough to sate our appetite for methodically ranked hits. We needed the whole Hot 100, plus access to the album, R&B, and international charts. Greg started subscribing, and every Saturday when the latest issue came, we would sit and discuss the new positions of our favorite songs for hours. To this day, I know that "Tarzan Boy" by Baltimora peaked at number 13, up from 16 the week before, no bullet.

Greg was the one person in the world I could really open up to. He told me tearfully about his parents' divorce, and I told him how badly I screwed up all my college interviews. We loved doing things together that teenage boys weren't supposed to do, like watching *Sesame Street* and laughing like it was *Saturday Night Live*. We made up silly songs with titles like "Will You Feed My Fish?" Then when we decided to get serious about songwriting, I suggested the title "Fish Out of Water." Greg knew that the tuneless mess we composed at his parents' piano wasn't going to get any airplay, but he went along with it because I clearly had an important personal statement to make.

If there was anyone I would ever share my big secret with, it was Greg.

Then one day, he said this:

"I could never be friends with someone who was gay."

I remember it exactly—his tone, his cadence, the way he didn't look directly at me when he said it. And the words. Just like that, so simple, so direct. And it came out of nowhere, like Greg just had his own important personal statement to make.

So there it was: my greatest fear emphatically confirmed, underlined, and bolded. If Greg ever knew I was gay, there'd be no more friendship. I'd be sitting alone in the cafeteria, with no one to discuss the prospects of Tony Toni Toné's new single.

And the thing was, you could say something like that back then and not be an asshole. I couldn't even argue with him, or I might invite suspicion. If there was no such thing as homophobia, then you couldn't accuse someone of it. There wasn't even anything to defend yourself against. "Yeah, I don't like gays. So what?" No one's going to feel guilty about that.

My best friend had just uttered the most hurtful words anyone had ever said to me, and there was nothing I could do but go back to playing The Legend of Zelda and hope he'd drop the subject.

One thing was perfectly clear: I could never tell Greg I was gay, no way, never, not in a million years.

College should have been where my coming-out story began. On the first day of orientation, the entire incoming class was treated to a sensitivity seminar to let us know that it was positively marvelous if someone was black, or Jewish, or even gay. I wasn't expecting to walk into a place that felt this way, and it seemed a bit cruel that they would create this kind of environment for a bunch of naive young kids who would then have to go into the real world where everyone hated everyone. Still, I was used to building bubbles around myself, and if Columbia University was going to put me in one where no one could call me a fag, then I was going to appreciate it while it lasted.

That first day, they split us into groups of ten so we could get to know each other. We were asked to state our name, where we were from, how we identified racially, what social class we were in and—holy shit—our sexual orientation.

It was obvious our group had been carefully assembled to represent the ideals of college diversity, like a snapshot on the cover of a recruitment catalog of a hot white girl, a nerdy black guy, and an Asian kid in a wheelchair sharing a laugh on the college steps. The upper-class advisers were clearly hoping to score at least one LGBT among our numbers, just to round things out.

A voice in my head told me this was my big chance. I was about to define myself for the next four years. I should take advantage of being in a blissful liberal utopia where being gay was just one special eccentricity that made me a unique individual. If I could just bring myself to say, "I'm Jerry from New Jersey, a white, middle-class homosexual," then all of this misery could be over.

As we went around the circle and introduced ourselves, I kept hearing Greg's voice in my head: "I could never be friends with someone who was gay." These people hadn't been here any longer than I had. The college could encourage them not to judge, but it couldn't force anyone to hang out with the queer in their orientation group. I wondered if maybe I could just omit the last part of my introduction, end on my economic status, and leave the rest TBA.

But what if someone called me on it? Just as we were moving on to the trust games, that working-class Korean girl from Kansas would shout out, "Hold on! Jerry from New Jersey didn't tell us where he falls on the Kinsey scale!" Then everyone would turn to me, gently encouraging me to just admit the truth as my face turned bright red and I crapped my pants. Yeah, it was better to just do it and get it out of the way.

"I'm Jerry from New Jersey. I'm white, middle class, and . . . heterosexual."

As the words came out of my mouth, I realized it was actually the first time I'd ever said that out loud, the first time I'd blatantly lied. As much as I'd been called a "fag" in high school, no one had actually questioned my sexuality, and I'd never had to proclaim to be straight before.

No one else in my group was gay either. It made sense because if the ratio is one in ten, well, then I was the one.

I had almost had the courage to test the waters, but unfortunately, that was the closest I would come to outing myself as an undergrad. It was my gay Groundhog Day. I'd poked my head out, seen my shadow, and ducked back down for four more years in the closet.

After college, I headed to California for film school, confident I would be in an even more accepting environment. Hollywood was the land of the gay mafia, after all. If I could get in with them, I'd be set.

I prepared myself mentally for the first day, when I'd meet all the other aspiring auteurs in my program. This time I was going to be honest. I might even lead off with the gay thing. "I'm gay Jerry. What else do you need to know? Hey hey!" Finger snap! My new friends would think I'd lived my whole life this way, the fun, happy, well-adjusted homo. Anyone who had a problem with it could just avoid me and hang out with the other douchebags. Screw 'em! I was ready. I was excited.

And then—no one asked.

There was no sensitivity training here. Orientation at the University of Southern California was about how to get an ID badge and learning where the bathrooms were. Nobody expected us to stake out our social position on the first day. Whatever icebreaking we did was all movie talk. Gay or straight was beside the point. The big divide here was Spielberg or Scorsese.

This wasn't college. It was more like high school, where sexuality, if it existed, wasn't discussed. We shared screenwriting template plug-ins. We passed along info about which coffee shops would let you sit for hours on the purchase of a single latte. We parsed Barry Levinson and Steven Bochco until we were blue in the face. Nobody expected me to confront my sexuality because nobody was gay here. I was back in the real world, where everyone assumed you were straight unless you went around limp-wristedly belting the Rodgers & Hammerstein catalog.

Sure, there were opportunities to out myself, like when someone would ask me if I thought Pamela Anderson was hot. But instead of being honest—a "no" would be sure to invite follow-up questions—I'd gently sidestep the issue. "Pamela Anderson? She's on *Baywatch* with David Hasselhoff, right? Hey, did you ever see *Knight Rider*?" It's amazing more people didn't see through my shuck-and-jive. I may not embody some of the stereotypes people hold about gays, but I definitely fit the number 1 job description, that is, not sleeping with women. No one ever asked me why I didn't have any psycho ex-girlfriend stories, let alone current girlfriend stories. They either thought I was really private—or really pathetic.

The way I saw it, I had two choices. Option One was to keep going like this forever. I could do what millions of gays, politicians, and gay politicians before me had done: find some naive, easily satisfied woman, get married, and have kids. After all, every family is messed up in its own way. Our little idiosyncrasy would be a complete lack of love between the parents and a cringingly unpleasant sex life. And some people are alcoholics. Big difference. It was the ideal family model that had been drummed into my head since I was a baby. Parents plus kids plus dysfunction. It's what people are supposed to do. It's what would make me happy. It's what Pat Robertson would want, right?

Or—I could take what was behind Door Number Two. Door Number Two was My Gay Life, and everything about it was a complete mystery. I didn't have any role models or road maps in the gay world. I didn't know what my goals would be or where

I would end up. San Francisco? Broadway? Jail? Maybe I'd find some nice guy and grow old with him, if I was lucky. Maybe I'd be that lifelong bachelor everybody feels sorry for. Or maybe I'd end up as the creep who hung out behind the middle school. One thing was for sure. Door Number Two meant no kids. There would be no Little League games, no vacations at Disney World, no one to pass my childhood toys on to. I'd just be that weird, sad old man who died with a box of Smurfs gathering dust in the basement.

Option One had so much more to offer—to me, at least—but I couldn't help wondering about the woman who would be my unsuspecting victim—or, rather, "wife." Let's call her Stacey.

Stacey's a sweet girl with a good sense of humor. I meet her in a chat room for Scritti Politti fans. She likes short guys with glasses who once collected Smurfs and who know the entire libretto to *Miss Saigon*. I'm the answer to her prayers, and we get serious fast, like in a romantic comedy montage. A shared milkshake. Fireworks above a Ferris wheel. A burned casserole at a candlelit dinner in my apartment. We snuggle and stuff, but that's about it. I play shy. Maybe she's super-religious, so that's all she asks for. "Jerry's so respectful," she tells her church friends, proudly. "I think he'd be willing to wait for me forever!"

Okay, so I marry Stacey. The sex is abysmal, but she doesn't really know what good sex is anyway, so she doesn't complain. I have to picture her hot brother Mike in order to get the job done. Oh, yeah. Stacey has a hot brother, Mike. I'm sure of it.

Soon, Stacey and I have a couple of adorable kids. Let's call them Zack and Stacey Jr. Zack thinks his dad is the coolest, even though he doesn't know how to fix a leaky faucet and he squeals like a baby whenever he sees a spider. Almost every week, Zack gets into a fight with some kid who mocks the way his dad throws a football. For Stacey Jr., I become the ideal male, the standard by which all the future men in her life will be judged. She ends up going to theater camp and dating her flamboyant leading man in *Spring Awakening*.

If I'm lucky, no one ever figures out my secret. We just each go on living in denial, satisfied with whatever fulfillment we can scrape out of life. And my kids never know their own father. In my best-case scenario, I bring two new people into the world just to lie to them the way I lie to everyone else.

Or—one day it all comes crumbling down. Zack finds some shirtless pictures of Scott Bakula on my computer. Stacey Jr. picks up on the way I ogle Uncle Mike. They compare notes. It all adds up. Now they pity their mom and resent their dad. My wife kicks me out and starts dating a series of abusive creeps. I've skewed her standards so the only thing she demands of men is that they be heterosexual, though not beating the shit out of her is a plus. Zack shuns me, humiliated that his hero has been exposed as a selfish, pathetic mess who chose to live a lie. Stacey Jr. becomes hopelessly clingy, terrified that my love for her is as fake as the love I had for her mom. All three of them rack up enormous therapy bills and write tell-all memoirs about how I ruined their life. Zack's is a graphic novel.

My elaborately melodramatic fantasy scenario was just too much for me to bear. How could I live with myself if I did any of these things to a woman I've never met plus two kids who wouldn't even exist otherwise? Poor Stacey, Zack, and Stacey Jr.! They deserve better! Plus, living that lie would mean denying myself the possibility of ever finding true love. Oh, and all that vaginal intercourse. Ick.

So Door Number Two won out. I came to terms with the fact that I would never have a "normal" family. I would never stuff a piece of wedding cake in Stacey's face in front of all our loved ones. I would never study the rules of baseball on Wikipedia so I could follow along at Zack's tee-ball games. I would never watch Stacey Jr. crowning in the delivery room and gazing upon the world for the first time with her tiny blue eyes. Come to think of it, I would probably never even see a vagina. In my mind, I held a little funeral for Stacey, Zack, and Stacey Jr. But it was a funeral for me, too—or at least the me I'd known until then.

After all my anxiety, the actual coming-out process was fairly anticlimactic. It was awkward, for sure. A couple of my friends expressed surprise or confusion: "But you love Drew Barrymore!" "But you don't dress gay!" No one shunned me, though, or told me I was going to Hell or asked me if I also raped dogs and little boys. There were no scenes out of a TV movie of the week, where Mom shouts "My baby! My baby!" as Dad shoves the last of my stuff into a U-Haul and slams the front door in my face. People just took it in, hugged me, and then we went back to our regularly scheduled relationship. Even my very Catholic extended family kind of shrugged at the news.

During all the time I had been struggling with my identity, homophobia actually became a bad thing. Everyone who cared about me just wanted me to be happy. And finally, I was. Not just because I no longer had to lie but because, for the first time, I could be honest—about my thoughts, my feelings, my fears. With very few exceptions, I felt closer to my friends and family, more comfortable around them, now that I could be myself. It was like my own personal Berlin Wall falling. Sure, it exposed the sad remnants of a repressed and doomed realm heretofore hidden from view, but at least people were eager to come in and spruce the place up.

The entire process took years, but by the time I was thirty-one, I had come out to every person in the world who mattered to me—with one enormous exception.

Greg.

More than a dozen years out of high school, we were still close. Greg lived three thousand miles away, in New York, but we talked on the phone regularly, and I saw him every time I went back East. We had outgrown our obsession with *Billboard* charts, but we now channeled our energy toward professional tennis. We memorized stats and rankings, and when the challenge ladder for a major tournament was released, we would go through round by round and make our predictions. We even took a trip to London together so we could attend Wimbledon. The one thing that remained from adolescence was our unspoken embargo on discussing our love lives.

Every time I spoke to Greg, it was definitely in the back of my mind. I figured he must have met some gay people in college, that he was probably on good terms with Ned from Accounting, that he still bobbed his head when an Erasure song came on the radio. I was sure he'd seen *Ellen* and *Will & Grace* and Tom Hanks's Oscar-winning performance in *Philadelphia*. The whole world's attitudes about gays had changed since we were teenagers. Surely his had, too.

In fact, he'd probably figured out my big secret. I was a single guy in my early thirties. I'd never had a girlfriend—or any interest in finding one. One day while we were at Wimbledon, I snuck off to a revival of *My Fair Lady* in the West End. It didn't take Stephen Hawking to do the math on this one. Greg was probably just dying for me to come out so he could fix me up with Ned from Accounting. Then again, if Greg knew I was gay and he was cool with it, how come he never brought it up?

Every time I considered having the big talk with him, I would flash back to that moment when we were sixteen. "I could never be friends with someone who was gay." Instantly, I'd lose my nerve.

Here I was, feeling like myself for the first time, happier than I'd ever been, and I was still afraid of being rejected by somebody I considered my best friend. I realized I hadn't come as far as I'd thought, that on some level I was still that scared teenager, full of shame. And there was only one way to change that.

I mustered whatever courage I had, and I dialed Greg's number.

Coming out of the closet is one thing at which practice never makes perfect. Though I'd done it dozens of times at this point, I still made all the rookie mistakes: being nervous, assuming the reaction would be bad, and, the worst, starting with the words "I'm sorry." In this case, it was "I'm sorry to do this over the phone," which, although true, was far too dramatic a setup, as was what followed: "Greg, I have something very important to talk to you about, something I've needed to say for fifteen years."

Greg knew something was up. He was totally silent. Too silent. Too long. Finally, I just said it. "So . . . I'm gay!" Still no response. Absolutely nothing. Just agonizing quiet that went on for, if memory serves, approximately six hours. I couldn't bear it, so I started talking again. "It's been a really long process, and I hope you're not hurt that it took me so long to tell you, but that's more a reflection on me than on you and, hey, have you seen *Philadelphia*?"

"It's okay. You can stop," he said. He took a long pause. "It's fine. I'm cool with it. I've . . . I've kind of been going through the same thing."

"Um . . . what?"

"I've been . . . you know, questioning."

I had prepared myself for a variety of reactions—the most likely being that he would convey a sense of caring and compassion, thus validating our long-term friendship—the least likely being that he would shout "Fag!" and hang up. But I hadn't quite expected this.

Greg was gay. He was every bit as gay as I was. Gayer, maybe. He might even be the gayest person in the entire world, but he couldn't even say the word. Here I was apologizing for being so slow in coming out, and it turned out Greg was even further behind in the process. He hadn't even accepted himself yet. His voice was shaking. He was petrified.

A few minutes earlier, he'd picked up the phone, probably expecting to discuss Monica Seles's comeback, and instead he was forced to confront the personal demons he'd been suppressing for three decades. I could see how that might have thrown him. It became clear that Greg had been "questioning" for years—and that his question had pretty much been answered. But he hadn't told anyone. Anyone.

Until now.

I had certainly considered the possibility that Greg might be gay. If there was one person I'd ever known who was even more secretive about his love life than I was, it was Greg. I think that's part of why we became such good friends, though I always assumed he was doing me a favor.

But somewhere along the way, I dismissed my suspicions. I mean, come on, the guy was in his thirties now. He had to be straight. The only other possibility was that he was gay and even more in the closet than I was. What were the odds of that?

I thought back to what he'd said that day when we were teenagers. "I could never be friends with someone who was gay." And then I remembered what he said next:

"Could *you*?"

Suddenly, I realized that his statement hadn't been motivated by hatred but by fear. It was a possibility I didn't even consider at the time. Back then, I was crushed. And I had to respond. But how? I was caught off guard. I was afraid. All I could say was, "I don't know."

"I don't know."

And what followed was fifteen years of "I don't know." It seems absurd now. All that time we were both struggling in private, and we could have been there for each other, had someone to talk to, someone to share with, someone to make us feel human.

Growing up gay was hell, and there's nobody I would rather have gone through that with than Greg. If only we'd known. If only we hadn't been so afraid.

I had called hoping for his support, but instead, I was the one being supportive of him. I told him how happy coming out had made me, how accepting everyone had been, how relieved he would feel if he could just be honest with himself. In the days that followed, we spoke constantly. Everything had changed, including the strength of our friendship, which was greater than ever. We cried, we joked, we teased. We talked about being in the closet, about coming out, and about how hot John McEnroe was. It turned out we had even more in common than we ever knew.

Within a week, Greg came out to his whole family. A few days after that, it was his birthday, and he gave himself the best present he could think of. He took a dozen of his closest friends out to dinner, and just before dessert, he made a big announcement to the whole table. In an instant, his hiding was over.

Greg didn't have any bad experiences either. No rejection, no hostility, no drama. Just like with me, the fear was so much worse than the reality.

During his whole coming out marathon, he had to make one really hard call, to his best friend from college. When Greg shared his news, his friend got quiet at first, and Greg started to panic. Then the friend cleared his throat, took a deep breath, and said, "It's okay. I'm cool with it. Actually, I've kind of been going through the same thing."

So this was Door Number Two. It wasn't lonely or depressing like I'd feared. It was kind of hilarious. I wasn't mourning my lost hypothetical family or my safe hypothetical life, just a past that was full of regrets. This wasn't a death. It was a rebooting. With the help of a great support team, I'd hit control-alt-delete on my misery and was flickering back to life, starting over.

I was Jerry version 2.0, and for the first time I could remember, I was excited to see what the future held.

2

THE ISLAND OF MISFIT GAYS

COMING OUT WAS EXCRUCIATING, humbling, endless—and, ultimately, one of the easier things I had to do in my twenties. Once I'd shared my lifetime of shame with whatever close acquaintance I had arranged to meet at Denny's for the occasion, that was it. It was over, and we could get back to our Grand Slam breakfasts and talking about last night's *Seinfeld*. Decades of hiding culminated in little more than momentary discomfort, repeated dozens of times. The real agony, it turned out, lay outside of those encounters.

World, meet Sweet Talk!

My *Porky's*-inspired alter ego had waited a long time to make his public debut. He was a little older, a little grayer, not quite as thin and sprightly, but hey, at least his Clearasil budget had gone down. At last, Sweet Talk was unleashed, free to ogle, flirt, and rack up some raucous conquests to share with the guys in the locker room—starting, of course, with the guys in the locker room. Yeehaw!

I finally felt thirteen at heart, only to learn the harsh truth that hits most people when they actually are thirteen: being thirteen sucks. It's not puppy love, milkshakes with two straws, and commingled vomit streams over the railing of the Tilt-a-Whirl. It's misery, rejection, and self-disgust. It's Sylvia Plath and the Smiths, learning to judge yourself by the most hurtful criticisms you receive from others, to know with unflinching certainty that no one has ever felt a pain as profound as the one known as "Being You." The only good thing about being thirteen is getting it over with when you're thirteen.

Unless you're me, goddamn it. I was stuck doing it at twenty-eight.

Add to that the twin boogeymen of gay dating in the late 1990s: AIDS and Jeffrey Dahmer. The only bright side was the bold new world of online dating, where I could hide behind words and the safety of a less-than-one-megapixel head shot. By reading profiles and checking the right boxes, I could even attempt to weed out the guys who were into random hookups and possibly eating their bedmates. Finally, I'd found somewhere I belonged.

It didn't take me long to figure out the most obvious rule of romance in the cyber age: dating is marketing. If you had killer pecs, you posted a shirtless pic. If you had a twelve-inch wiener, you made that your user name. (And in the likely event that 12InchWiener was already taken, you got creative. FootLonggg-Salami or 12Inchez2ThrillU would make the point just fine.) You might have only a few seconds to snag the interest of a handsome stranger, so it was important you always put your best foot forward, a rule that went double for foot fetishists.

Lacking a killer gym bod, I settled on a strategy more within my reach: be funny. Everyone says they're looking for a mate with a sense of humor, from ShyGayJedi1138 to PlugMyHungreeBottomNow!!!! Well, hey, I won the comedy award in my graduate screenwriting program. I could do this. I answered my essay questions with schtick, packed my profile with punch lines, and made a big joke of the whole thing.

Within hours, my in-box was bursting with responses.

"Your profile is hilarious! I'm sure you'll get lots of dates!"

"Thanks for making me laugh. Good luck!"

"lol your funny. l8r!"

There was one thing missing from all these emails: any interest in hearing back from me. Everyone wanted to compliment my sense of humor, but no one wanted to date me. This being a dating site, it did seem like I was doing something wrong.

There was one exception. He didn't mention my humor, but he said I was cute. His user name was Poohger, and his picture was a shot of his bare torso, shoulders to waist. It wasn't a particularly impressive torso, but there it was, offered for inspection. Bony, hairless, and freckled, it could easily have belonged to a twelve-year-old girl or a Calvin Klein model. It seemed an odd choice for a photo, but maybe this man thought torsos were a major turn-on. Then again, what did I know? I was the newbie. Maybe the torso was a nice change of pace for guys on this site. Maybe Poohger's in-box was full of emails that began, "Hey, nice torso!"

Still, a torso is better than nothing, so I wrote back. Over the course of a few emails, we discovered a mutual addiction to MTV's candidly trashy docusoap *The Real World*. I'd started watching when I was still young enough to be one of the spoiled cast mates living in an IKEA-festooned palace and given a platform to tell the world about their feelings. Now I was too old to be on the show and probably too old to be tuning in. But Poohger didn't see my point. After all, he was eight years older than I and just as hooked.

We set up a phone call. He didn't want to share his number just yet, so I gave him mine. The call came in right on schedule, and the ID was blocked. This guy was so guarded with his identity that I was starting to wonder if he was a spy—or, better yet, Tom

Cruise. But his voice suggested neither. It was thin and meek, like his torso. He sounded nervous, starstruck even, like a squealy tween thinking, "Omigod, it's that guy from the Internet!" He stumbled for interesting things to say. "So you're really from New Jersey, huh? Wow . . ."

"So why the screen name Poohger?" I asked. It seemed an appropriate icebreaker.

"I was just trying to think of something. You know, everything's taken," he said, and I, StinkyLilWeasel28, agreed. "But I have this Pooh doll on my desk . . ."

I felt the need to clarify. "*Winnie* the Pooh?"

"Yeah. So I started trying Pooh with different combinations of other characters. Eeyore, Piglet, finally Tigger. That's how I got Poohger."

"Okay. So it's not really a Winnie the Pooh thing."

"No, it was just the first thing I could think of that wasn't already in use. Don't get me wrong, though," he added. "I love Pooh."

I could suddenly see why he didn't feel too old for *The Real World*.

We didn't talk long because the reception, like his chest, was spotty. Instead, we agreed to meet for dinner.

He lived in Encino, a thirty-minute drive from my apartment in West Hollywood, but he offered to meet me in between, in Sherman Oaks, a twenty-five-minute drive from my apartment in West Hollywood. He picked a Mexican chain restaurant and gave me detailed directions how to get there, as if concerned I might not show up. He didn't know he was my only offer.

I purposely arrived twenty minutes early and parked across the street. I sat in my car, eyes trained on the restaurant, dying for a sneak preview of the man I was about to date. Granted, I didn't have much to go on. But I studied every torso that went in, unbuttoning each shirt in my mind to see if the mental picture might match the JPEG he provided. It wasn't exactly a blind date, but it was blind from the neck up. And the waist down.

As early as I'd arrived, it turned out Poohger had been there even earlier, and when I walked in, he looked up at me instantly. His eyes flickered with a hopeful excitement that said, "Wow, it's really him!" I have to admit, it was flattering.

My first glimpse of him was a relief, mostly. He wasn't some hideous freak with a tattooed forehead and a bullring-pierced septum. He was a regular guy, someone who, in any other circumstances, I would have walked right past without noticing. Average height, fair skin, slightly bumpy nose. He wasn't gorgeous, but he wasn't ugly either. His face was exactly as appealing as his torso, no more, no less.

The timing of our date was perfect. Earlier that week, a new season of *The Real World* had premiered with an extended one-hour episode. We had plenty to discuss.

"You know who I can't stand?" he said. "Coral! What a bitch!"

"I love Coral," I confessed.

"Well, I mean, she's good TV," he backtracked. "Nicole is the really annoying one. Coral's okay." It was a stunning revelation for me. I had the ability to make a man nervous.

Halfway through the date, Poohger's cell phone rang. "Hello . . . ? Yeah, I'm here right now. No, it's okay. It's good. Yeah, he is. Thanks for calling." He hung up.

Holy shit. It was a check-in call. It was so obvious. His friend was prepared to rescue him if he was having a miserable time—and I'd passed the test. This was a successful date!

"Sorry," Poohger smiled. "He won't bother us again."

When we finished dinner, Poohger asked me if I wanted to see a movie. He went to his car to get a newspaper, but the only one he had was out of date. So we went directly to the theater, only to learn we had just missed most of the starting times. The only film we could see was the latest in the *Scary Movie* franchise.

"I kind of liked the last one," he offered.

"Ugh," I groaned.

"Shoot!" he swore. "I'm sorry. I should've had the right damn newspaper!"

I assured him that even if he'd had today's paper, we still would have missed the movies. I checked my watch and realized that, if we wrapped things up fast, I might make it home in time for *Saturday Night Live*.

As we walked to our cars, Poohger invited me back to his place, but I said no. *Saturday Night Live* seemed like the better option.

"You're really cute," he said.

"Thanks."

There was a long pause. "Now it's your turn," he prodded.

"Well, you're . . . nice," I said. I tried to sound coy, but the truth was I couldn't pretend I had any physical attraction to him.

He moved in to kiss me, but I jumped in my car just as his eyelids began to droop. "It was really nice meeting you," I said. It wasn't a lie.

Should I have just kissed him? I wasn't sure. Still, I was pretty confident that if I changed my mind, I'd get another chance.

Now we would play the waiting game. I'd seen straight people do it so many times in romantic comedies. You measure your interest against your date's and figure out how long you should wait to call again so as not to seem too desperate. I figured a week was reasonable, but knowing how eager Poohger was, I guessed he'd crack at about the three-day mark.

As I opened the door to my apartment twenty-five minutes later, my phone was already ringing. I let my answering machine pick up.

"Hi, Jerry. I just wanted to say again what a great time I had tonight. You're a terrific guy, and really—really cute. I just—I feel like I blew it. I'm sorry I didn't have today's newspaper. Really, really sorry."

I wanted to cry for him. I also wanted to cheer for myself. This guy has a pretty serious case of the Jerries. Yay me. Who knew I had the power to turn a normal guy into a blathering fool? He was really beating himself up. It was kind of cool.

"It won't happen again. I promise. I stopped on the way home and got a new paper—two papers actually, just to be safe."

Now it was starting to get painful. It felt cruel to let him go on like this. I contemplated picking up the phone, but what would I say? I'd probably end up making a second date with him.

"I got the *L.A. Times* and the *Daily News*, so next time I'll be prepared. We can check them both. I thought maybe we could see a movie tomorrow night. You pick. But not *Scary Movie*. I know you don't like those." Chuckle.

He didn't stop. Why couldn't he stop? He gave his phone number and his cell phone number. "Or you can email me," he added. "If I don't pick up, leave a voice mail. I'm probably just in the shower or something, and I'll call you right back."

OKAY. STOP. STOP. STOP!!!

It was too much to bear. I left the room and waited until he hung up, two minutes later.

I'd been so worried before meeting him that Poohger would be a nut job or an Elephant Man. What I'd found was a perfectly amiable guy who thought I was awesome. As it turned out, that wasn't quite as appealing as I would have hoped.

I never called him back.

For quite a while afterwards, Poohger was one of my better dates.

One day my in-box lit up with an excited email from a guy who was quick to point out how much we had in common. "My name's Jerry, too! LOL!!!!!" He loved that I was five feet five inches because he was five feet four, and "us short guys need to stick together LOL!!!!!!!!!!" We were both from New Jersey, "but different Turnpike exits LOL!!!"

We arranged to meet for Chinese food. I was waiting outside the restaurant when I heard him call my name. "Jerry! JERRY!" It was an eager bark, unnecessarily loud, like he'd just spotted his old college roommate on the opposite end of the Superdome. When I looked over, I saw a cluster of people crossing the street toward me. I scanned all the faces but couldn't find the one from Jerry's profile.

"Jerry?" Finally, as the crowd reached the corner, the masses dispersed, and one guy was left standing there. It then became clear why I hadn't seen him—because he was nowhere near five feet four. Perhaps he meant to say four feet five.

He looked up at me and said how nice it was that I actually resembled my picture. "You know some guys . . . !" He then let rip a tremulous cackle that literally snapped my head back. It's no wonder he ended every sentence of his emails with "LOL." When this guy L'ed, it was majorly OL.

It turned out Jerry and I had more in common than just our names. We were the same age, practically had the same birthday. We both liked *Ally McBeal* but thought it was getting too wacky. We both drove black Nissan Altimas. We both ordered the lemon chicken.

If that had been enough, I don't believe his height would have mattered. But not only was Jerry considerably shorter than I, he was also considerably gayer. He snapped his fingers for emphasis when he talked, something I thought gay guys only did in sketch comedy. When a finger snap didn't add enough punch to his punch line, he lunged forward and stamped his foot, like a mule. And that laugh . . .

While we were seated, it was the laugh that made me self-conscious. But when we stood up again, it was the height. I didn't have much experience being the tall one on a date, and I couldn't help worrying that we looked ridiculous, like Abe Lincoln standing next to a poodle. I had to reach down to shake his hand, to bend over to hug him. I knew I had no right judging anyone based on their height, but at the same time, I was now more forgiving of people who judged me. So this is why so many guys would limit their matches to men five feet ten and up. To them, I was the poodle.

Jerry let me know he was leaving town that night for a wedding, so it would be a few days before we could hang out again. Already, he was better at the waiting game than Poohger.

The next day, he called from out of town. "I just saw another black Nissan Altima, and I thought of you. Maybe next time we go out, we can carpool!"

I never called Jerry back either.

This was my gay adolescence, a series of uncomfortable dates, each of them tragic in its own way. There was the lap band guy, the massive head injury guy, the guy with eight pet rats, the voice-over actor with the lazy eye, the professional paid audience member on infomercials. (He described his job to me as follows: "Sometimes, they want you to clap. But you can't just clap. You have to get really excited, like this . . . WOOOOOHOOOOO!!!!!") No matter how adequate they seemed at first, there was a painful vulnerability lying just below the surface, waiting to be discovered. All of them were incredibly nice guys, but none of them was right for me.

The gay world wasn't at all like I'd imagined when I'd grown up so in fear of it. The men I met weren't the scantily clad party boys from gay pride floats, nor were they handsome and self-confident like the characters I saw on TV shows. They weren't even like the creepy closeted Republicans who'd occasionally be featured on the news after getting caught in a sex sting. They weren't media-friendly. They didn't dress in the latest fashions or have five-hundred-dollar haircuts. They worked in banks, P.F. Chang's, and H&R Blocks, where they ate microwaved Hot Pockets for lunch and tried to remember if tonight was the night for *CSI: New York* or *CSI: Miami*. Many of them were brand new to the dating scene. They were regular guys—timid, awkward, and frequently terrified—just like me.

There was nothing unique about my angst after all. With that realization, my postponed puberty began to wind down, and I started to relax.

I'd come across Drew's profile many times, but he scared me more than anyone. Handsome, successful, smart—he was too perfect. Either he was a big phony, or his fatal flaw would turn out to be particularly lurid, like he'd done jail time or he liked to be barfed on during sex. He described himself as a "TV executive," whatever that meant. He probably installed cable boxes for Comcast. There was another possibility, of course—that he really was as good as he seemed. That would be even worse. If that were true, there's no way he'd have any interest in me. I didn't bother writing.

Then, one day, the unthinkable happened. Drew wrote to me.

His email was funny, sweet, and confident. Everything was spelled and punctuated correctly. He showed genuine interest in the things I'd written about myself, and to learn more, he asked questions that were thought provoking but not intrusive. I promised myself to be cautious. This was too good to be true.

I wrote back more than I knew I should. I labored over every word. I spell-checked and re-spell-checked. I read my email aloud to hear how it sounded, then I read it again in a British accent to make sure it didn't come across as pretentious. I carefully measured how much interest to show at this stage. I didn't want to scare him off. When I hit "Send," I stayed within a five-foot radius of my computer for hours, until I heard the new email ping and saw it was from him. He was still interested. Success!

We set up a lunch date at the Grove, LA's magical outdoor mall, the most romantic place in town if you're into blatant commercialism and upscale kitsch, which clearly, we both were. I got there ten minutes early so I could see him before he saw me. But like Poohger, Drew beat me at that game. As I strolled up, he was already sitting outside the restaurant, staking me out.

He smiled in a way that let me know he was relieved by my appearance. He looked just like his picture, as I'd hoped.

Any fear I had of us having nothing to talk about was gone before the bread arrived. If Drew was nervous, it didn't show. He was the Batman of conversation, slick, unstoppable, with an endless supply of cool tricks at his disposal. The way he lobbed probing, thoughtful questions made me feel like one of Barbara Walters's most fascinating people. It wasn't that we were talking about anything extraordinary. He just had this warmth that made me want to open up, and it made me want to know him better, too. He was a talk show host—and not a mere Maury or Montel. Drew was pure Oprah.

He'd been at MTV for eight years, rising from an administrative assistant to someone who *had* an administrative assistant. He was a legitimate big shot, who spent his days hearing pitches from Mark Burnett and Puff Daddy and his nights on location, calling suggestions into a headset. Randy Jackson was a fan of *his*, and the rapper Chamillionaire once let him try on his jewelry. From anyone else, it might have seemed far-fetched, but it was easy to see why famous people would open up to Drew. He wasn't the typical ass-kissing Hollywood douchebag. He was humble, considerate, and genuinely interested in people other than himself.

Drew had a gift for elevating conversations, even with our waitress. When she asked if she could take our plates away, he responded with, "If I were you, Amanda, I would've dumped that penne alla vodka in that old bat's shitty blue wig."

The waitress groaned. "I mean . . . right?"

I had no idea how Drew remembered our server's name. I vaguely recalled her introducing herself when we first sat down, but that was an hour ago. Besides, what the hell were they talking about?

"What old bat?"

"That Botoxed grandma two tables over." Drew motioned with his fork. "Did you not hear her complaining about her expired coupon?"

Somehow, while fully engrossed in our own conversation, Drew had also picked up on a spat between Amanda and this other customer. As I was still trying to piece together what had happened, Amanda opened up to Drew about her lousy day. She wasn't supposed to be working, but she agreed to cover for a friend who had an audition for a commercial. That meant dropping her six-year-old son off with his dad for the afternoon—and her two-year-old with *his* dad.

"Slut!" Drew shouted, wagging his finger at her. My jaw hit the floor, but Amanda cackled and high-fived him. It was then that I realized how truly special this guy was. He could not only get complete strangers to share their life stories with him, but he could make fun of them, and they'd only like him more.

It all put me so at ease, I would've given Drew my PIN if he'd asked. It was a great feeling to have on a first date, the notion that nothing was off limits, any topic, no matter how potentially awkward, was on the table. I suddenly felt the freedom to pose the one query I'd been holding back throughout lunch.

"So you work at MTV. What can you tell me about *The Real World*?"

I had promised myself I wouldn't raise the subject, for fear of coming across as the fawning *Real World* fanatic I really was. I didn't want to give this guy the impression I was only interested in his cool job or make him worry that I was some crazed blogger looking for a scoop on the next *Battle of the Seasons*.

I had nothing to worry about. Drew was flattered, proud of his work—and full of gossip Poohger would have killed to hear.

The MTV talk gradually led to something deeper, the discovery of a mutual obsession with all things television. Unlike anyone I'd ever met who worked in TV, Drew actually liked TV. If he were ever to win public office, he would be sworn in not on a Bible but on the *TV Guide* Fall Preview issue. There was no reference I could drop that went over Drew's head. We knew the same Saturday morning cartoons, the same forgotten flops of the 1980s, the same lame reality stars. It was so refreshing to share a bit of news like, "Did you hear Glen Scarpelli came out of the closet?" and not have to explain who Glen Scarpelli was. We played our own TV geek version of *Jeopardy*. I'd throw out an obscure title like *I Married Dora*, and he'd reply, "What was the greatest show *ever*?" Correct answer.

Neither of us considered any of this trivia. It was part of who we were, vital to our discovery process.

The longer we sat, the more we bonded. We got dessert—and about fifteen refills on our Cokes. I worried about dragging the date out too long and sapping all the excitement. Still, there was one question I had to ask before we left. It had been nagging me all through lunch, but I chickened out at every opening in the conversation. It was really big for a first date, the kind of topic that could ruin an otherwise perfect encounter. But I just had to know. As the check came, I finally summoned the nerve and blurted it out.

"So what do you think of Coral?"

Drew stopped cold. He looked up and me and took a deep breath. "I fucking love Coral!" he exclaimed.

It was at that moment that I knew I fucking loved Drew, too.

3

OUR DAUGHTER, FU-LING

I'VE BEEN ON TWO TV GAME SHOWS, but neither of them showered me with as many fabulous prizes as Drew. On our first date, I offhandedly mentioned a type of British candy I'd liked when I visited London. The next time we met, he showed up with a box of it, along with the new Pet Shop Boys CD, which, for gays, is just kind of a given. When I told him I'd never seen the original *Nightmare on Elm Street*, he immediately went out and bought me the DVD. He once saw me playing Mario Kart, and even though he couldn't stand video games, he messengered a copy of the newest installment to my apartment the day it came out to make sure it reached me before I bought it for myself. Every date with my new boyfriend was like a Showcase Showdown. It left me wondering whether he would one day pick me up on a catamaran or in a brand new car!

I wasn't the only one who benefited from Drew's generosity. He drove across town to Best Buy every Tuesday, when new releases arrived, and bought absolutely anything he could give away to anyone he even remotely knew. He thought nothing of dropping

$90 on an *X-Files* box set for the nerdy receptionist at his office or $40 on the limited premium edition of the direct-to-video title *Aladdin 3* for his goddaughter, who kind of liked the first one.

For a while, I thought Drew must be a millionaire, but then I saw his apartment. His dump was just a few blocks from my dump on the dumpier side of West Hollywood, not far from where Eddie Murphy and Hugh Grant were busted for picking up prostitutes. In many ways, Drew's building was indistinguishable from a prison, right down to the bars on the windows. There were no curtains, no decorations on the walls, and where a dining room table should have been, Drew had a large cardboard box with the leftovers of last night's pizza on it. Anyone who equates being gay with fastidiousness and design skills has clearly never been his houseguest.

It's not that Drew is a slob. He just prefers to spend money on other people rather than himself. If the guy who cut his hair had lacked a dining room table, Drew would've had one express delivered to the salon, with assembly thrown in. Asked why he didn't just buy himself one, though, Drew shrugged and asked, "What's wrong with the box?"

People were always trying to repay his kindness, but as beneficent as Drew was with others, he was miserly about accepting gifts in return. He still took a clunky first-generation iPod with him to the gym. As his birthday approached, I figured I'd get him the latest model, until I saw that he had a closet full of iPods, unopened in their original packaging. It turned out most of his close friends and business associates had the same gift idea at one point or another, but Drew felt uncomfortable accepting something so expensive. Instead, he held onto all the iPods until Christmas, then regifted them to his family. "Does Matt have an iPod?" he'd ask.

"You gave him one for his birthday."

"But does he have a Nano?"

It wasn't just Apple products Drew tossed aside. After I moved in with him, I started finding unused gift cards everywhere in his apartment. They were buried in drawers or amid piles of receipts on top of his bureau. $25 to Bed, Bath & Beyond, $50 to AMC movie theaters, a $100 spa voucher.

"Why don't you spend these?" I demanded.

"I don't like to. I feel weird."

He had enough Cheesecake Factory gift cards to eat Crispy Caramel Chicken for a month, enough Gap cards to buy the same bland sweatshirt in nine different colors. He had $300 in Best Buy cards. Best Buy! He was there every week! My new boyfriend was probably the first hoarder in history who stashed items of actual value.

One day, in frustration, I scoured the apartment, with the goal of finding every last unused gift card. Over the course of one afternoon, I turned up untold stashes of store credit and amassed them in a massive plastic Matterhorn on top of his dining room box.

The grand total was $2,255.

"We have to start spending these," I told him.

Drew rolled his eyes. "But I have money."

As his birthday approached, his friends started calling and emailing me. "He's so hard to shop for. Any idea what he wants?"

"Geez, if I knew, I'd get it for him myself."

Then they'd sigh. "Fine, I guess I'll just get him a boring gift card."

I wanted to tell people not to waste their money, but then I realized something. *I* had no problem spending gift cards. "Great idea," I'd say. "I think he really likes Restoration Hardware."

I told everyone the same thing. "Get Drew a gift card to Restoration Hardware. He'd love that." Did I feel a tiny bit guilty? Sure, but I had a plan.

On his birthday, he arrived home from work, arms laden with iPods from people who hadn't bothered to contact me. "Ugh, I hate these things!" he groaned as he walked in. He went to dump his bags on his dining room box, when suddenly he stopped short.

The box was gone. I was sitting instead at a brand new, gleaming oak table. "Where did you get that?" he asked.

"Restoration Hardware. Happy birthday."

He gave me a giant hug, then backed up and looked around, just a tinge upset. "What did you do with my box?"

It wasn't long before Drew and I started hearing the question all young, committed couples are hounded with: "So . . . are you guys planning on having kids?" Given that we were gay, the topic was usually broached delicately or with a wink, like they knew it was a long shot. "That'd be so awesome!" people said. Often, the query was followed up with, "Because you *can*, you know?" or with a reference to Rosie O'Donnell's family. "She has, like, ten kids," people would remind us.

I imagine we got the question more than most gay couples, simply because Drew connected better with kids than anyone I had ever met. If we found ourselves in line behind a father and son at the movies, it was a given that Drew would start talking to the kid about what he was going to be for Halloween or complimenting his cool Power Rangers T-shirt. Personally, I feared strangers' children because talking to them in public can quickly get you earmarked as a perv. Drew never made anyone uncomfortable, though. His interest in kids was so pure and sweet.

If we were having dinner with our friends Marcel and Deborah, we would arrive an hour early so Drew could squeeze in some play time with their daughter, Charlotte. When it was time to go, it was his leg Charlotte would cling to. "Don't leave!" she'd wail. "Read me a story, Drew!"

Older kids loved him because he worked at MTV, and he was happy to share the behind-the-scenes scoop on *Jackass* and *Pimp*

My Ride. Younger kids loved him because he was silly and imaginative, unafraid to play princesses with them or wrap a diaper around his head for a cheap laugh.

In another generation, Drew would've been the host of a kiddie TV show, an asexual clown with a puppet on his lap and a mid-afternoon time slot. When people asked him why he never had a family, he'd put down his ukulele and motion to the hordes of screaming toddlers at his feet. "Aw, these are my kids," he'd grin.

This was the twenty-first century, though, and all those well-meaning friends were right. We *could* have kids of our own. We *should* have kids of our own. If anyone deserved to be a dad, it was this garrulous man I'd fallen in love with.

As much as we liked the idea, it did seem like a long shot—at least until we found an adoption agency that accepted gift cards. That didn't stop us from having fun with the idea.

I would suspect that overall, I'm a pretty kick-ass guy to be in love with. I'm not controlling or aloof. Not commitment phobic or necrophilic. Not an alcoholic, chocoholic, or rage-oholic. My loyalty is strong; my body odors, weak. I'm too small to abuse you physically, too conflict averse to beat you up emotionally. I don't have a lot of bad habits like smoking crack or stabbing Federales. I'm equally comfortable making conversation with your parents, your grandparents, and your special needs cousin. I'll never tell you you look fat, old, or confused, but I will tell you when you have a full broccoli floret stuck in your teeth. You can even leave the toilet seat up with me. When I need to sit, I'll know what to do. But if you do plan to date me, there is one tremendous catch you should be aware of.

I play pranks.

Not often and not haphazardly but when you least expect and with cunning precision. I prank the way some people bite their fingernails or speak French. I can't help it. April Fool's Day is my Kwanzaa.

Drew and I met on February 1, so our bi-month-iversary seemed like the perfect time to introduce him to my dark side. Cue evil laugh.

He'd been developing an MTV series with Paula Abdul, who brought the requisite dose of crazy to my favorite TV show, *American Idol*. She once left Drew a rambling, tearful voice mail message, which we played about a hundred times, laughing and laughing. Paula had been trying to get Drew to attend a taping of *Idol*, and now that he had a boyfriend who was slavishly devoted to the show, Drew finally took her up on the offer.

On the very morning we had tickets, April 1, 2003, a scandal rocked the entertainment headlines. A finalist named Corey Clark had been booted unexpectedly off the show by producers. For weeks, Clark had been making waves by serenading Paula at the judges' stand. Now he would become better known as the dude who'd been arrested for allegedly beating up his sister.

It was a juicy story, but it deserved to be even juicier. The stars had aligned, and conditions were ripe for a perfect storm of pranksterism. I typed up a phony news story, slapped a *Daily Variety* logo on it, and emailed it to my trusting boyfriend.

Ousted "Idol" Fights Back—Alleges Affair with Host
Tues Apr 1, 1:06 PM ET
LOS ANGELES (Reuters)—Disgraced "American Idol" contestant Corey Clark has lashed out against the show, claiming producers are hiding the real reason for his expulsion. Clark alleges that two months ago, during the show's semifinal round, host Paula Abdul "made advances of a sexual nature, after which we had sex."

Clark claims the former pop princess isn't kidding around when she declares her crushes on the competitors. "She's a predator," he says. "She's pushing 40, she's lonely and she hasn't had a hit in years.

She's doing the show for two reasons. To revive her career and to meet men. Period."

Throughout their fling, Clark says Abdul lavished him with expensive gifts and gave him tips on his image, encouraging him to wear a sheer mesh shirt during last week's show. "I didn't want to wear that," he says. "It was skanky." He claims he was often absent from the Hollywood Hills mansion that houses the other contestants because he was at Abdul's home with her and what he describes as "her ugly dogs."

I worried that I'd gone too far. It was so absurd, and the quotes were particularly nonsensical. Drew was smarter than to fall for this.

Within seconds, he responded. "HOLY SHIT!" he emailed. "HOLY SHIT! HOLY SHIT!" As any prankster knows, this was a rave review. Three "Holy Shits"! Kudos to me!

There was just one thing I hadn't expected: Drew had a dark side, too. My good-natured boyfriend, it turned out, was a super-gossip. Before he replied to me, he forwarded my email to half his address book. His coworkers, his boss, the MTV press department.

Then, suddenly, he called me in a panic. "Tell me you didn't just burn me with an April Fool's joke."

I snorted with glee. "To a crisp!" I cheered.

But Drew wasn't laughing. He let me know that my email was currently circulating throughout Hollywood—among his agent friends, his producer friends, page 6 of the *New York Post*. Any second, Kurt Loder might break into TRL with an MTV News special report.

"I could lose my job!" Drew said. "Thanks a lot." *Click.*

Of course, he didn't get fired. He just had to send an embarrassing retraction and make a couple of crow-eating phone calls to reign in the hoax before anyone took it seriously. It turned out that no one other than Drew believed the story anyway. As I suspected, it was too ridiculous.

We went to the taping that night as planned. I got to meet Paula Abdul. She was extremely nice. She called me "Jimmy." It was a great time.

Did I learn my lesson? Yes. April Fool's Day is fun!

The following year, I cast my net wider. My target: everyone.

I spent months planning my ruse. It had to be elaborate. It had to be believable. It had to be perfect.

Then, first thing on the morning of April 1, the following email hit the in-boxes of just about everybody I know.

From: Jerry Mahoney
To: [recipients]
Subject: Big News!
Date: Thu, 1 Apr 2004 05:59:12 -0800
Dear friends and family:

Drew and I have a very big announcement to make, and I hope you'll forgive us for doing this via email, but it really was the best way to reach all of you at once. A few months ago, we began the process of adopting. We have lots of love to give, and if we can piss off a few right-wingers in the process, so much the better!

After exploring several options, we decided on an agency that specializes in Chinese adoptions. It seems fitting for us to take in an Asian kid. I mean, Drew and I both love Chinese food and Jackie Chan movies. (Ha, ha. Geez, if that's my level of cultural sensitivity, I feel sorry for this kid already.) Maxine, our agent in America, knew of a particularly distressed orphanage in the Siyue Hunong region. We submitted our application, had it professionally translated, wrote about a thousand checks, and submitted to a very long, awkward, static-filled phone interview. Then, finally, just last night, we signed the papers. In three weeks, we'll be flying to Shanghai (and then taking a nine-hour train ride) to pick up our daughter!

Out of respect for her heritage, we've decided to keep her given name, Fu-Ling. We deliberated whose last name to give her, weighing all the implications of each, how our families would feel, and, of course, whose name sounded better with Fu-Ling. And in the end we flipped a coin. Welcome Fu-Ling Tappon. (Dammit. Should've picked heads... Well, at least the next one will have my name.)

And since I'm sure everyone wants to see the newest member of our family, her picture is attached below.

Love,

Jerry and Drew

>———-Original Message———-

> From: Maxine Rablish

> To: Jerry

> Sent: Tue Mar 30 13:29:21 2004

> Subject: Fwd: Re: [no subject]

> hey, guys!!! well, i had to say five chinese prayers to buddha and sacrifice a goat

> (sorry, sick joke!!!!!!!!), but we finally got a picture out of that crazy woman!! i

> have to say, in all my years of doing this, you prob. scored the cuuuuuuuuutest

> baby ive ever seen!!!!!!!!!!!!!!!!!!!!! congrats again and again, kids!!!!! can't wait

> til you bring her home and i can take you and little fu-ling out to lunch!!!!! xoxox

> >——- happy baby adoption china siyue wrote:

> > Date: Mon, 29 Mar 2004 18:43:57 +0100

> > Subject: Re: [no subject]

> > From: xin-xian xiang

> > To: getchababyhere323@yahoo.com

> >

> >Attachment is pictur of you baby for arrange to pick up china 23 apirl. Too

> >welcome Fu-Ling too happy familiy!

Below all of this was a picture of China's absolute most adorable baby. Thank you, Google Image search.

Then came what, in the Internet age, marks the official start of any good prank, hitting "Send." It was out of my hands now. My baby was off on its own, out in the big world, sowing mischief far and wide, and I left Drew behind to deal with the fallout.

I was on my way to meet up with Greg in New Orleans.

The trip was his idea. In the time since our fateful phone call, so much had changed for both of us. Drew and I moved in together, and Greg embarked on the world's fastest-ever coming-out spree. Friends, parents, baristas. Most of the Tri-State Area heard the news. What it took me ten years to do Greg accomplished in about two weeks.

Along the way, he learned not one but two of his two best friends from college were also gay. Back in school, the three of them shared a house together, but apparently, little else. We all felt the same—shocked, confused, and full of regrets from years spent in the closet. Greg thought the answer was to pack everything we missed into one wild three-day jaunt to the Sleazeville of the South. A good, old-fashioned Repressed Gay Summit.

The timing was purely coincidental, but it did keep me from giving my April Fool's joke the follow-up attention it deserved. This was back during that brief period of several weeks in the early 2000s when cell phones could ring with a polyphonic rendition of "Baby Got Back" but not yet book your round-trip tickets to Orlando or turn your sprinklers on. Or, for that matter, email.

The only indication I had of how people were reacting was a voice mail I heard from my friend Adam during a layover.

"OHMYGOD! I'MSOHAPPYFORYOU!! OHMYGOD! SHE'SBEAUTIFUL!! I'MEXPLODINGWITHJOYANDLOVEAND-HAPPINESSFORYOU! I'MSOSOOOOOOOOTHRILLED!!! ICAN-NOTIMAGINEBETTERPARENTS! OHMYGOD! IT'SSOFUCK-INGGREAT!!!!!!!"

So far, so good. I turned my phone back off for the connecting flight.

Soon, I was sitting with Greg and his two college friends in a restaurant that served gator fricassee. If you're in a group of four gay men, it's inevitable that you'll compare yourselves to the ultimate group of four gay men, the gals of *Sex & the City*.

One of Greg's friends repeatedly demanded, "I want to be the Miranda! Let me be Miranda! Come on, please can I be Miranda?" We said yes because, really, only a Miranda would want to be Miranda. (Although if he'd brought it up one more time, we were going to make him Stanford.)

Miranda branded Greg's other friend the Charlotte. Charlotte had never seen the show, so Miranda had to explain his reasoning. "She's a prude."

"Oh. Okay."

One thing nobody debated was that Greg was Samantha. Since his metamorphosis, he'd been slutting it up all across Manhattan. With this trip, he was expanding his conquests to below the Mason-Dixon Line. He arrived the night before the rest of us, bravely ventured into a gay bar, and hooked up with a guy he met there. It was that easy—and so was Greg. I'd spent my delayed adolescence as the shy wallflower. Greg had actually become Sweet Talk.

I was labeled the Carrie, the protagonist, the moral center. Lest I be too flattered, Miranda reminded me it was only because all the other roles were taken. Bitch.

While we were breaking the ice and eating okra, I sent a couple of phone calls through to voice mail, but when Drew called for the fifth time, I decided I should probably pick up.

He was practically hyperventilating. "Have you checked your email?" he asked.

"I'll have to do it back at the hotel. Are people falling for the Chinese baby joke?"

"Hard," he said. It was just as I'd hoped. My prank was weaving its delicious black magic. I let rip the delicious cackle of April Fool's triumph.

"It's not funny!" Drew shouted. "I've had people come into my office in tears! They're so happy for us! I feel sick!"

"Wait," I said. "I didn't send it to anyone you work with."

"I forwarded it to them. Now I wish I hadn't. They want to throw us a baby shower!"

The more he told me, the more I exulted. My caring, trusting friends had taken little Fu-Ling into their hearts. It was an April Fool's Day miracle!

Too bad my boyfriend was on the edge of a nervous breakdown. I tried to calm him. "Look, I knew I was going to be out of town, so I composed an email to let everyone know they'd been had. If you want, you can send it on my behalf."

"Where is it?"

I gave Drew instructions how to find the message on my desktop computer, back at our apartment.

"All I ask is that you hit 'Send' precisely at the stroke of midnight tonight!"

"Fuck that!" Drew replied. "I'm going home and sending it now. This has gone too far!" He slammed down the phone.

I was dying to check my email back at the hotel, but first, I had a date with the undead. Our Miranda had signed us up for a "haunted" tour, which seems to be the only kind of tour they offer in New Orleans. He wanted to save a few bucks, so he booked us with some no-frills outfit he found in a tiny ad in the back of a tourist magazine. Such a Miranda move!

Our guide ended up being a bitter grad student named Mitch. He asked us to meet him at a bar, and he arrived forty minutes late, with a backpack, three days of facial scruff, and no apparent interest in the history of his adopted hometown. He checked the four of us out, sighed, and rolled his eyes. "Do you really want to do this?" he asked.

We followed Mitch lazily around town. At times it felt like we were leading the tour because it was impossible to walk any slower than he did; thus, he was always trailing behind us. He didn't say much, and when he did, it was something like, "This is one of the most haunted houses in the city. There was a guy who used to live here . . . I'm blanking on his name." Most of the ghosts he told us about were vengeful former slaves, which was kind of a buzzkill. Who wants to go on a ghost tour where you root for the ghosts?

We kept having to step aside to let the more popular tour groups pass us by. Dozens of tourists would crowd around a guide decked head to toe in vampire gear, with pasty white makeup and the raspy voice of the undead. They clung to each other as he intoned chilling tales of spirits rising from the bayous. "I know that 'vampire,'" Mitch said under his breath. "He's from Cincinnati."

The walking tour ended abruptly when we realized Mitch was no longer with us. We weren't sure how long it had been since he'd disappeared, and we couldn't tell whether he snuck away or had just fallen behind and gotten lost. But we didn't look too hard.

We had more important plans, plans far more frightening than anything on Mitch's tour: it was time to go to a gay bar. Greg had arranged to rendezvous with the guy he'd hooked up with the night before, and he wanted to introduce us all. "He can't wait to meet you," he assured us.

The way Greg talked about him, this guy sounded purely magical. He was older, confident, and dashingly handsome. He was passionate but tender, strong yet sensitive. They talked about their lives. They wondered about the future. They ordered room service. Greg had already invited the dude to visit him in New York. Was our Samantha in love?

We knew when we lost sight of Greg amid the sweaty, strobe-lit room that he'd found his man. And if there was any doubt, it was erased when we saw Greg's tongue eagerly probing some strange guy's esophagus. We casually strolled over and waited a long time to get their attention.

Greg's new man was not what I'd expected. I'm not one who describes people as lithe, but it seems like the most appropriate word in this case. "Petite" would be another fitting description, as would "revolting." He was small and twig-like, about half the weight of a third grader, with jeans so tight, he seemed like a plastic doll. He was ten years older than we were but dressed ten years younger. As we moved in for introductions, he threw his arm around Greg's neck and plopped sideways across his lap.

He smiled and told us his name, but what I heard was, "Hi, I'm Sex."

Sex sat with Greg all night, like a dutiful puppy—a puppy perennially searching for food inside its master's mouth. He was the kind of guy who seemed to exist solely to shepherd guys like Greg through that potentially unpleasant "first fling" phase. I couldn't imagine Sex outside the context of a pickup scene. Sex at the Laundromat, waiting for his clothes to dry. Sex at the dentist with cotton balls tucked into his gums. Sex at work, standing on the corner of a downtown intersection, twirling a Quizno's sign.

Charlotte, Miranda, and I knew from the instant we met him that Sex was going to break our friend's heart. He wasn't interested in falling in love. He got everything he needed out of the relationship the night before. Sex would never be coming to New York.

When Sex stood up to get another Corona, Greg turned to the rest of us and smiled. "Well . . . ?" he asked.

I was as speechless as I'd been when the torso told me I was cute. I searched my brain for something nice I could say convincingly. Looks—no. Personality—no. Think, Jerry, think.

"You seem very happy with him," I said, finally. Whew, not bad.

"I don't like him!" Miranda snapped.

"What? Why not?"

Greg was devastated, but rather than retreat, Miranda doubled down. "He's gross!"

Greg looked at me. "Do you think he's gross?"

In truth, I thought "gross" was far too mild, but I couldn't say that. "He's . . . not someone I would be interested in myself."

"Great, so you all think he's disgusting. Thanks for your support!" Greg stormed off. It was the last we saw of him that night.

A little while later, I returned to the hotel, disheartened and exhausted. As I passed by the business lounge, I realized there was something inside that might cheer me up: my emails. Though I could barely keep my eyes open, I logged into my Yahoo account.

I'd never seen so many messages in my life, without half of them being for cheap V_1AGRA. The "HOLY SHIT!"s were off the charts. I even earned a few "OH MY FUCKING GOD"s, which is like a prankster's Pulitzer. My friends' euphoria burst from the screen with every word.

"This is the best news of the year! I have a smile a mile wide."

"Wowee, I can't be more excited for you guys!"

One buddy offered his sister as a translator. (She'd minored in Chinese at college.) Another said that Fu-Ling kind of looked like Drew.

It was just what I'd been hoping for—until I saw the responses that came in after Drew revealed it was a joke.

"Hope you had a fun time with this. Know you made me feel like an idiot!"

"Please tell Jerry that I fully CRIED!!! You guys are dicks."

"I don't think this is funny."

"You a**hole."

It was hard to gauge people's tone from responses like these. I wanted to believe they reacted out of bemused appreciation, but I couldn't be sure, especially when I saw this note from Drew: "You need to call Pam and apologize. She says she's never talking to you again."

I decided to call my friend Adam, the one who had gushed so delightfully on voice mail. He was a great friend and a good sport. His reaction would be fair.

I remember two quotes distinctly from that phone call. One was "I will never be happy for you again." The other was "Everyone is going to hate you for the rest of time."

If one thing was clear, it was that people loved the idea of Drew and me having a family. People weren't upset because they'd been fooled. They were upset because they wanted so badly for my news to be true.

I realized I'd broken one of the golden rules of pranksters: never prank the things you dream about, because when you're done, all you're left with is the realization that they were just a joke. We weren't going to China, we weren't visiting an orphanage, and we weren't going to have a sweet little girl falling asleep in our laps on the plane ride home. Man, that would have been incredible.

By the next morning, at least one person had forgiven me. Greg was disappointed that we didn't give Sex a more positive review, but he rejoined our group for our airboat tour of the bayou. Soon, we were joking like we always did. I think we both knew the Sex thing was fleeting. What we had with each other went much deeper.

As time passed, most of my friends grew to have at least a grudging appreciation for my prank. I even got a few delayed compliments on pulling it off. Everyone else just stopped bringing it up.

Then, months later, a shocking story hit the entertainment world. A former *American Idol* contestant, Corey Clark, was claiming that he and Paula Abdul had been having an affair, and that was the real reason he had been kicked off the show two years ago. Drew called me instantly when he saw it, speechless.

That's the other thing about my April Fool's jokes. They have an uncanny tendency of coming true.

4

CAN WE BORROW YOUR
LADY PARTS FOR NINE MONTHS?

W HEN IT COMES TO THE REQUISITE baby-making equipment, vaginas are further down the list than you might imagine. As long as Drew and I had clean criminal records and a checkbook, we could start the process of becoming parents. What baffled and terrified us was the process itself. I had no idea what would happen between now and the day an Elmo-loving munchkin started clomping around our house in Crocs. My mind tended to wander toward the darkest possibilities.

I'd read plenty of books and feature articles about gay parenthood, but for the most part, they were propaganda, designed to convince Middle America that gay families were Just Like Everyone Else. "Doug and Waldo remember the day little Leticia Rose came back with them to their Park Slope brownstone. With a pink bow on her nearly hairless head and the tiniest pair of shoes Prada makes, she was doughy, she was perfect, she was *theirs*." Yes, but was Leticia Rose born addicted to PCP? How many arms did she have, more or less? Was some sixteen-year-old girl from Idaho bawling her eyes out back at the maternity ward of New York Methodist while Doug and Waldo were parading Leticia Rose (nee Beyoncé Miracle) around Brooklyn in a Moses basket?

The stories tended to focus on the happy endings, but I had a feeling that what came before was hardly fairy-tale material. War, poverty, drugs. Adopted babies had some badass backstories. Drew and I assumed foreign adoption would be the quickest and easiest way for us to go, if not the most cheerful. We'd jet off to another continent to score some sad sack kid who'd been orphaned because Ethnicity A was determined to rid the world of Ethnicity B or because a misreading of some well-meaning religious book made a band of heavily armed basket cases think women who bared their elbows were put on Earth for sport hunting. As much as I wanted to be a dad, there was something disconcerting about the prospect of finding ourselves in the "win" column of a genocide. Would we start rooting for international strife? Bloodshed in the Congo? Time to call our travel agent!

It turned out the Third World was more afraid of Drew and me than we were of them. There tends to be an inverse relationship between the size of a country's orphan pool and their tolerance of gay rights. Even in the most depressed places on Earth, there's a feeling that unwanted babies are better off languishing in a killing field than thriving in West Hollywood. It was hard to get too upset about it. The less gay-friendly a country is, the more trouble they seem to have providing clean drinking water for their people and staving off diseases that were eradicated decades ago. Go tackle tuberculosis, Cambodia. We'll work on gay adoption in a few years.

That meant Drew and I could either wait for a new genocide to spring up somewhere more gay-friendly—C'mon, Denmark!— or we could focus instead on domestic adoption. Plenty of gay couples find their offspring in *America's* Third World, the places in the Midwest and the Deep South where abstinence-only education and ever-tighter restrictions on abortions are producing unwanted babies by the bucket load. You could argue that Rick Santorum had created enough gay families to fill one of Rosie O'Donnell's cruise ships from stem to stern. Finally, a reason to vote Republican.

Best of all, domestic adoption for gays has its own bible, Dan Savage's book *The Kid*. It's a moving, hilarious, and somewhat unsettling account of how Dan and his boyfriend Terry adopted a baby from what he describes as a "gutter punk," a young homeless drifter and occasional addict who struggled to keep her shit together for nine months for her fetus's sake. It was exactly the gritty, candid true story I'd been dying to hear. There was no sugarcoating. This is what we had to look forward to—gutter punks, tragedy, late-night phone calls from desperate social workers looking for someone to love a two-pound preemie who'd been dumped at a fire station. If that's what I was in for, I wanted to prepare myself.

It was in *The Kid* that I first learned of "Dear Birthparent" letters. Prospective parents are required to put together a biographical packet full of pictures, stats, and a letter addressed to the women trying to pick homes for their unwanted fetuses. Instead of some random overseas bureaucrat assigning babies to families the way they assign roommates in freshman dorms, the big decisions with private adoptions are made by the birth moms themselves.

This is where Dan and his partner scored big. The birth mother chose them specifically because they were outside the mainstream, like her. If she couldn't provide her kid the life she felt he deserved, well, she didn't want him to go to a couple of lame-o's either. *The Kid* convinced me that domestic adoption might actually work for Drew and me. All we needed was to convince one birth mom, somewhere in the U.S., that we were grade-A daddy material. It sounded doable.

I was feeling more confident than ever. Being a writer, I loved the idea that I got to make my appeal in essay form. I was already composing my profile in my head. In search of inspiration, I typed "Dear Birthparent" into Google. The number of hits was staggering. Some were posted by adoption agencies, others were pasted onto blogs or Facebook profiles. There were YouTube videos and Twitter feeds. I half expected to find an eBay fetus store or an "I Can Haz Baby?!" Tumblr. These were real people, going through the same process we were contemplating. They were our competition.

And they sucked.

The profiles were all the same. They started off by complimenting the birth mom on the difficult choice she was making. Ahem, ass-kissing! Then they'd introduce her to their family and talk about how amazing they were. Bragging. They'd wrap up by musing about the special moments they might share with her child—helping him with math homework, holding her hand on a roller coaster, letting him pick out a rescue puppy to take home. Cloying. Predictable. Alongside the text would be a few pictures of them looking family-like, sitting by a fireplace, having a picnic, dressing up as Santa and an elf for the neighbors' kids.

What a snooze. Standing out in this crowd would be easier than I thought. Drew and I were fun. We would have no problem putting together a zany letter that would win birth moms over by the hundreds. I imagined us having our pick of fetuses. If we weren't feeling like a redhead, no biggie. We could custom order whatever kind of kid we wanted. We'll take the prom queen with early acceptance to Harvard who got knocked up by some slimy politician she was interning for. Ah, a scandal baby! The brass ring!

Instead of composing our letter, though, I kept reading. I couldn't stop. It was a peek into a side of people's lives they don't normally show you. There was an ocean of Joes and Belindas out there baring their souls, turning their tears into words and posting them for strangers to see. It was like the world's best reality show but with real people! Who to root for?

Mike and Teresa were in their mid-forties and had baby fever for nearly twenty years. They had a big house in the country, a gated swimming pool and a golden retriever named Effie who loved kids. They even had the perfect names picked out—Byron for a boy, like the poet, and Hope for a girl, because hope was what had kept them going through Teresa's nine miscarriages. Two years ago, her doctor finally forbade her from trying again, for her own safety. That's when they started saving money so they could adopt. Teresa took on a second job tutoring, and Mike did some carpentry for friends. Once they had a baby, Teresa planned to stay home full-time.

Then there were Monica and Al. Monica wanted to share her love of baking with a child, and Al wanted someone he could pass his autographed Mickey Mantle rookie card down to. Monica was adopted as a child and always knew she wanted to build her own family through adoption. Al was deaf, so he had a soft spot for disabled kids. They had already taken in two other kids, so the new baby would have two sisters, one who was paraplegic and the other who lived in a bubble. This time, they were hoping for a boy, special needs a plus.

Luke and Sylvia married young, eager to start their family. She was a registered nurse, he was an eighth-grade history teacher. But when Sylvia got cervical cancer at twenty-five, their story nearly came to an abrupt end. It was only thanks to a hysterectomy that Sylvia kicked the disease. Now she was healthy but would never know how it felt to have a baby grow inside her. Their faith kept them going, and they were convinced their misfortune was a higher calling. When the right woman read their letter, they would have the family God always intended for them.

It was hard to feel superior to any of these people. We weren't any more worthy than they, any more capable of loving and providing for a baby. From reading their stories, I could see them as a birth mother might, and they were fantastic. They all deserved babies. I wanted to gather every one of them in a big room and surprise them, like Oprah. "Look under your chairs, everyone! You get a baby! And you get a baby! Everybody gets a baby!"

How many of them would actually be chosen? There was no way to know. The curse of Dear Birthparent letters was that there were no happy endings to be found. If a couple successfully adopted, they simply took their letter down. The only couples you could find online were the ones who were still waiting, still coping with that baby-sized hole in their hearts.

There were so many would-be families out there, so many people at the same place as us. I couldn't help feeling that, by entering this pool, we would also disrupt it. What if we took Mike and Teresa's kid? Would they get Luke and Sylvia's—or none at all? Or maybe we'd be the ones who never got chosen.

The other thing that surprised me about all these letters is that there was a shitload of gays. It seemed like every male couple in the country had read *The Kid* and wanted in on the action. There was no way we would stand out in this crowd the way Dan Savage and his partner had years earlier. We were as ordinary as anyone, as likely to make a birth mom yawn and click "Next" without a second glance.

If we couldn't adopt internationally or domestically, where would our baby come from? Mars? The black market? Kidnapping?

It was Drew's therapist who came up with the answer: Mindy Stanhope, M.A. Mindy was a colleague of his—a specialist in family planning. If anyone could help us sort through our options, it was she. When we met Mindy, she seemed incredibly childlike herself—young, outgoing, chirpy-voiced. She was small, too. The top of her head was roughly level with my Adam's apple. I wanted to shout, "We'll take her!" and sign the adoption papers right there. There was something overly mature about Mindy, though.

She was alert and interested, smart and inquisitive. She asked probing questions like, "How did you two meet?" "Tell me about your families." "Where do you see this relationship in five years?" Within a few minutes, I realized this meeting wasn't quite what it was presented to be. I'd been tricked into couples counseling.

Thankfully, we aced Mindy's pop quiz. Most people she met probably came to her out of frustration because something in their relationship was horribly broken. They were glum and desperate, on the brink of splitting up. Drew and I were beaming with optimism, eager to move our couplehood to a deeper level, envisioning a future together that lasted well into a shared room at a nursing home.

Without even trying, we won Mindy over to Team Us. "You guys are awesome!" she raved. Drew and I were feeling great. We had the official Mental Health Seal of Approval.

Mindy agreed that foreign adoption was unlikely in our case. She also acknowledged the perils of domestic adoption. But she saw another, more promising route. "Have you considered gestational surrogacy?"

"Oh, no," I said. "We couldn't."

We knew plenty about surrogacy. That's when you hand some strange lady a turkey baster and a contract and hope that when the kid comes out, she sticks to your deal. We'd seen enough soap operas and daytime talk shows to know how that can end up. No thanks.

Mindy explained that gestational surrogacy was different. Embryos were created in vitro, using another woman's eggs, so the surrogate bore no genetic link to the baby she carried. This weakened any emotional tie she might feel to the newborn, as well as any legal claim she might have should she decide she wanted to keep the kid after all. That, combined with intensive psychological screening, had pretty much wiped out the surrogacy horror stories that kept the Lifetime Movie Network in business. The ideal candidate had already given birth to her own children; thus, her uterus had a proven track record. But more importantly, she had completed her family. She had enough kids of her own, so she had no interest in keeping yours for herself.

Not only was surrogacy unlikely to end as tabloid fodder, but there were plenty of advantages to making a baby that way. In an adoption, a birth mother can't sign over custody of her child until after it's born, usually following a forty-eight-hour waiting period. So even if she picks you, you have no say in how she cares for the fetus. She might chain smoke in her SUV all the way to her ob-gyn appointments, and you can't even ask her to roll down the window. Plus, there's always the chance that once she holds her offspring in her arms, she'll have a change of heart and decide to keep the baby for herself. Of course, every woman should be afforded that opportunity, but it takes a major emotional toll on the intended parents, who play a tense, high-stakes waiting game until they can finally take a baby home.

A surrogate baby, on the other hand, would be legally ours from conception. We could attend all of the surrogate's prenatal appointments, watch our baby grow on the ultrasounds, even cut the umbilical cord in the delivery room. And there would be no fears about how the surrogate would take care of her fetus. Surrogates were professionals who took pride in their work. Before they were approved for the task, they were screened for drugs, alcohol, and nicotine. They had to pass mental and gynecological exams. It was the perfect route for control freaks like us.

There was another benefit, too. Unlike adoption, as amazing and generous as that can be, with surrogacy we'd actually be creating a life. Our baby would exist only because, against all odds, Drew and I met and fell in love. It just seemed so beautifully ordinary.

Mindy knew a man named Wes, who ran a surrogacy agency specifically for gay couples. It was called Rainbow Extensions, and Wes wasn't just the president; he was also one of their first clients. He and his partner had two surro-kids. We called him that afternoon.

"You two are doing something very few people before you have done," Wes began. "You're pioneers!"

Throughout our call, we could hear Wes's kids in the background—playing, fighting, requesting juice. It was a glimpse into what we hoped our future would be. Wes was very patient as we lobbed questions at him.

"Where do you find your surrogates?"

"Are they doing this for the money or because they love the idea of helping gay dads?"

"How do we know the surrogate isn't pounding back cosmos and binging on sushi all weekend while our baby mutates into a sloth-like monster inside of her?"

He'd heard them all before, and he had all the answers we were hoping to hear—at least until we got to the issue of what happened after the baby came. We wanted to know if the surrogate would stay a part of our lives.

"We send our surrogates a card at Christmas," he explained. "That's really all they want."

He thought he was reassuring us, but we were disappointed. So the woman who brought our child into the world would be nothing to them but an address label?

"Okay," I asked. "But what about the egg donor?"

"What about her?"

"Can we find one who'll stay in touch?"

"Absolutely not! You'll never hear from her again, and I assure you, you don't want to!" He was starting to get testy.

"But don't kids ask questions about her?"

"All they need is a first name and a picture, which Rainbow Extensions provides. Our kids are perfectly satisfied with that."

"Your kids are still young. As they get older, won't they . . ."

Wes cut me off. "All they need is a first name and a picture."

"Come on. It's only natural they'll be curious about their biological mother."

It was at about that moment that Wes achieved spontaneous combustion.

"Okay, let me stop you right there," he said, trying his best to stay calm. "I want to make one thing perfectly clear. Your child will have two fathers. He or she will have a surrogate and an egg donor. But there will be . . ." He took a long pause for dramatic effect, or perhaps to pinch his diaphragm for maximum volume. ". . . NO! MOTHER!!!!!"

It turned out I'd uttered the dirty word of surrogacy. The M-word was strictly verboten. It was more than a matter of semantics. It was an issue of pride. With so many people questioning whether two dads were qualified to raise a child, some felt it was crucial to designate who was doing the heavy lifting and whose commitment was over after a few trips to the doctor. No one in this arrangement was worthy of the M-word, the thinking went, especially not egg donors. Most egg donors wanted nothing to do with the M-word anyway.

Unlike surrogates, who'd finished having their own babies, egg donors tended to be younger and unattached. They were happy to help strangers start families, but only on the condition that the kids they made would never track them down and weird out their real kids or, for that matter, their husband. They were often students working their way through college, and they wanted to collect their fee without amassing any baggage. All we would have would be a first name and a picture.

It didn't seem fair. We wanted to be totally up front with our kid about how we made him or her. We were pioneers after all. Who doesn't love a good adventure tale?

No matter who you are, you deserve to know where you came from. It's Your Story. Your Story starts with how your parents met and fell in love, how they found out they were pregnant, the rush of pure joy they felt when they brought you home for the first time—something to counteract the clinical sperm-meets-egg stuff and make every kid feel special.

Adoptive parents may have to gloss over a few unpleasantries in the first act of their Your Story—the ethnic cleansing perhaps—but they've got a killer climax. "We had some love to share, and you needed a home. Out of seven billion people on this planet, we found each other, and we knew right away we were meant to be a family."

In contrast, what Your Story would we tell our kid? "Well, we found a couple of total strangers who needed some cash, we completed a series of business transactions and bam, the doctor worked his magic in a petri dish." Then we'd give them a first name and a picture and shut down any follow-up questions with, "Sorry, that's all Rainbow Extensions says you need."

"Don't worry about it," Drew assured me. "You can't plan a kid's birth story beforehand. The story is what happens as you go along."

"What if it's like Wes says? 'You have no mommy. Stop asking.'"

"It won't be like that."

"How do you know that?"

"Because it's us. Our surrogate and egg donor won't be mommies, but they're not going to be business partners, either. We'll get to know them. We'll let them into our lives. They'll be as close to us as we want them to be."

"And we'll stay in touch?"

"You think a surrogate is going to spend nine months with us and then walk away?" Drew put his arm around me. "We're awesome, remember?"

5

UM, SPERM

"SO WHOSE SPERM are you going to use? Yours or Drew's?"

I knew coming out of the closet would mean sacrificing some privacy, but I never expected that a few years later, I'd be having this conversation with my mom.

This was an unforeseen downside of surrogacy—the spermification of my life. Once Drew and I decided to give surrogacy a shot, suddenly everyone I knew felt comfortable discussing the flagellating residents of my man junk—friends, neighbors, bosses.

"You given a sperm sample yet?"

"What's your sperm count?"

"Better hope your boys are swimmers!"

No one dropped more S-bombs than our caseworker at Rainbow Extensions. She spoke a language that sounded much like English at first, until you realized that in her native tongue, every fifth word was the clinical name of the male reproductive cell.

"Who's sperm we gonna use?" she asked. "We need to collect your sperm, test your sperm, sperm your sperm, and enspermanize your spermological spermograms." This was what SpermEnglish sounded like.

Her name was S'mantha. S. Apostrophe. Mantha. In her picture on the Rainbow Extensions website we could see she had frizzy red hair and elongated brown-white teeth that looked like unwaxed snowboards. Her blouse appeared to have been made from the sofa cushions my parents had growing up, and if I told her that, she'd probably be flattered. "How nice! I recycle everything!"

On our very first phone call with her, S'mantha informed us that she'd already booked a visit for us to the Westside Fertility Center. "Nothing to worry about," she assured us. "They just need a bit o' sperm!"

It was then I discovered a topic even more awkward than sperm itself: what you have to do to produce the sperm. Sure, I knew the procedure pretty well, but it was never something I'd done in a doctor's office.

Into a plastic cup.

While a nurse waited outside for me to finish.

As if all that pressure wasn't enough, I'd have to make do without the standard accoutrements to which I'd become so accustomed—tender mood lighting, a can of diet A&W root beer, and a faded VHS of *Dances with Wolves*, cued up to the skinny-dipping river bath scene.

Or would I?

"You might want to bring your own materials," S'mantha informed me.

"Materials?"

"You know? Materials. To assist in collecting your sperm." Surprisingly, the word "porn" didn't seem to exist in SpermEnglish.

S'mantha explained that Westside Fertility catered to a mostly straight clientele, so she couldn't guarantee the availability of the particular genre of "materials" that would help Drew and me produce our sperm.

As much as I resented that our fertility clinic couldn't accommodate us with the appropriate smut, I was kind of pleased to have a good excuse to buy porn. How often does that happen? All of my porn shopping memories were so bleak and demoralizing.

For one thing, buying a dirty magazine was the most blatant way of announcing my sexuality, before I was ready to do that. When I purchased my first stroke mag, it wasn't just an awkward step toward becoming a skuzzy grown man. It was a giant leap out of the closet. You could argue that the first person I ever truly came out to was the cashier at Newspaper Nirvana on 75th and Broadway.

I was a senior at Columbia University, about two miles uptown, and I was doing what I always did at newsstands, reading *Billboard*. It was kind of an exciting week. Color Me Badd was proving they were no one-hit wonder with "I Adore Mi Amore" up nine spots to number six, and a hot new rap outfit from East Orange, New Jersey, was making its debut at number 85 with "O.P.P." I predicted a bright future for Naughty by Nature.

That's when I noticed something even more shocking than the staying power of "Everything I Do (I Do It For You)" by Bryan Adams—a shelf of glossy magazines with chest-bearing men on the cover.

It was porn, there among the general magazine population. Sure, like most newsstands, this one had its porn prison, secreted away behind the cash register. Each sleaze rag was sealed in plastic and partially obscured so that if you wanted to buy it, you had to ask for it. "Pardon me, my good man, but might you sell me a copy of the latest *Big Black Asses*?"

There was no way I could ever utter a sentence like that aloud, even to a complete stranger, so I had resigned myself to a porn-less life. But for some reason, this store's porn prison featured only straight smut. The gay stuff was filed under "Men's Interest," adjacent to the "Music" section, where I was standing. It seemed the nice older gentleman in the turban who owned this particular establishment was oblivious to what was displayed in the pages of *Honcho*, *Torso*, and *Latin Inches*, all of which shared shelf space with *Details* and *GQ*. I stole nervous glances from behind my *Billboard*, my eyes zeroing in on a particular periodical called *Freshmen*.

The cover featured a blond, blue-eyed frat boy in a wrestling singlet and mouth guard. To a straight, possibly Sikh, newsstand owner, it could have passed for a workout magazine, but my sperm knew that its objective wasn't just to get your pecs hard.

Jerry, my sperm whispered. *It's porn!*

"Shut up, sperm! It can't be! You can't just leave porn out like that! There are laws!"

But my sperm was persistent. *I bet they never even opened a copy before they shelved it. Ha ha! The fools!*

"Just let me look at *Billboard* in peace!"

Heyyyyyy . . . that wrestler on the cover looks a little like the guy from Color Me Badd, dontcha think? Without the goatee and earring? You ever wonder what a guy like that might look like . . . naked?

Well, yes. I couldn't lie to my sperm. Yes, I had thought about what the guy from Color Me Badd might look like naked, clean-shaven, and unpierced—perhaps even in a wrestling singlet and mouth guard.

Buy it!

"It's dirty!"

You're a grown man!

"I'm a nice boy!"

Buy it! C'mon, let's raise the stakes! We're tired of freeze-framing Costner's ass!

"I want to . . . but I can't! Not now! I need to psyche myself up, get in the right frame of mind. Maybe in a couple of months . . ."

A couple of months? This isn't like buying something else you'd be humiliated to ask for—like cigarettes or a Michael Bolton CD. This is easily accessible porn! How long do you think it'll stick around?

My sperm had a good point. This was the lucky break of a lifetime. There were no other customers in the store, no one to fear but the cashier, who, let's face it, was a professional man. He wasn't going to say anything to me. Why would he care what type of naked pictures I liked to look at? My money wasn't gay. And who was he to be high and mighty anyway? He'd already bought gay porn, too—from the distributor. Maybe he'd judge me quietly, but so what? I wasn't getting into his Nirvana anyway. Then again, why would he judge me at all? He didn't even know it was porn!

I was already holding the perfect porn shield. *Billboard* was twice the size of *Freshmen*. With the *US News* college rankings on the other side, my filth would be virtually incognito. Just to be safe, I also picked up *Time, Newsweek,* the *New Yorker, Rolling Stone, Spin, TV Guide, People,* and *Nintendo Power.* This way, I wouldn't arouse any suspicion at all.

The cashier rang me up methodically. He didn't even look at what I was buying. He just slid each magazine in my stack enough to see the price of the one below it, then moved on to the next one.

It's working! We're buying porn!

Then, when he got to *Freshmen*, he stopped cold.

He dug it out of the pile, held it up, examined it.

Oh shit, I thought. He knows. He's going to ask for ID. He's going to spit on me. He's going to call me a fag and make me cry.

Hahahahaha! My sperm laughed maniacally. *You're so busted!*

"Shut up, sperm! This is your fault!"

The cashier flipped *Freshmen* over and examined the back, which featured a Speedo-clad hunk in an ad for a phone sex line. There was no hiding anymore. It was possible the cover model existed in some kind of gray area between wholesomeness and gay fantasy. But 1-900-HOT-SPUNK did not.

As the cashier stood holding the magazine for what seemed like the entire fall semester, a woman entered with her eight-year-old daughter in tow. They scanned the candy racks for gum. Any second, they'd be right behind me in line. The little girl would giggle innocently, and the mom would inquire, "Daisy, what are you looking at?" Daisy would point up at the leering wrestler, and her mom would scream, "Police! Police!" I thought about making a break for it.

Then the cashier's finger tapped the wrestler's knee. He nodded knowingly and opened his mouth. Oh, shit. Here it comes. "Five ninety-five," he said, gesturing toward the bar code. Then he rang up my porn and put it back in the pile. He stuffed my purchases into a clear plastic bag and slid it across the counter to me.

The see-through bag proved it. He had no idea this was adult material, or he would have hidden it in a brown paper bag inside another bag inside a third bag, then directed me to exit quietly out the back. That's what I imagined happened when you bought porn, at least.

Instead, I found myself descending the steps to the 1/9 subway line, on my way back to my dorm room to peer beyond the singlet. I had gotten away with the scam of a lifetime, and it only cost me $50 in magazines I had no intention of reading. As the train came screaming into the station, my euphoria ebbed, and I realized where I now stood. I was forty blocks from campus, six subway stops from home. And the only thing protecting me from total exposure was a clear plastic bag, weighed down with enough magazines to fill the waiting room at the Mayo Clinic.

Buying porn was now the number two scariest thing I'd ever done. Getting it back to John Jay Hall Room 1117 was number one with a bullet.

I stood in the crowded subway car, with one hand on a railing and the bag squeezed tightly between my legs to keep it from falling over. I prayed I wouldn't lose my balance, that the bag wouldn't break open, and that no one would see inside and say, "Hey, can I check your *Billboard* for a second? I hear the Scorpions are making a comeback." Any jostling could bring *Freshmen* to the fore and expose me to the world.

As I walked across campus, I clasped the bag tightly with both hands, like a bank robber shielding a satchel full of hundred-dollar bills as he searched for his getaway car. By some miracle, I didn't see a single person I knew. Maybe it's because I had my head down and refused to make eye contact with anyone. But soon I was in my dorm room, enjoying my prize.

My sperm had been right. *Freshmen* was porn—beautiful, glorious porn. It was relatively new, an offshoot of a magazine named *Men*, whose models were, presumably, not quite as fresh. It was kind of a classier gay version of *Barely Legal*. Each issue featured four models, ranging in age from their late teens to their late-late teens, old enough to vote but not to buy Zima. They were a diverse array of types, like the members of a boy band. There was one baby-faced innocent, one jock, one ethnic, and one guy with a single tattoo, the token rebel. If the pictures could speak, he'd probably be rapping, poorly.

Each dude was posed to suggest some activity that young people were known to engage in, only with an unexplained emphasis on his genitalia. You'd see a hot guy with his schlong draped over a soccer ball or splayed out on a professor's desk while resting his balls atop an apple. It was sexy, it was exciting, it was totally fucking absurd. You really expect a teacher to eat that apple? Gross! There was no way to attach a narrative to these photo spreads. Most just fell under what I considered an "Oops! I Forgot My Pants!" scenario.

"Hey, just thought I'd come shoot some hoops . . . and Oops! I forgot my pants!"

"Yo, I swung by to study for our Econ final tomorrow . . . and Oops! I forgot my pants!"

"So I cleaned out the filters, checked the chlorine levels and . . . hey, what are you looking at? Oh, man, this is embarrassing."

It was silly, but that was what I needed. I wasn't ready to take sex seriously. I just wanted to imagine a world where regular dudes occasionally forgot to wear pants. *Freshmen*, you'd found your newest fan.

Sixteen years later, I stood in a sex shop on Melrose Avenue. I didn't have to look hard to find the gay shelves here. There was bear porn, grandpa porn, weird fetishistic import porn. Glossy pro porn as polished and glam as the latest *Vanity Fair* and home-made porn zines that looked like they came off a dot-matrix printer in a cave somewhere in Idaho. All the oiled, throbbing dicks on display would have given twenty-one-year-old me a nervous breakdown.

The choices were virtually endless, but I decided to make my decision easy and picked up a *Freshmen*. I loved how easy it was to buy it this time. I just walked to the counter and paid. If the cashier had asked, I was prepared to shrug and say, "Yeah, I like cock. Do you validate parking?" But of course, that didn't happen. And this dude knew just where to find the price: $8.99.

A few days after that, I brought my purchase with me to the West-side Fertility Center, safely stored in a brown paper bag inside another bag inside a third bag, just in case. The receptionist seemed confused when Drew and I told her our names. She scanned her desk for our file, but it wasn't there.

So we dropped the secret password. Ahem. "We're with Rain-bow Extensions."

She groaned audibly. Clearly, she was familiar.

"Did they give you some paperwork to bring us?"

"No, they never mentioned . . ."

"Of course not," she sighed. "They never do. Well, you're going to need to call and have them fax it. I'm sorry."

I got S'mantha on the phone. "You're at Westside right now?" she asked, puzzled. "But I have your appointment down for tomorrow. Is that right?"

"Well, no. That's not right. We're here."

"Are you sure?"

"I'm sure we're here. I'm also pretty sure it's today. That's what you told us."

"Hold on. Lemme check." She dropped off the phone for a minute. "No, you're right. It's today. Is that what I said?"

"Yes. And I think they're going to take us, so that's not the problem. But they don't have our paperwork."

"Oh, that can't be right. I'm eighty percent sure I sent it over. Have them look again."

"Okay." I put my hand over the receiver for ten seconds and pretended I was having them look again. "No luck. Can you refax it?"

"I guess so. Oh, gosh. Where is it? Gimme a few minutes."

Drew and I sat in the waiting room, which was roughly the size of a middle school auditorium, with about thirty chairs arranged in rows. It was almost big enough to stage a touring production of *Les Miz*. But instead of head shots of whatever *American Idol* runner-up was playing Marius, the walls were covered with pictures of infants. Hundreds of them, smiling, sleeping, bathing. At the Westside Fertility Center, business—and babies—were booming.

There were single babies, twins, triplets, and quadruplets, but thank God, no Octomom. Some shots were in color, some black and white. There were probably at least a few taken by Annie Leibovitz as a family favor. Some had that slightly creepy smooshed-tush naked sitting shot. New parents and old ladies think this is cute. The rest of us wonder, Why would we want to see half your baby's ass?

I wondered if our family photo might someday grace this baby museum. Suddenly, Drew poked me and gestured toward the entrance. Two gay men had sauntered in, peering excitedly around the room. They jogged over to a thirty-ish Latina woman with the first stages of a baby bump. They presented her with flowers and cheek kisses. We realized we were looking at our future.

She was their surrogate, pregnant with their child. And she was Latina! It was the first time I'd considered that our surrogate might be a different race than we are, and I couldn't think of anything more awesome. I started picturing the day when our pasty white baby might emerge from a massively dilated African American vagina in a goopy testament to the miracles of modern science and the United Colors of Benetton.

At last, the receptionist called us over. "Okay, you can give your samples now."

It was go time. A nurse set me up in a plain, windowless room with a TV, a DVD player, and a little half bed, half couch that was covered in a surgical sheet to guard against mess.

She handed me a plastic cup. "When you're done," she said, "mark down the time you finished and circle yes or no to indicate whether you spilled any."

"Spilled any?"

"You know, your sperm."

She closed the door, and I locked it behind her.

Ewwwwwwwww.

I dug into my fortress of bags and unsheathed *Freshmen*. It was kind of exciting, like being back in college. I opened it up and saw a flashy new layout but models that looked pretty much the same. The baby-faced innocent, the jock, the ethnic, and the rebel. The only difference was that now the rebel had three tattoos. Ooh, his parents must be so pissed!

But as I flipped through the pages, I didn't get the same thrill as I did when I was in my early twenties. I wondered if it was all the college imagery, the messy desks, and the generic pennants on the walls that read, simply, "STATE." Maybe I needed scenarios more geared toward my current life stage. "Okay, I brought over that mortgage paperwork for you to sign . . . and Oops! I forgot my pants!" "I can get you three-point-nine percent APR on that Camry . . . and Oops! I forgot my pants!"

But it wasn't just the silly pretenses for the nudity. It was the eyes. Sweet, shy, pleading. The Freshmen seemed lost. Those adorable young faces reminded me of the boy I used to be, so innocent, so unsure. Even the rebel seemed like a nice kid, if he would just be a little more careful about what fell through the holes in his torn jeans. I didn't relate to these guys anymore, and seeing them naked only made me feel creepy. That's when I had an even spookier realization. This magazine was never intended for college kids just poking out of the closet. It was for dirty old men!

I wanted to talk to these boys, to encourage them to make better life choices, to protect them from the readers of this magazine. While I'd spent the last fifteen years growing up, they hadn't changed at all. I had morphed from Freshman to Man, and they were still too dumb to put on some fucking pants.

As disturbing as it was, there was something reassuring about my epiphany. Seeing *Freshmen* as a thirty-six-year-old hadn't been the turn-on I needed at that moment, but it did something even more important for me: It gave me a sneak preview of how it must feel to be a dad. If my kid ever posed for a magazine like that, I'd kill him.

6

THE WOMB OF STEEL

AMONG THE MANY USELESS TOPICS discussed in high school algebra that nonetheless stuck with me was the subject of imaginary numbers. An imaginary number is what you get when you try to take the square root of a negative, because such a number couldn't possibly exist. As Drew and I took our place on the waiting list for a surrogate, I learned a new imaginary number: $109,728. That was the estimated cost of having a baby with Rainbow Extensions. For an estimate, it sounded awfully precise. $109,728—or $109,731.46 if you stop for Starbucks.

There were no financing options, no coupons in the Sunday paper, no deals for free delivery. $109,728 was due in full, in advance—or no baby. Drew and I didn't have trust funds or stock portfolios or access to a ragtag team of professional thieves who could help us pull off some wicked casino heist. What we had was about $40,000 in the bank and a lot of blind optimism. We had originally earmarked that $40,000 for a down payment on a house, a new car, and a future, none of which we would ever have now.

The only other thing we had on our side was time—one year on the surrogate waiting list to amass the small fortune this baby would cost us. Luckily, our finances had taken a sudden unexpected uptick. Drew found a new job that paid him $1,000 more a week, and I got a promotion that grossed me an additional $500. I did the math, and if we put all that money aside, our imaginary number started to look astonishingly plausible. We still had a long way to go, but *la la la everything's going to work out la la la!*

One of the benefits of working with a surrogacy agency is that, as long as you can produce the money, they'll handle how to dispense it. We wouldn't need to fork over any direct payments to doctors, lawyers, or, God forbid, the surrogate. All we had to do was enjoy the wonder of creating life while S'mantha handled the icky financial stuff.

The problem was that we couldn't get S'mantha on the phone. The results from the sperm analysis were supposed to come in on a Tuesday, and she promised to call us the minute she had them in hand. We waited all day, but we never heard from her. On Wednesday morning, we left her a voice mail. We tried again on Thursday and Friday. We sent emails, but we never heard back. This was the woman we were going to entrust a six-figure sum to?

"Rainbow Extensions. How may I direct your call?"

"Hi, this is Jerry Mahoney. I haven't heard from my caseworker in a week now, and I'm a bit concerned."

"Who's your caseworker?"

"S'mantha."

"Oh." The receptionist sounded grim. It was an "oh" as in "Oh, you haven't heard?" The plot thickened.

She put me on hold. Then, someone else picked up. "Who are you holding for?"

"Well . . . S'mantha, I guess."

"Oh." This was an even graver "oh." It was an "I don't want to be the one to deal with this" "oh."

I went back on hold for what seemed like an eternity. I'd been to the Rainbow Extensions offices. It was basically one big room with about ten cubicles. I pictured the entire staff popping up like prairie dogs in a panic. "S'mantha call on line one!"

"I'm not answering it!"

"Not my turn!"

"They're still holding!"

"Someone needs to deal with this!"

"Anyone picked up line one yet?"

Then, finally. "Oh, Christ! I'll get it!"

A slightly annoyed voice came on the line. "Hello?"

"Yes, I'm calling about S'mantha."

"Is there something I can help you with?"

"Can you tell me where she is?"

"She's fine. What is it you need?"

"I need to know what happened to S'mantha!"

Drew was pacing frantically behind me as I spoke. "Are they not telling you? Give me the phone!" I waved him away.

"She's no longer with Rainbow Extensions," the voice said, sighing as if my tortuous interrogation had finally broken him.

"We kind of figured that out. Was she fired?"

"She was presented with a career opportunity she couldn't turn down." I laughed until I realized he wasn't intentionally quoting *The Godfather*. This seemed to be a legitimate Rainbow Extensions talking point.

"Why weren't we assigned another caseworker?" I asked. "We feel like we don't matter to Rainbow Extensions."

"What are your names again?"

About a week later, we received a call from a new woman, Linda. She sounded like she was about eighty years old, hard of hearing, and easily confused. She informed us she would be our interim caseworker until a permanent replacement could be found. Linda gave us a checklist of paperwork and phone consults we needed to complete. We diligently took care of all the outstanding issues, then called Linda to let her know.

She never called us back. She didn't return our emails. Her phone was always forwarded to voice mail. It was time to give Rainbow Extensions another call, but this time Drew insisted on doing the talking.

"THIS IS FUCKED UP!" he shouted. "This is the worst service I've ever dealt with! Don't you know how much we're paying you? We're entrusting you to help us have a baby, and people keep disappearing under mysterious circumstances."

"There's nothing mysterious about Linda's departure. She retired."

"Without notice? In the middle of the week? Bullshit!"

"That's what happened."

"Then why didn't she tell us she was retiring?"

"You'd have to ask Linda that."

"I'd love to . . . but I can't get her on the FUCKING PHONE!"

"Is there something you need?"

"Yeah, I need a supervisor. You're an idiot."

A few days later, a man named Maxwell called and introduced himself as our new caseworker. He seemed like a nice guy, but he had clearly drawn the short straw around the office if he had to deal with us. Our first phone call consisted of Drew lecturing him on the proper way to deal with clients and demanding that, if he decided to leave Rainbow Extensions, he had to let us know in writing, in advance, rather than by forwarding his phone to voice mail and never returning.

Over the next nine months, Drew and I built up our savings to around $80,000. I was finally starting to feel at ease with the price tag. We knew Rainbow Extensions might call any day with a surrogate for us, and $80,000 seemed within a comfortable stalling distance of the total.

One day, an email popped up in our in-boxes. "Great news, guys!" Maxwell began. The email included five attachments containing an encyclopedic summation of a human being named Kristen Lander. There was a psych clearance, a medical clearance, a financial accounting, her surrogate application, and a file marked "Photos." I opened that one first.

She was Caucasian, damn it.

Other than that, she seemed perfectly suited to carry our children. She was stocky and stern and, from the looks of her, could easily kick our asses. She had big blue eyes and a sarcastic smile that just dared you to mess with her. I imagined her voice being gruff and business-like. "Grrr! Baby goes here!" she'd grunt and point to her belly.

A few of the pictures showed her with her three adorable kids. One shot was of her and the twins she'd delivered in a previous surrogacy. There was also an image of her in a T-shirt that read, "Yes, I'm pregnant. No, they're not mine." A surrogate with a sense of humor? I was sold.

There aren't many instances in which you know everything about a person before you even meet them, but whatever the pictures didn't tell us, Kristin's application did. Her entire life unfolded in front of us as we read. She worked part-time as a human resources assistant. She was the bassist in a Bangles tribute band. She had a nose piercing and three butterfly tattoos.

Kristen's husband Paco was a boxy Latino man with large hoop earrings and a goatee. He worked for a moving company. We even saw how much money they made. Together, Kristin and Paco grossed $3,000 a month. The $25,000 surrogacy check would almost double their annual income.

There was nothing overtly gay-friendly about them on the surface, so it was a relief to see that Kristen's previous surrogacy had also been for a gay couple. I'd always wondered how our surrogate would cope with explaining the gayby in her belly. She'd constantly be answering questions, defending herself to homophobic family members and clergypeople. Having our kid meant opting into the world of homophobia Drew and I took for granted. As she wrote in her application, though, her previous pregnancy was a breeze. Everyone supported her, even her church. She welcomed the prospect of creating another gay family.

Best of all, Kristen's lady parts were at the top of their game. Her uterus was easier to get into than the University of Phoenix. All of her children had been conceived without much effort, carried full term, and delivered healthy. Her surrogate twins were born at thirty-seven weeks, impressive for a multiple birth. She was the perfect baby incubator.

She was the Womb of Steel.

Maxwell set up an appointment for us to meet Kristin on February 1. It was the five-year anniversary of the day Drew and I first met. It was kismet. We were building the perfect fairy tale to tell our future kid. We read Kristen's application about ten thousand times, memorized every bit of trivia. We would have killed on Kristen Lander Jeopardy.

"This was Kristen's course of study in college before dropping out."

"What is sign language?"

"This is the only medical condition Kristen checked 'Yes' to."

"What is hemorrhoids? Teehee!"

Maxwell asked us if we'd selected an egg donor yet.

"No."

"Oh." He sounded concerned. "You should do that before you meet with the surrogate."

"We were told we'd have plenty of time to do that after we met the surrogate."

"Oh no," he said. "Who told you that?"

"S'mantha."

"Who? Nobody by that name works here."

7

THE WOUNDED BIRD

I'D NEVER GIVEN MUCH THOUGHT to what my ideal woman would be. It had always been kind of a moot point. As I sat down at my computer to search the Rainbow Extensions egg donor database, I was confronted with a page full of check boxes. Hair color, eye color, height, weight, hobbies. All I had to do was map out Ms. Right and hit "Enter." I wouldn't even have to worry if she was out of my league. I could click on any picture and be confident that the stranger I was looking at would willingly entwine her DNA with mine. It was a straight guy's fantasy—and my worst nightmare.

Drew wanted nothing to do with it, so I offered to weed through the contenders and compile a short list. I hovered over my mouse. She should probably be tall, just to balance out my Smurf-like stature, should I be the sperm donor. She should be smart, happy, and fun. Her essay questions should be free of obvious grammatical and spelling errors. (No child of mine was going to inherit a disrespect for the language!) And I figured she should be at least kind of somewhat moderately physically appealing.

Of course, I had no idea what that meant. I'd spent my entire adolescence wondering what made women attractive, why certain ones made the cover of *Vogue* while others ladled Salisbury steak onto my Styrofoam lunch tray at school. The worst question one of my guy friends could ask me growing up was, "You think she's hot?" I knew the wrong answer would be tantamount to confessing, "No, but you are." But as hard as I tried, I couldn't tell what separated Chrissy from Janet—or, hell, even from Mrs. Roper. Betty versus Veronica, Ginger versus Mary Ann, Nancy Reagan versus Barbara Bush. I just didn't have a horse in the race, and it was so hard to pretend otherwise. It was such a relief when Julia Roberts came packaged with the title "Pretty Woman." It was like having the teacher's edition to the "You think she's hot?" textbook. "I'll tell you who's hot!" I could say with confidence. "That chick who played Tinkerbell in *Hook*!" High five!

It's not that I don't appreciate female beauty. I just think all women are Julia Robertses, the same way that all art is nice to look at, but please don't ask me to explain the deeper meaning behind those Jackson Pollock splotches.

As I stared at the search page, wondering how to make my own personal Kelly LeBrock materialize, I decided the best thing to do was just describe myself, only taller and with boobs. Brown hair, blue eyes, fair skin. I hit "Go," and the screen went nearly blank.

"0 hits," it read in tiny print. "Return to search page."

It turns out there was one big problem with finding the perfect woman: Rainbow Extensions had only sixty-six to choose from.

Their photos were taken by the agency's donor coordinator, poorly lit head shots all framed against the same drab blue wall. From the looks of things, it was a strictly one-take affair. These nervous young girls shuffled into an office and got shoved in a chair, and before they knew what they were doing, a flash went off in their face. There were no reshoots for crooked smiles or half-closed eyes. How they looked at their most vulnerable was exactly how I saw them.

For the most part, they were merely girls, some as young as nineteen. If Drew and I had been straight and foolish, we could have had a daughter this age by now. They had bad hair, freckles, and acne. They weren't chosen for their emotional preparedness to donate. They were chosen because their ovaries were clown cars cram packed with eggs. These were the women nature deemed most suitable to get pregnant, but if they actually came home knocked up, their parents would have been furious.

As I browsed their profiles, I felt like I was looking at the more sensible, slightly older sisters of the Freshmen. "Xander, I'm totally telling Mom and Dad about that magazine you posed for!" "Go ahead, Kaitlyn! I'll just tell them you're selling your eggs to gay dudes." Oh, Mom and Dad, if you'd just given Xander and Kaitlyn a bigger allowance, none of this would have happened!

If their photos weren't clear enough indicators of their youth, the essay questions drove the point home. They discussed their poli sci majors, their fondness for indie rock bands I'd never heard of, and, eyes wide with optimism, the corporations they'd be running in five years. They all loved "hanging out" and *One Tree Hill*. Every single one of them described their sense of humor as "random," like their generation had secretly convened and decided that "random" was a thing. Some wrote in that shorthand text speak that drives us thirty-somethings nuts. "Wood luv 2 help u."

Each profile came with a video. Almost without exception, they were like hostage videos. Nervous young girls uttering tightly rehearsed self-promotional pitches fed to them by the interviewer in front of that bare blue wall. "Hi, my name is X and I am Y years old and I go to the University of California at Z." "My personal interests include snowboarding and . . ." "I want to be an egg donor because . . ." Isn't this the generation that grew up with MySpace, reality TV confessionals, and sexting? Why were they all so webcam shy?

Dud, dud, dud. I was going through the sixty-six options so fast, I was afraid I would never find The One.

And then I saw her—Kellykins88.

It was love at first click. She was perfect years old, perfect feet tall, and a sophomore at UC Perfect. She had a bubbly voice and a hearty laugh. She had long blonde hair, oversized blue eyes, and a smile that withstood the requisite mention of her ovaries. For the last few years, she'd been volunteering with autistic kids at a local youth center. Now she dreamed of being a special education teacher. She spoke of herself assuredly but humbly. She was just a girl making a video for a boy, asking him to reproduce with her. She had me at "Do I look at the camera while I talk?"

Kellykins88 was the first candidate I could imagine telling our kid about someday. "We chose her because she was a good person," I'd explain. "Just like you."

When Drew got home, I dragged him to my laptop. "I've found her!" I squealed.

Drew took a deep breath and waited for me to pull up Kellykins88's profile.

"This is so weird," he said. "It's like I'm getting my first look at our kid!" He was right. It was one of those truly special, totally twenty-first-century moments I'd cherish forever.

"Ewwwwwwwwww!" Drew snarled. "Her?!"

His capsule review was not what I'd hoped for.

"What? She's hot! Isn't she?"

"She's Shrek-ish!"

"Just wait till you see her video. She's so sweet and charming and . . ."

"It talks?!"

"Oh, come on. She's not that bad."

Drew waved his hand. "Next!"

There was no point trying to convince him. If I sold him on someone he didn't like, then I'd always be the one who picked the crummy egg donor. Kid got a D in social studies? Drew could shrug and say, "Well, you picked the egg donor." No date for the prom? "Blame Daddy Jerry, sweetie. I preferred the cheerleader's eggs."

Drew wasn't any kinder to my list of alternates. "Buck teeth, twelve chins, walrus whiskers!" he moaned as he went through the options.

I fought for a few. "But Missy spends her school breaks distributing mosquito nets in Senegal!"

"Pfft! You sure that's a woman?"

I realized we were approaching this process completely differently. As a writer, I'm drawn to characters with intriguing quirks and heart-tugging back stories. But for Drew, who spent twelve years overseeing reality programming for MTV, this was just another casting session. If she wasn't good enough for *Date My Mom*, she wasn't good enough for us.

I'd never felt so shallow before, but then again, a certain amount of shallowness seemed necessary for the task at hand. If some physically flawed donor gave our son or daughter Spock ears or a cauliflower chin, the poor kid might never forgive us. It's not like I'm under the illusion that Drew and I have such pristine genes. All the more reason we needed someone above average to balance things out.

There had to be other options out there. I pleaded with Google for help: "egg donor tall smart pretty" . . . *I'm feeling lucky!*

0.11 seconds later, Google answered my prayers.

A company called Grade A Fertility promised eggs of a higher pedigree. Each listing boasted of the woman's SAT scores and alma mater. Almost every girl was an Ivy Leaguer, but if she went to a safety school like Tufts and she looked like a cast member from *Gossip Girl*, they let her squeak through.

Each head shot looked like a Neutrogena ad, a medium close-up of some fresh-from-the-salon stunner lounging on a jetty and staring wistfully into the sunset. The essays read like excerpts from *New Yorker* profiles of particularly fascinating individuals. Their credentials were impeccable. You got the feeling that the first through fifth female presidents were all listed on this Web page.

There was just one big catch: the cost.

The federal government recommends an $8,000 fee for egg donors. It seems like a fair amount of compensation for the time and discomfort required to donate eggs, and most companies, Rainbow Extensions included, charge exactly that. But it's merely a suggested retail price. It's not legally binding, and individual agencies are free to mark up as much as they choose. Only a few are ballsy enough to do so. Grade A was the ballsiest of all. Along with each woman's remarkable resume came an eye-popping price tag.

Heather graduated summa cum laude from Dartmouth. She was a Rhodes scholar and a second-year student at Harvard Business School. She was also blonde and blue-eyed and had an absolutely perfect figure. Price: $25,000.

Monica was a Junior at Princeton and a violin prodigy who'd played with the Pittsburgh Philharmonic at age ten. She got a perfect score on her SATs, spoke four languages, and translated ancient Greek poetry as a hobby. She bore a remarkable resemblance to the actress Scarlett Johansson. Price: $30,000.

Diane was tall with perfect bone structure and flawless skin. She was an editor of the *Yale Law Review* and had clerked for the Supreme Court. She was a member of MENSA and an alternate on the Olympic shotput team. Diane was African American. Price: $12,000.

Each listing boasted how many times that particular young woman had donated successfully. Heather had done nine transfers and was ready for number ten. This statistic was supposed to assure you she was up to the job, but it made Heather seem kind of easy. Like naming your kid Madison, having a Heather baby was a sure way of ensuring there were three other kids in the preschool class just like her. Growing up, we played shirts versus skins basketball. Kids today probably played Heather DNA versus non-Heather DNA.

Not that Heather cared. She'd earned almost a quarter of a million dollars passing on her genetic material to strangers. Unlike at Rainbow Extensions, there was no pretense that she was in this to help infertile couples. It was a get rich quick scheme, nothing more. You wondered why she even needed business school anymore. She'd struck gold with her genes. If she kept this up until she was thirty, she could retire comfortably and still have time left to make ten kids of her own.

Still, it was hard not to be sucked in by the stats. We all want our kids to have the best, and being beautiful and intelligent gives you a big head start in life. There are no guarantees that a Rhodes Scholar's eggs are going to make your kid smarter or that Scarlett Johansson's DNA will make your kid prettier than Kellykins88, but it sure couldn't hurt. This was possibly the most important decision we'd make about our child. How would we feel if we cheaped out and, as a result, our kid's dreams were always frustratingly shy of his reach?

Then again, did we really want a miniature reflection of stuck-up Heather's snotty little face gazing up at us from our Baby Björn? Who was she to think she was better than Kellykins88? If we used Heather's $25,000 eggs, we could just as easily be saddling our unborn child with the greed gene. And how would we explain it to him? "Your egg donor was top of the line, son. We got you, and she got a Porsche." Or, "We wanted you to be taller, but anything over five-foot-nine was out of our price range." Was that what we'd have to substitute for, "We picked your donor because she was a good person?"

We'd already made our peace with the ethical gray areas of surrogacy, but these so-called premium eggs were a minefield of moral dilemmas. It was like eugenics or something. No, it wasn't like eugenics. It was eugenics.

Even Drew was turned off by the idea. He would have killed to get any of these girls on *The Real World*, but he didn't want one as his daughter.

Plus, of course, we didn't have the money.

Grade A was out, and so was Rainbow Extensions. I wasn't sure we'd ever find someone who satisfied us.

"We should just ask Susie," I said one night, in frustration.

Drew's answer was not what I was expecting. "I've been thinking the same thing."

Susie was as close to the ideal woman as I could imagine. She was kind, beautiful, smart, a gifted artist, and, at twenty-eight, practically at the peak of her fertility. She was pretty enough for Drew and good-hearted enough for me. She was somebody we could proudly tell our kid about someday. She was what we dreamed of finding, and she was right under our noses. Susie was Drew's little sister.

Despite being nine years apart in age and on opposite sides of the country, Susie and Drew couldn't have been closer or more alike. They talked on the phone nearly every day, laughed at the same dirty jokes, had the same mercurial temper. Their mother was constantly remarking about how similar they were, how Susie made the same facial expressions Drew did, how she had the same attitude he did at her age, the same frustrations. They weren't just brother and sister. They were kindred souls—and best friends.

We thought of Susie as our princess because nobody deserved a fairy-tale life more than she did. Unfortunately, she seemed permanently trapped in the part of the story where she was stuck doing menial chores while everyone else went to the Prince's ball. Instead of scrubbing the castle floors, she was stocking shelves part time at Lord & Taylor. She liked having a position where she didn't have to think and where she could listen to her iPod all day. When she went home at night, it was to her childhood bedroom in her parents' house. She had a phobia about driving, so she walked miles back and forth to work, even in the harshest winter weather. She spent most nights at home because she simply couldn't get to wherever her friends were hanging out. Drew called her a wounded bird.

Susie was too proud to accept anyone's help. She turned down rides, job leads, cash, and gifts, just about anything that had the whiff of charity. But at the same time, she was outrageously generous in return. It was yet another way she resembled her brother. Each holiday season, she turned her family's attic into her own version of Santa's workshop, using her creative skills to make gorgeous gifts for everyone on her list. She once loaned a boyfriend thousands of dollars to buy furniture, money none of us even knew she had and which he flaked out on repaying after they broke up.

This was another running theme in Susie's life: loser boyfriends. Everyone in the family remembered the stoner who came over for dinner and sat down in the dining room barefoot. We all witnessed the pretentious jerk who ruined Christmas by mocking a painting she'd made for him. Her dating history was a who's who of Rochester's Least Wanted.

She was the kind of young woman parents worry about—She's so wonderful, why can't she meet a man worthy of her? Then, a year ago, it finally happened. Prince Charming breezed in from out of town and swept her off her feet. His name was Jack, and he was sweet, handsome, and loving. Susie was a perfect fit for his glass slipper, and he never treated her like less than his queen. Jack had the most family-friendly career imaginable: nature photographer. He got paid to fly around the country and take pictures of animals. His idea of a fun date was to take Susie bird watching.

To Drew's mom, who'd had their suburban backyard declared a wildlife preserve, he was better than a doctor or a lawyer. He was a nice man, who had arrived to rescue our wounded bird.

Susie and Jack talked about moving in together, and pretty soon, that became talk of moving away together. Jack wanted to go to Berkeley, on the other side of the country, to start a new life, just the two of them. It was exactly the Happily Ever After that Susie had been dreaming of.

They didn't like being away from each other, so when Jack went home to Iowa to visit his family, he promised to call every day. Her phone never rang. At first, Susie figured he was just busy catching up with old friends and spending quality time with his family. A day went by, then another. Jack didn't return Susie's voice mails or reply to her texts. She was heartbroken, terrified, and completely paralyzed. She didn't know how else to contact him. All she could do was wait.

Finally, an email arrived. It came from Jack's mailbox, but it was written by his father. He used Jack's cell phone to compose a message to everyone in his son's address book. The list of recipients went on for pages. Susie was as unknown to this man as any of these miscellaneous contacts. "To all those who knew my beloved son," it began. She couldn't bear to read further.

Instead, she looked up a phone number for Jack's best friend and frantically dialed him to find out what the hell had happened. It took all of Susie's strength just to keep the phone to her ear as he told her the story.

In Iowa, Jack had been hanging out with some of his old buddies from the neighborhood, guys he hadn't seen in years. They convinced him to partake in one of their favorite pastimes from back in the day: shooting heroin. Susie had no idea Jack used to be a junkie. It was the kind of detail someone might hide if they were enjoying the rush of a new love and trying desperately not to mess it up. Apparently, when he was using, Jack had built up quite a tolerance to the stuff and needed a really strong dose to get sufficiently high.

Nobody told Jack that, after you've been clean for a while, you can't go back to that same dosage. While his friends floated away to their happy place, Jack's body began to shut down. He O.D.'ed.

Susie's worst fear was confirmed: Prince Charming was dead.

Susie never suspected a trip back home could end in her boyfriend's funeral. She was stunned, furious, and heartbroken, all at once. She kept a tiny picture of Jack taped to a corkboard in her bedroom. He was standing in the woods, a camera bag slung over one shoulder, a weathered brown hat on his head, laughing. It reminded her of the way she knew him. Keeping it up was a necessary torture for her. The pain reminded her of the joy, and that was all she had left of the guy who was going to change her life. Months after Jack died, Susie still cried every day. All you had to do was ask her how she was doing, and she might tear up.

Years earlier, Susie had told Drew and me that she'd give us her eggs if we ever wanted them. She blurted it out casually, the way people say, "When I win the lottery, I'm going to buy you a house." It was natural, as we were searching for a donor, that her offer would spring to mind, but the timing just didn't seem right. How would the conversation go? "Hey, Susie, you know all that happiness you deserve and have been struggling so hard to find? Well, great news. We've figured out a way you can have it . . . and immediately give it away to us."

We knew exactly what would happen if we popped the question. Before we even finished asking, Susie would answer yes. Whatever Drew might need from her, she'd be happy to give. Her own emotions were secondary at best. She'd always been more interested in other people's happiness than her own. But was it really the right thing for her to do?

It was the night before our meeting with Kristen Lander that we finally forced ourselves to decide. To ask or not to ask.

"I'm leaning toward yes," I admitted, smiling nervously.

Drew sighed and closed his eyes, struggling with his conscience. "I've made up my mind," he said, finally. "I can't do it."

With that, the decision was made. Drew knew his sister, and I trusted his judgment. I dreaded the thought of returning to the online databases. Maybe I could think outside the box—place an ad on Craigslist, set up a "Men Seeking Egg Donor" blog. There had to be a solution.

All of that would have to wait, though, because we had a meeting to prepare for. We opened Kristen Lander's file for a quick refresher course on a woman we'd come face-to-face with in just a few hours.

8

HOW WE MET YOUR M-WORD

ON THE MORNING of my fifth anniversary with Drew, I woke up with a strange man in my bed.

"She's going to hate us! She's too perfect! Why are we doing this?"

He looked like Drew. He smelled like Drew smells in the morning. He was even wearing that pit-stained, torn-up English springer spaniel shirt Drew wore to bed every fucking night. But this was not the man I'd fallen in love with.

"I'm such an idiot! I've built my hopes up too high! We want this too much!"

Over the last five years, I'd seen Drew hit this level of panic a few times before. When we bought our condo. When he left MTV to start a new job. When he left that job to start another new job. He didn't handle major life changes well, and I'd made the mistake in the past of trying to talk him down. The best thing to do was to stay calm, agree with everything he said, and be the one thing in his life that's not aggravating the hell out of him. That was my surefire recipe for an anxiety exorcism.

The problem was, we didn't have much time. In four short hours, we would be face-to-face with the woman who might someday make us dads. So it was that we kicked off a milestone day in our relationship with a trip to couples counseling.

"What if she finds out we can barely afford this? What if she learns what a shitty school district we live in? Do you know Matthew Broderick and Sarah Jessica Parker are having a baby with a surrogate? Why would anyone pick us, when they could have a celebrity baby?" Drew clutched his hands so tightly around a throw pillow that I was sure I was about to get hit with flying goose feathers.

Thankfully, this was Mindy Stanhope, M.A., we were talking to, the woman who gleefully declared the first time we met her, "You guys are awesome!" She listened patiently while Drew voiced his ten bajillion fears, not at all concerned for her upholstery.

"I can't do this. Let's adopt! Let's just be uncles! Why are we having kids at all? I'm not sure I believe gays should have kids. There, I said it!"

"How much do you know about her?" Mindy asked, calmly.

"Everything! It's all on her application!"

"And don't you think she learned a lot about you from your application?"

Drew shrugged. "I don't know. He filled it out."

As Mindy tamed Drew's demons, I zoned out. I had too much on my own mind, like wondering if we'd get to meet Matthew Broderick and Sarah Jessica Parker at the Rainbow Extensions family picnic. That would be so cool.

By the end of the fifty minutes, Mindy had worked her magic. Drew was back to his old self, still nervous but ready to turn on the charm and win Kristen over.

On our way out the door, Mindy wished us luck, then scooted back to her desk, giggling. "One more thing, guys!" she squeaked.

She handed us a box of fancy chocolates, wrapped beautifully with a decorative bow. "Happy anniversary!" she beamed.

I threw my arms around Mindy and squeezed her tiny frame. It was so generous, so thoughtful. It was the edible equivalent of, "You guys are awesome!" For the first time in therapy, I almost cried—and I started to wonder: Had we overlooked the most obvious egg donor of all? It seemed so unethical, but if a therapist could gift us with candy, why not an ovum or two? I had to shake myself out of it. This wonderful woman had done something nice for us, and here I was mentally fertilizing her with my eyes. What had I become?

Drew and I shook our heads as we got into the elevator. "That was so sweet of Mindy," Drew said.

"The sweetest."

"I just fucking love her."

I looked down at the box. No one had ever given me fancy chocolates before, and I never knew how happy it could make me feel.

"How'd ya know I's a chocaholic?" Kristen warbled, as I handed her the box in the conference room of Rainbow Extensions. She tore the ribbon off and started poking around inside with her index finger. "Any rum nuggets in here?"

We had just sat down in the Rainbow Extensions conference room. Kristen looked just like her pictures, only less smiley, slightly thinner, and her mouth less perfectly formed to say, "Cheese."

She sat beside her husband, Paco, who slumped so far backward in his chair he was practically using it as a bed. He said hello with a barely perceptible nod of the head and a rhino-like grumble. He steadfastly refused to get up, as if to let the gay guys know there would be no hugging whatsoever.

Oh, poor Paco. He didn't know the effect Drew and I had on people. Maybe Kristen's previous gays had bought into his baller act, but we were going to scoop out the teddy bear that was surely lurking below the surface and make him love us. In a few months, every visit with us would be a hug-a-palooza. By the time our baby was born, we'd be the guests of honor at his familia fiestas, where his relatives fly up from Mexico just for a taste of his famous homemade hot sauce. "Viva Drew y Jerry!" they'd all shout as they raised their glasses of Tecate and spiked horchata.

Sure, sit on your hands now, Paco. I know where this is headed.

Our caseworker Maxwell glanced down at a clipboard, which contained detailed instructions on how he was supposed to conduct this meeting. "Kristen," he said, resting his finger on item number 1. "Tell us why you decided to become a surrogate."

Kristen shrugged. "I like havin' babies. I'm good at it." There was a slight pause and then, "I know how happy it'll make 'em." She motioned toward us to indicate who she meant by "'em."

Then it was our turn. "Drew and Jerry, why do you want to be parents?"

That was the question, at least. All Drew heard was, "You can talk now."

"First of all, thank you for driving up here from San Diego to meet us," he began. "I know the 405 is hell at this hour. I'm just blown away thinking about what's brought us together today. I mean, did you ever think you'd be driving up to Los Angeles to have a baby for a couple of gays? Paco, are you the husband of the year or what?"

Maxwell cut him off. "Guys, we have a lot to cover in this meeting."

Drew just kept yapping. "By the way, your kids are gorgeous. Okay, what grades are they in, starting with Joshua?"

Maxwell glanced at the clock. "We usually suggest that everyone go out afterward to get to know each other better. This meeting is primarily intended to discuss the implications of . . ."

Kristen cut him off, assuring Drew, "We'll talk at lunch."

I realized Drew never addressed Maxwell's original question, about why we wanted to be parents. "I'm terrified of kids," I confessed. I immediately realized that was probably not the best way to start, but it got everyone's attention. "What I mean is, the way people get tongue-tied when they meet a celebrity, I sometimes get that way with kids, because everything we take for granted is something new and amazing for them. I'm so impressed by the things kids do. I think, 'Wow! He knows all the Pokemons!' or 'She can count to ten in Spanish!' You know how a kid at the playground will say, 'Mommy, watch this!' and then they hang upside down from the monkey bars or something? And the mom doesn't even look up from talking to her friend or sending a text? I'm sitting there thinking, 'That's awesome! Do it again!' I told myself when I have a kid, I'm always going to watch them on the monkey bars.

"But Drew—you should see him with kids. I've never met anyone as good with kids as him. He gets them. It doesn't matter how old they are, whether they're shy or outgoing, geeks or jocks, he knows just what to say, just how to make them laugh. Put him in a room with a kid, and he'll be their best friend within thirty seconds. I don't know how he does it. But any little boy or girl who has Drew as a dad is going to be the luckiest kid in the world. He needs to be a dad, and I need to be a dad with him because I wouldn't want to do it with anyone else."

Drew clutched my hand tightly. Kristen smiled. Maxwell made a check mark on his clipboard. "Okay, next question."

I soon realized we'd just been asked the only two icebreakers on Maxwell's list. The meeting then took an immediate and very dark turn. The real purpose of this introductory session was to make sure the surrogate and the intended parents were all on the same page regarding any issues that may arise during the pregnancy. What if the fetus tests positive for a genetic disease? What if there are birth defects? Down syndrome? What tests would we be willing to perform, and what actions would we be willing to take?

They were just hypotheticals, but we needed to provide definitive answers. The only thing worse than learning your fetus had health issues would be to find out your surrogate had different views on how to handle them. Every decision parents face in only the worst-case scenario we had to make up front.

It was terrifying—to us, at least. Kristen had been through a meeting just like this the last time she'd been a surrogate, so she was quick with her answers.

"No, no, oh yeah, yeah, I don't care, fine, whatever, you bet, it's the IPs' decision."

"IPs?" I asked.

"Intended parents," she muttered. "That's you." She laughed. "Forgot you're first-timers." Nothing phased her—until we got to the subject of multiples.

"I'm not havin' triplets!" she barked. "Twins, okay, because it's not mandatory bed rest. But triplets is mandatory bed rest, and I'm not goin' on bed rest, so I'm not havin' triplets."

It was the most we'd heard come out of her mouth since we met her, and we soon learned why.

Kristen's last surrogacy had begun with three embryos successfully attaching to the wall of her uterus. Out of a mutual agreement with the intended parents, she underwent a process called "selective reduction," in which one of the implanted embryos was unimplanted. So it came to pass that she gave birth to twins.

The procedure was painful physically and emotionally, but as much as she wanted to avoid going through it again, it was preferable to the alternative. "I'm not havin' triplets!"

Kristen's aversion wasn't just a matter of comfort. We'd been warned about the risks of higher-order multiples ever since signing with Rainbow Extensions. Having three fetuses greatly increases the chance of extremely premature delivery, cerebral palsy, breathing problems, low birth weight, and a host of other complications. The Rainbow Extensions insurance company refused to cover pregnancies involving more than two fetuses. If you took the risk of triplets, you were on your own.

It was hard not to think about parents who chose to have even more than three kids at one time. Didn't anyone warn them they were playing Russian roulette with their uterus? We had to agree with Kristen. Two fetuses, tops.

On the other questions, we deferred to what we came to consider the Golden Rule of IPs: our fetus, our choice; her body, her choice. If a doctor recommended an amnio, that was about the health of the fetus, so we'd want Kristen to comply. But when Maxwell asked us how we felt about epidurals, we didn't hesitate. "She can have all the drugs she wants."

We were well aware of the controversy surrounding epidurals and how the neonatal Nazis come out and judge you if you dare to get one. But we were men. We could only imagine what the pain of delivering a baby was like, and if sitcoms were any indication, it was hilariously extreme. Who were we to force a woman to undergo the maximum agony of childbirth because we'd read a few articles in *Newsweek*? Allowing our surrogate an epidural if she so desired seemed like the feminist thing to do.

Unfortunately, the Golden Rule didn't always apply so neatly. There was one topic in particular that rested directly at the awkward intersection between Kristen's body and our fetus, and it was a biggie. Abortion. No one actually said the A-word, of course, but we recognized its euphemisms, like "termination" and "selective reduction."

Drew and I are both pro-choice, but that's easy to say when you know you'll never have to make the choice yourself. We were gay men. What were the odds we'd ever be faced with an unwanted pregnancy? Surrogacy would allow us into a woman's body and give us a say in how she handled it. The thought of telling her to terminate a pregnancy made me queasy.

Maxwell ran down his list of nightmare scenarios, asking us over and over to make the choice that's fueled a thousand court decisions. When is a life no longer worth living? What risks are we willing to take with our child's well-being? When would we decide what this woman should do with her body?

I don't know! I just want a healthy baby!

We'd gone in expecting a friendly meet-and-greet, but it turned out to be the most emotionally draining hour of my life. Drew and I were practically shaking. In just under sixty minutes, we'd mourned our hypothetical fetus dozens of times. But through it all, Kristen never cracked. She was so professional about everything, so straightforward and confident in her choices. As we left the room, we thanked her for helping us stay calm. She just shrugged. "It's all the same questions from last time."

Our next stop was lunch. The place we picked was exactly the place the last guys had taken her the first time they'd met. Kristen remembered it well and didn't even need a menu. "I'm stickin' with the tuna salad," she bellowed. "It's pretty good."

As her iced tea arrived, Kristen noticed we were still reeling from the barrage of nightmare scenarios, so she shook her head and laughed. "None of that shit's gonna happen, guys," she said. "Can ya pass the Splenda?"

Pretty soon, we'd managed to lock the meeting away in our memory dungeons. There was important business at hand, namely, getting to know the woman who would change our lives.

Drew barraged Kristen and Paco with questions. "What are your kids like?" "What do you do for fun?" "Have you been to Legoland?"

Kristen handled it just like she had the meeting. Calmly, methodically, using the bare minimum of words required to answer. There were a few things she loved in life. She loved Paco, who she described as warm, sensitive, and so much nicer than her previous husband. She loved to hit the clubs. "I'm a dancer!" she declared and waved her hands over her head.

But most of all, she loved her kids. Being a surrogate allowed her to stay home and raise them, which made it the best job in the world. She loved her surro-kids, too. They lived up here in L.A., so while she was here, she planned to swing by and see them. She pulled a picture up on her phone. "The one dad's Japanese," she said, as if their ethnicity needed explaining. "They used a Japanese egg donor so the kids'd be half Asian."

Drew nodded. "Half Asian babies are gorgeous, aren't they?"

Kristen was very active in the surrogate community. She was a fixture on message boards, frequently offering advice to "the other girls." That morning, she'd logged on, and all her surrogate friends had sent her encouraging messages for this meeting. She stressed to us how she couldn't wait to be pregnant again. She was hoping to get started right away.

"That's so sweet," we told her.

It turned out there was a special reason for her rush. "Only got two more years 'fore I'm too old, and I wanna have two more babies." We hadn't realized it until then, but Rainbow Extensions had an upper age limit for surrogates. Once you turned thirty-eight, you were forced into retirement. Kristen's surrological clock was ticking.

We tried to include Paco in the conversation, but for the most part, Kristen answered his questions for him. Drew would say something like, "How do you like your job, Paco?" Paco would shrug and grunt, then nod his head toward Kristen. She'd swallow whatever was in her mouth and say, "Pays the bills." It became clear that this wasn't some act Paco was putting on to intimidate us. He was extremely shy and awkward, and he believed fully in Kristen's ability to handle the conversation for both of them. Paco was like the me of their relationship.

I could picture us taking a kind of secondary family portrait that included them so that our kid would always know how he or she came into the world. We'd do it every year on their birthday, when Kristen's kids would mingle with ours in a bounce house in our backyard. By year three, Paco might even put his arm around us.

We were getting ready to pay the bill, when Kristen asked the only question she had for us. "What's your egg donor like?"

Drew and I glanced at each other nervously.

"We're still finalizing our decision," I said, diplomatically.

Kristen seemed concerned. "Ya don't have a donor?"

"It's the agency's fault," I assured her. "They told us we didn't need one until after we found a surrogate."

"They only gave us access to their database a week ago," Drew added.

Kristen leaned in and lowered her voice. "Don't tell anyone I said this," she whispered, gazing over her shoulder as if someone might be listening in. "But you gotta watch 'em."

"Who?"

"Rainbow. Watch 'em close. Watch 'em real close."

It was serious and a little chilling, like we were in a bad spy movie. What was she talking about?

"Let's say they got a habit of double billin' ya for stuff."

"Did they do that?"

"I'm just sayin', check yer invoices. I don't think they do it on purpose. They're just kinda . . ."

Drew nodded. "Total fucking morons?"

"HA, HA, HA!" We all glanced over at Paco, who was actually laughing. Loudly. Oh, Paco. I knew we'd break through.

Drew turned back to Kristen. "I feel like I can really trust you," he said. "So I'm going to tell you something we haven't told the agency yet. We're thinking about asking my sister to be the egg donor."

I didn't know if Drew was serious or just stalling. I thought we had taken Susie off the table.

"We just need a week or two," I assured Kristen. "We'll have it all sorted out."

Kristen nodded and slurped the last of her iced tea.

9

MORE THAN AN AUNT, LESS THAN A MOM

"**F**UCK KRISTIN LANDER! Fuck her and fuck her husband and fuck her fucking womb!"

Drew was on the phone with his mom.

"You know what she is?" he shouted. "A piece of trash!"

Kristen dumped us.

It was Monday morning, and Maxwell had just dropped the bomb. The Womb of Steel had spent the weekend on the surrogate message boards, and all her cyber friends told us that Drew and I were IP poison. Their concern was the same as hers: our lack of an egg donor. They warned Kristen that we could keep her uterus locked in limbo for six months or more while we flailed about for our personal vision of perfection. If she moved forward with us, she could forget about her goal of getting pregnant two more times before she turned thirty-eight.

All of that we could understand. But what really upset Drew was that Kristen had betrayed our confidence.

"She said something about one of your sisters possibly being an egg donor?" Maxwell asked.

Drew snarled. "I told her that was private information!"

"Well, if you could lock her in fast, you might get Kristen to reconsider."

When we got off the phone, I delicately raised the topic. "Should we think about asking Susie? We don't want to lose Kristen."

Drew was furious. "I wouldn't let her have a baby for us if she paid us a hundred million dollars!"

It was an odd choice of words, given that Kristen had just turned us down on terms that were considerably more favorable to her. But I got it. Drew had already moved on from denial to rage. It was time for me to join in the fun of the Kristen Pile-On.

Drew: "I'm going to tell Rainbow Extensions she's been trash talking them."

Me: "Yeah, and tell them to stop double billing!"

Drew: "Can you imagine having to break it to our kid someday that he came out of that wench? She's disgusting."

Me: "What does Paco see in her?"

Drew: "Did you notice they didn't even offer to chip in for lunch? I mean, of course, we were going to pay, but they could've offered."

Me: "They didn't even say thank you."

Drew: "They're assholes."

Me: "They're rude!"

Drew: "I'm sending her a bill! I want that $40 back!"

"I want those chocolates back!" I shouted. "Those were an anniversary gift from Mindy!"

Drew's mom took the news pretty hard. Well, not as hard as Drew.

"Fuck fuck fuck fuck fuck!" he screamed into the phone. "I love you, Mom." And he hung up.

Less than a minute later, his phone rang again.

"Hello?"

"You know you can have my eggs if you want them, right?"

"What?"

It was Susie. "I said you can have my eggs if you want them."

It was that swift, that casual. Something we'd quietly debated for months she blurted out in an instant. "You can have my eggs if you want them," as if she were offering to loan us her hair dryer or Ani DiFranco CDs rather than a part of her womanhood.

"I have to go. I'll call you later." Drew hung up, stunned.

Only a few minutes later, an email arrived. "I was serious about supplying eggs," Susie wrote. "And it would be a matter of me handing the eggs over and washing my hands of the situation. And if for some reason the kid turns out unattractive, we could blame that cunty egg donor that nobody knows."

Among the many things Susie shared with her older brother was a tremendously foul mouth.

Her offer changed everything. Our fear was that if we asked her, she would have felt pressured to say "Yes." Now she was kicking off the conversation with "Yes."

We were equal parts excited and terrified. Was this really in Susie's best interest? Thankfully, we knew one person who could help us sort this out, someone who had counseled egg donors before, who knew all the issues that might arise and could help talk Susie and us through this enormous decision. We made an appointment with Mindy, and within minutes, Susie had booked her plane ticket.

"You're fuckin' with me!"

This was yet another Tappon, Drew's brother Peter. We had him on speakerphone so we could share the good news.

"No, seriously, Susie's going to donate her eggs," Drew explained. "Jerry would obviously donate his sperm, so the kid will be a bit Tappon and a bit Mahoney. It's kind of exciting."

"You're fuckin' with me!"

We realized Peter wasn't being playful. Drew took the call off speaker.

"Peter, I'm serious. Susie offered us her eggs, and we said yes."

"You can't do that!" Peter shouted. "That's fucked up! Seriously. Fucked! Up!"

Drew ended the call, shaken. His little brother's opinion meant a lot to him.

The Tappons were an unusual family, to be sure. Drew was gay. His younger brother Matt was gay. Susie was a free-spirited college dropout. Peter was the straight man, in every sense. A good, hardworking heterosexual and a productive member of the community, he was the white sheep of the family.

Peter knew a lot about families. He was a social worker in Philadelphia. When he explained his job, you could see the pride he felt. He was one of the good guys. The government would come in and take kids away from their parents. His agency helped the parents get their shit together so they could resume custody, under the philosophy that the best place for a kid was with his own family. Peter had dedicated his life to helping families stay together.

Now he was telling us that our hypothetical kid deserved better than we were offering.

It certainly didn't come from homophobia. Peter had earned his cred all through adolescence, when he was constantly forced to defend his gay brothers to his tough-guy buddies. He was fully behind us becoming dads, and he was excited to be an uncle. But our plan to use Susie's eggs struck him as incestuous and weird. I'd never heard him this worked up before.

If Drew's own brother felt this way, surely strangers would, too. Our family was going to be unusual enough with two dads, and now we were heaping on an extra helping of odd. It's like if the Addams Family also did Civil War reenactments. You'd want someone to step in and tell them they were overdoing it in the creepy department.

Would everyone we met secretly be thinking, "That's fucked up"? Would people look at our kid with pity, or derision? "You aunt's your mom, huh? Sucks to be you!" Would our own kid resent us for the choices that led to his birth? Would she feel like an outcast forever?

We'd allowed ourselves to get so excited. Now we were having major doubts again, and Susie was on her way to see us.

Whenever Susie would visit, it was like summer vacation from school plus Christmas multiplied by puppies to the power of Disneyland. It was easily the thing Drew and I looked forward to the most all year—and we usually only got one Susie visit a year, so we did our best to cram 365 days of bonding into a week or so. Drew would take time off work. We'd play Wii and go shopping and see Harry Potter movies with large popcorns and extra, extra large drinks. We'd go to all our favorite restaurants, show Susie off to all our closest friends. Drew was never happier than when he was with his little sis.

We were determined to make this just like any other Susie visit, but Rainbow Extensions had their own plans. They set up a meeting to put Susie through their standard screening procedures. While she was there, they subjected her to a battery of psychological exams—even, against our wishes, an IQ test. They gave her a contract to sign, which said, in legalese, about a hundred different ways, that she would have no rights over any fetus created from her donated eggs. She couldn't come anywhere near the baby without our express permission. The language was far harsher than anything we would have allowed if they had shown it to us first, but Susie signed it.

Things went smoother at Westside Fertility. We were eager for Susie to meet the head physician, a jovial middle-aged man named Dr. Saroyan, whom we'd grown especially fond of. We admired his honesty and his expertise. Drew and I waited while he gave Susie an ultrasound, and then he sat the three of us down to share the results.

"Your ovaries are perfect," he began. "You have beautiful, beautiful follicles. You are perfectly ready to make babies, but are you sure you want to do it for these guys?"

One other thing we loved about Dr. Saroyan was his dickish sense of humor.

"I mean, you could do a lot better than them," he went on.

"Yeah, but he's my brother," Susie played along. "I kind of have to."

With a plaster replica of the female reproductive system and a tiny wand, Dr. S explained to Susie exactly what she was signing up for. Every month, a fertile woman produces dozens of eggs from her follicles. Typically, only one of these eggs will become viable. All these budding eggs duke it out, until one becomes so dominant that it absorbs all the others. That egg gets sent to the uterus for possible fertilization. This was sounding less like what I'd learned in high school health class and more like an ovarian cage match.

In vitro intervened at the point in the process before any one egg could be crowned champion. All the egglings were nurtured and allowed to grow to the point of viability. Typically, Dr. Saroyan would harvest upwards of thirty eggs from a single cycle. Then we'd stir in my 107 million sperm and hope to get a dozen or so fertilized embryos. Of those, we'd take the healthiest one or two and transfer them to our surrogate.

To get all those eggs, Susie would have to take hormones. A lot of them. And they had to be injected. By her. In her butt. The side effects could include nausea, abdominal pain, and general moodiness.

"How bad are the injections?" I asked.

"I've never had anyone drop out because of the drugs," Dr. S assured. "But it's a pain in the ass."

Susie only had one question herself: "When do we start?"

Dr. S smiled, then he leaned in for a rare moment of seriousness. "What you're doing for your brother is a beautiful thing, Susan, and you are a clearly very special person. I'm going to take good care of you."

While Susie was at the fertility clinic, a nurse took a blood sample to test for genetic diseases. The only hurdle left was making sure Susie and I weren't predisposed to any of the same horrendous maladies.

Well, there was one other hurdle, too—Mindy.

"So what do you expect out of this arrangement?"

Susie shifted in her seat across from Mindy. "I just want to make my brothers happy."

I was kind of hoping when Mindy met Susie that she'd jump up and shout, "She's awesome!" like she did with us, but clearly, it wasn't going to be that easy, even if Susie was prepped for all the standard questions. She'd talked so much about donating her eggs this week that she stayed composed and confident through even the toughest queries.

"It'll be their kid, not mine."

"I'm not ready to have a kid. But I'm ready to be an aunt."

"Because I love them. They're my brothers."

Susie aced the interrogation, but Mindy was suspicious. She started digging deeper.

"Why is it you never learned to drive?"

"I guess I just don't want to grow up," Susie confessed.

"Really? Because this is a very grown-up thing you're doing for Drew and Jerry."

Pretty soon after that, the Kleenex came out. We talked about Jack a little, but mostly we talked about Susie. Her life and her dreams. Her pride and her sadness. Her desires and her demons. I was so impressed with how she handled herself—and so nervous about the decision we were making.

Mindy had the right idea. If we wanted to be sure Susie was doing the right thing, we had to play hardball.

"We're going to need boundaries," I said, "and we should talk about them. Susie will be more than an aunt but less than a mom. I love you, Susie, but if we have this kid, you're going to have to watch us make a lot of mistakes and know that you don't get a say in it. We'll decide where he goes to school, what she wears, whether we circumcise, how to discipline, what to buy them for Christmas, all the billion decisions parents have to make. And you're not going to like everything we do. We'll probably screw this kid up a million different ways, but they'll be our million ways."

All I wanted was for Mindy to give us her thumbs-up, but as the clock ticked away and our session came to an end, she conspicuously avoided saying "yes." She didn't say "no," either, which was just as frustrating.

What she said was that it would be complicated. Forever. We were entering into a gray area. Like Rainbow Extensions had told us, we were pioneers. Sometimes, pioneers got lost.

On our way home from the appointment, we were more con-fused than ever. That's when Peter called—for Susie. They talked for a long time. He asked her questions even tougher than the ones Mindy had asked. He knew just what to say because he knew Susie so well. She cried some more. And gradually, Peter came to under-stand. He'd grown up in an unusual family himself, and he loved them all dearly. He would get used to our unusual family, too.

Peter let Drew know that his opinion had changed. "I think what you're doing is pretty cool," he said. "I'm really happy for all of you."

I realized that other people might share Peter's initial response. There would always be strangers who would think we were a bit fucked up. But that didn't mean we shouldn't proceed. It just meant we'd have to educate people, to show them what a functional family we had and demonstrate that our family, like any other, was built out of love.

For Susie, nothing had changed. She had made up her mind, and she was going to help her brothers. Drew and I decided we were ready as well. We were going to make a baby with Susie.

It was time to hitch up the wagon and head into uncharted territory.

10

WHAT'S-HER-WOMB

SUSIE FLEW HOME. It had been an emotionally raw week, full of tears, laughs, and the kind of squinty-eyed, staccato wheezing that's hard to identify at first but that usually ends up being tears. We had discussed every aspect of Susie's home life, her work life—and, with toe-curling awkwardness, her sex life. In meetings with doctors and shrinks, I learned everything I never wanted to know about Drew's little sister and was terrified somebody might ask. I heard about her ovaries, her hormones, and the glorious womanly flow of her menstrual cycle, all the murky female potpourri being gay was supposed to exempt me from. I listened as the doctor described how he planned to retrieve the eggs by lubricating a rubberized wand and inserting it gently into her—okay, I couldn't handle any more. This wasn't how I'd expected making a baby would be. It was all so intimate.

Thankfully, we could put that behind us now and start imagining what our baby might look like. A little kid who was biologically related to both Drew and me. The possibilities fascinated me. Would she be tall like a Tappon or mousy like a Mahoney?

Would he have Drew's handsome brown eyes and warm smile or my cowlicks and swirling freckle patches? How would our unique features merge into one warbling little miracle?

Project Infant had evolved. For the first time, we could imagine having a kid with roots in both our family trees. We could hold up our own baby pictures and marvel at the resemblance. The feeling was overwhelming, a mixture of euphoria, curiosity, and more than a little narcissism. It was a feeling, we realized, that straight couples experience all the time.

Choosing our egg donor was a major step for sure, but thanks to Kristen Lander, we were still in a holding pattern. There was no way Susie could carry the baby for us. That was just too complicated, too emotional, and besides, she wasn't interested in being knocked up. So we were back to womb hunting. The excitement of making our huge decision was muted by the reality that we were still missing a gigantic piece of the puzzle. Even with three adults ready to make a baby, we remained one short.

My mind wandered to Kristen. For all I knew, she regretted dumping us. Maybe she thought about us every day, stared at our application photos, and pined for our embryos, ever more convinced she'd passed up on her Messrs. Right.

The solution was obvious: crawl back to her in tears, a broken man begging for a second chance.

"But we've chaaaaaaanged!" I'd wail. "We have an egg donor now. C'mon, baby! It'll be different this time!" Maybe I'd hold up a boom box on her front porch or rush to intercept her in an airport, something bold and psychotic like in a romantic comedy.

It could work. I knew it could. But just to make sure, I did what any snubbed ex would do: I cyber-stalked her. Using an assumed identity, I logged onto a surrogate message board that I knew Kristen frequented. Yes, it had come to that.

And there it was, at the top of the screen. An item titled "Finally matched!" Kristen bragged to her surro-friends that she'd found the world's greatest IPs and was prepping for her embryo transfer.

It was too late. She'd moved on. If I was a spurned ex-boyfriend, then I had just read the love of my life's wedding announcement.

Then came the worst part, Kristen's sign-off: "I'm so excited to be working with guys that have their act together." Aw, so she was still thinking about us.

Maxwell from Rainbow Extensions had more bad news. Susie's blood tests were in, and it turned out she was a carrier for Tay-Sachs disease, a gruesome genetic affliction whose sufferers had a typical life expectancy of four. My blood would now be tested, and if I was also a carrier, that meant no baby with Susie.

Maxwell told me not to worry, that Tay-Sachs wasn't common among people of Irish ancestry, like me. He actually seemed to know what he was talking about. He was thoughtful and empathetic. Maybe Rainbow Extensions finally got their act together.

Maxwell promised to call me with the test results in two weeks. When I didn't hear from him, I started to worry.

"Rainbow Extensions. How may I direct your call?"

"Yes, can I speak to Maxwell please?"

"Who?"

"Maxwell."

"Maxwell who?"

Oh, shit. Was this really happening again?

"Maxwell Denver, my caseworker. Is he there?"

"I'm sorry. He no longer works here."

This couldn't really be happening. For a moment, I wondered whether this entire episode of my life was a prank, someone's elaborate revenge on me for Fu-Ling. Maybe Rainbow Extensions was an accounting firm my friends converted into a surrogacy agency during the boss's lunch break. Maybe the actress portraying "Kristen Lander" had a hard time keeping a straight face during our "meeting." Maybe I was being *Truman Show*'ed. It seemed more plausible than the next most likely theory, that Rainbow Extensions was run by the absolute dumbest people on Earth.

Eventually, I got someone on the phone who explained why Maxwell had left. It seems the upper management had finally realized that a shake-up was in order, so they were moving their corporate headquarters away from the L.A. office and asking all their caseworkers to relocate. And where had this gay surrogacy agency decided they could operate most efficiently?

Alabama.

Maxwell refused to move there, probably because he was gay himself and probably because it was insane. But that left me with a big question.

"So who's our new caseworker?"

"You won't be assigned a new caseworker until you're matched with a surrogate. Until then, you'll have the same caseworker."

"But you just told me our caseworker is gone."

"Well, you're kind of in between stages, so I think you're going to have to wait until you're matched to be assigned somebody new."

It was frustrating, but I'd almost forgotten the reason I called. "Can you tell me the results of my blood test? I need to know that I'm not a carrier for Tay-Sachs, or we'll need a new egg donor."

"I'm sorry. Only caseworkers are supposed to give out that kind of information."

Yes, without a doubt, Rainbow Extensions was full of idiots. "I don't have a caseworker!" I shouted.

"Well . . . I guess it's okay." She put me on hold for a minute. When she returned, her voice was grim.

"Mr. Mahoney. I have some bad news. You tested positive."

"What? Are you serious?"

"I'm afraid so. You're a carrier for cystic fibrosis."

"What?"

"It's very common among the Irish."

"I wasn't calling about cystic fibrosis."

"It's okay. As long as your egg donor doesn't also carry it, you're fine."

"She doesn't have that. She has Tay-Sachs!"

"Oh, well then you should get tested for that."

"I did! That's why I'm calling."

"Oh. It must be negative or it would say here. I'll have your caseworker look into it."

I hung up the phone.

I didn't hear much from Rainbow Extensions for the next couple of months. Not only were we in caseworker limbo, but we were three thousand miles and two time zones away from their new main office.

When we did manage to speak to someone, they assured us we were on the waiting list for both a surrogate and a caseworker and that an appropriate person would call us at an appropriate time. Until then, we should just go away.

So I decided I would go away.

To Iceland.

Everyone tells you when you're having kids to do all the things you won't be able to do once you're up to your neck in bibs and butt cream: dine in nice restaurants, see movies, hit the beach in Cabo. So I made an inventory of goals I wanted to accomplish before becoming a dad, a baby bucket list. And at number 1 was Iceland.

A few years earlier, I had been looking for an exotic setting for a screenplay I was writing. The more I learned about Iceland, the more perfect it seemed, not just for my story but for me. It was a tiny, untamed nowhereland, only a small fraction of which was inhabitable. The rest was made up of mountains and glaciers, volcanoes and lava fields, geysers and waterfalls—one breath-taking freak show of nature after another. There were only three hundred thousand people in the entire country, yet they had their own language, currency, and culture. And all of it was positively adorable.

Icelanders socialize by soaking in outdoor pools heated naturally by red-hot magma, even in the chill of Arctic-adjacent winter. Everyone's last name consists of their father's first name along with the suffix "-'s son" or "-'s daughter." If I had been born in Iceland, my name would have been Jerry Jerrysson. Instead of Santa Claus, Icelandic children believe in the Yuletide Lads, thirteen mischievous gremlins who traipse across the country each December perpetrating holiday shenanigans. They include Hurðaskellir, who gets his jollies slamming doors, and Bjúgna-krækir, who hides in the rafters of your house to steal smoked meats. And, cutest of all, a majority of the population believes in elves. Elves! After learning that, I wanted to pinch the entire country's cheeks until its pudgy little face turned blue.

If none of that sounds the least bit interesting to you, then perhaps your name is Drew Tappon.

His ten gajillion Facebook friends would never know it, but my boyfriend is a closet agoraphobe who is truly comfortable only within ten feet of the living room couch. Three years earlier, I dragged him to London, and even that was too foreign for him. Money he didn't recognize. Streets he couldn't navigate. "Mind the gap" and "Way out" and "Cheers." Aero bars. Shepherd's Bush. Sir Cliff Richard. We spent the entire week looking for an IHOP. It is international, after all.

At least England could pretend they spoke the same language as we do. In Iceland, every word is required by law to be at least eighty-three letters long, with a minimum of four umlauts per syllable. For my boyfriend, it was an über-non-starter.

If not for the baby bucket list, I probably would have shrugged off the whole idea. But I thought of the old adage about why the man climbed the mountain: because it was there. Well, Iceland wasn't going to be there much longer, at least not for me. My youth and my freedom were rapidly vanishing. The time for adventure was now. Before Drew could talk me out of it, I went online and bought myself one round-trip ticket from LAX to Keflavík International Airport. I was set to leave the first week in June, just in time to enjoy the annual puffin migration.

It was outrageously expensive, but so what? I was buying much more than one week of travel. The 331,000 Icelandic krona also provided an extended treatment for my baby fever. Instead of *What to Expect When You're Expecting*, I began reading tour books, searching for hot spots both social and geological. I reserved a single room in "The 101," Reykjavik's hip downtown district. I mapped out the local McDonald's just in case I had trouble finding a restaurant that met my narrow dietary preferences (i.e., no puffin). I even learned how to pronounce those weird letters that exist only in the Icelandic alphabet, like ð and þ, both of which, it turns out, are variations on "th."

I barely thought about Rainbow Extensions, the surrogate, or the baby Drew and I might someday have. I skimmed or ignored emails, like the one that assigned us a new caseworker, Andrea. Andrea assured us of two things: one, in the next few weeks, we would be matched with our replacement surrogate, and, two, shortly thereafter, we would be assigned yet another new caseworker. I didn't even bother getting annoyed. I was too busy corresponding with a man named Borkur to set up a day trip to Landmannalaugar and the volcano Hekla.

Sure enough, Andrea was a woman of her word. Three weeks later, she sent an email titled "Profile for Your Review." Attached was an encyclopedia of trivia about a new woman, neatly organized and illustrated with her personal photos. Unlike with Kristen, I didn't feel any panic this time. I just flipped through the application to make sure this candidate met our main qualifications. She was within two hours' drive. She was drug free. No visible swastika tattoos. Sold.

I'm not sure Drew looked at the application at all. It wasn't that we didn't care. We wanted so much to believe this new surrogate was The One, but we were petrified of having our hearts broken again. No matter what, we weren't going to let ourselves get attached this time.

Andrea told us the surrogate was dying to meet us. She'd already taken an afternoon off from work and arranged to have a neighbor watch her son, freeing up a few hours in her hectic life to drive to L.A. Of course, we assured Andrea, we would do whatever we could to accommodate the woman who was offering us the use of her lady parts. There was just one problem. At the time of the appointment, I would be in Iceland.

Andrea wouldn't even consider rescheduling. The match was made, the meeting was set, the wooing of the womb had commenced. Did we really want to risk turning off another surrogate? If we blew this one, we were going to start getting a reputation around the office. I called the airline, which was perfectly happy to change my flight for a fee of $800. Not a lot of planes fly to Iceland, so those that do can pretty much charge whatever they want.

To my surprise, Drew was firmly in my corner. He still didn't quite "get" my need for this frosty vision quest, but he "got" that it mattered to me. He was willing to turn down the meeting, even if it meant letting the surrogate slip away.

We called Andrea's bluff. I left her a message, letting her know that if she couldn't make the meeting work around my vacation, then we'd just have to go back on the waiting list.

The next morning, my phone rang. We had a new meeting time, the Friday before I left for Iceland. The surrogate had changed her plans.

The night before our big meeting with the surrogate, I was 100 percent ready—for Iceland. My bags were packed. My tour books were precisely stacked atop my suitcase. Day trips were booked. Receipts and confirmations were sorted in a folder in the order in which I would need to reference them. My camera, laptop, and Nintendo DS were fully charged, extra batteries and international voltage converters tucked away in easily accessible pouches. I would have no problem filling my seventeen-hour travel time with Mario Kart, the Legend of Zelda: Phantom Hourglass, and, of course, the Iceland Playlist on my iPod.

To prepare for the surrogate meeting, I brushed my teeth.

Drew and I decided we wouldn't bother bringing an ass-kissy gift this time. Kristen walked off with our fancy anniversary chocolates, and what did we get? A tab for her lunch and the cold sting of rejection. Screw that. Our new policy was baby first, candy second.

It was only as we walked out the door that I realized we were missing something.

"Did you print out her application?" I asked Drew.

"Why?" he grunted wearily.

He was probably right, I figured. It was too late to read it now.

We were in the car, halfway to Rainbow Extensions, when I finally thought of the obvious follow-up question.

"Do you know her name?"

"I think it's Andrea."

"No, not the caseworker. The surrogate."

Drew practically swerved off the road. "Ohhhhh," he moaned. "Shit."

Now, finally, we freaked out.

This was embarrassing. Helen? Hortense? Hezekiah? They were all equally valid possibilities. I wanted to scream. My memory was positively bursting with names: Ruth Bader Ginsburg, Maddox Jolie Pitt, Arantxa Sánchez Vicario, Peter Scolari, Brigitta Von Trapp, supporting actress nominee Sophie Okonedo, *Survivor* runner-up Kelly Wigglesworth. I could name my state comptroller, everyone from my tenth-grade homeroom, and all three of the Thompson Twins, pretty much everyone except the current most important woman in my life.

We had practically earned doctorate degrees in Kristen Lander. We pored over her application, devouring every detail, visualizing each anecdote, etching the outlines of pages and pages of photographs into our minds. But Surrogate number 2 was a blank, a shadow, a stack of unread papers. She was What's-Her-Womb.

We entered the agency to find two women staring at us. Pop quiz, hot shot: one was the surrogate, the other was the company assistant assigned to take us into the meeting.

I looked back and forth between them. One was smiling professionally. The other looked confused and out of place. It was almost too easy.

"It's great to finally meet you," we said to the smiler.

Ding ding ding! Right answer.

I sized her up in an instant. She seemed petite, but she was taller than I was. Thinner and prettier, too. There was nothing phony about her, at least none of the usual fake things you encounter living in L.A.: boobs, skin, smile. Maybe she dyed her hair. I wasn't sure. But she didn't look like she was overly concerned with impressing people, and to me and Drew, that was the most impressive thing about her.

Very meekly, she extended her hand. She opened her mouth and said something but at a volume too low for human ears to record. She was sweet, she was curious, she was terrified. Where Kristen Lander was a tiger, this woman was a kitty cat.

Beside her was her husband, a tall, skinny, clean-cut dude whose look and demeanor screamed California cool. His clothes were preppy, his hair spiky, his footwear flip-flops. He spoke in a voice even softer than his wife's.

It was the worst-case scenario: They were nice. Now we really felt guilty.

The assistant introduced herself as Becky, then led us to a conference room. There, Andrea waited on the other end of a speakerphone call from Tuscaloosa. Becky let us know she'd be taking part in the call just so we'd have a human connection in the room. It was the last time we heard her speak.

"Is everyone there?" Andrea asked from the dimpled triangular doodad on the table. The four of us couldn't help feeling like Charlie's Angels, although the twenty-something couple next to us was probably picturing the 2000 remake with Cameron Diaz and Drew Barrymore, damn them. "Drew? Jerry? Tiffany? Eric?" Whew, Tiffany and Eric, I thought. Remember those names.

Tiffanyanderic. Tiffanyanderic. Tiffanyanderic.

Andrea lobbed the first question at Tiffany.

"Tell us why you want to be a surrogate."

Silence. It was the standard icebreaker, but Tiffany stayed frozen. She looked to her husband for support, then she looked at us with a half shrug. It was a query that was simultaneously too easy and too deep for her to answer.

If Andrea had been in the room with us, she would have noticed how overwhelmed Tiffany was. She might have been able to smooth things over, to rephrase or transition to a less weighty topic. Instead, she mistook the silence for a bad connection.

"Hello? Hello? Are you still there?"

Nobody was sure what to say. Becky squirmed uncomfortably in her seat. Only Andrea was talking. "Hello?"

It was then that the sky opened up, dramatic music played, and a superhero swooped in to save the day.

It was WonderDrew.

"We read Tiffany's application," he insisted. "We already know this."

It was masterful. It was magical. It was a complete lie, but so what? It ended the agonizing silence and got Andrea to move on. The crisis was over. We were in good hands now.

Andrea launched into a drawn-out statement about the sensitive nature of the questions she would be asking and the importance of covering difficult topics up front blah blah blah.

Those of us in the room all knew who was in charge now. As our so-called moderator yammered on, Drew leaned over and muted the phone.

"Here's the deal," he explained to the frightened couple beside us. "This is a horrible way for us to meet. They need to tell us everything that could possibly go wrong, and it's fucking terrifying. But none of it matters, none of it's going to happen. They just have to go into it for legal reasons. Once we get through this bullshit, we'll go to lunch and just talk."

Becky averted her eyes, unsure how to respond. Drew hadn't forgotten she was there. She didn't scare him one bit.

At last, Tiffany warmed up—to us if not to Andrea.

The questions were all repeats from our Kristen Lander meeting, an increasingly chilling and absurd rundown of prenatal horror stories. What would you do if we implant an embryo and then learn the fetus has no toes? What if the eggs split ten times and there are a dozen babies? What if one of those twelve babies is part wolf?

This time, though, the roles were reversed. Now Drew and I were the old pros tasked with setting the newbies at ease. We responded calmly to each nightmare scenario. We'd mute the phone when saying something that was not for Andrea's ears. We bonded with Tiffany and Eric over how annoying this woman was. We'd answer her questions, then shoot each other eye rolls or make gagging motions.

That was how we got through it. The inquiries were designed to break us, to coldcock our optimism and ensure we were prepared for the bumpy road ahead, to confirm that, at the lowest points of this journey, we would all be on the same team. And it was Coach Tappon who held us all together.

We passed the test, and Andrea sent us on our way. For the four of us, this meant the beginning of an even more daunting challenge: getting to know each other.

We went to the same restaurant where we'd lunched with Kristen and Paco. Tiffany and Eric were as shy as I was, if not more. Twelve wolfen babies was nothing. Chitchat was our true fear.

Thus began the Drew Tappon Talk Show. Instantly, my boyfriend transformed into that gregarious TV host I fell in love with on our first date. He warmed up with a monologue, some snarky cracks about the agency that set us all at ease. Then he delicately shifted the spotlight to our dining companions, starting with every parent's favorite topic: their kid. Tiffany and Eric smiled, bragged and showed us pictures of their two-year-old son, Gavin. Drew was our Oprah—fascinated, caring, and oozing warmth through it all.

Within minutes, this scared young couple was sharing their life stories. When Tiffany was nineteen, she heard a report about surrogacy on the radio, and it made her cry. She swore to her mom that someday she would be a surrogate herself. Her mother probably figured this was just a good-hearted, impulsive young girl's fantasy, something she'd move beyond as soon as she heard the next radio report, about the Olympics, and decided she wanted to take up the javelin.

Years later, Gavin was born, and Tiffany had a living reminder of her pledge. She bonded with him instantly in the delivery room, the moment the doctor placed her son in her arms for the first time. She wanted to share that experience with someone who would never experience it otherwise, even if it was a complete stranger. After talking to her husband, she went online and googled surrogacy agencies. The first hit in southern California was Rainbow Extensions.

It seemed so funny to us. Here was a company that spent countless thousands of dollars in outreach, placing ads in local papers and doing who knows what else to try to recruit potential uteri. And then, one day, this sweet young woman just calls them up and asks for an application.

It was beautiful. It was also the perfect answer to Andrea's very first question, about why she wanted to be a surrogate. We wondered why Tiffany didn't share her story then. She just shrugged. "I didn't like her."

Tiffany thanked us for taking control of the conference call. She couldn't believe how relaxed we were through all those awful questions. We fessed up that it wasn't our first time hearing them. We told her about the Womb of Steel, about how we'd had lunch with her at this very restaurant, practically at this very table. How we were ready to have a baby with her, how excited we were when we left the meeting and how devastated we were when she rejected us.

"No pressure or anything," we laughed. It was a risky joke, but Tiffany and her husband both chuckled. Whew.

Tiffany told us the agency had sent her a stack of intended parent profiles, but she knew right away that we were the ones she wanted to meet.

"Why us?"

She giggled like a young girl. "Duh. Disney."

It turned out Tiffany was a major Disneyland freak. Huge. She took her son there a couple of times every week. The way most people might swing by the park down the street to climb the jungle gym, Tiffany and Gavin were queuing up for the Jungle Cruise. She boasted how, at two, her fearless little guy was already riding the Matterhorn. Tiffany's dream was to give birth on Mouse property, earning her newborn a lifetime pass to the Happiest Place on Earth.

Drew and I shared a puzzled, very nervous glance. What gave Tiffany the impression that we were Disney people? We certainly never mentioned Space Mountain in our application. Truth be told, Drew didn't even like Disneyland, and if you waterboarded me, I could maybe spit out the names of two or three dwarves, tops. Dopey, Sneezy— um, was there a Twitchy?

We had forgotten about the pictures.

Among all the photos you include with your application, the agency suggests you throw in a couple of you having fun with kids—smiling, laughing, not touching them inappropriately. So we tossed in a shot of us with my sister's three daughters, standing in front of a shrub trimmed into a Mickey Mouse shape somewhere in the Magic Kingdom. It was purely coincidental, but apparently that was what won Tiffany over.

"Sure," we said. "We looooooove Disney."

Eric, to say the least, was a supportive husband. As long and lanky as he was soft spoken, he had spent several years as a minor league pitcher. It was clear what had drawn Tiffany to him. In addition to his charm and good looks, he worked nights as a roller-coaster mechanic at Disney's California Adventure. While most of us slept, Eric was hanging upside down like Spider-Man, hundreds of feet off the ground, checking pressure and tightening bolts on California Screamin'.

He was as sweet and polite as his wife. Although towering and muscular, he was one of the nicest, least intimidating people I'd ever met.

Yet Eric scared the shit out of me. He was a jock, a straight guy, the kind of dude who got his varsity letter in fag bashing. Back in high school, guys like Eric threw spitballs at guys like Drew and me while we performed our exhaustively rehearsed selections from *Bye Bye Birdie* at the mandatory assembly. Even if Eric agreed to this arrangement, even if his wife got pregnant with our baby, I could imagine spending nine months in constant fear that he might one day just leap up and flush our faces down a toilet, like a pit bull who was always so good with children—until the day he snapped and snacked on a second grader.

Sure, that was one possibility. But even if things never rose to the level of a hate crime, how would a professional athlete tell his drinking buddies that his wife was having a baby for a couple of queers?

I knew the subject was nagging at Drew, too. It was the elephant in the womb. I had to say something.

"So, um, Eric . . . how are you going to tell your drinking buddies that your wife is having a baby for a couple of queers?"

Eric was taken aback. Was it possible he was just now realizing that we were gay? Then he laughed. "I don't really know anyone who would care." He displayed a very laid-back, surfer-like mentality. We seemed cool to him, so, like, whatever. It turned out he was only six years younger than we were, but he made us feel ancient, like homophobia was a problem of our generation, not his.

We realized Eric wasn't the kind of guy who got in a lot of fights—first of all, because he was bigger and stronger than most other guys, so no one would dare to challenge him. But second, he was too darn sweet. He was a puppy—a giant puppy but a puppy nonetheless.

Now that we were asking tough questions, Tiffany had one for us: Why did the Womb of Steel reject us?

And that led us to Susie. Drew choked back tears as he told the story of his sister and her offer. Tiffany teared up, too. "She sounds amazing. What's she like?"

"Well," Drew said, taking a long pause, "she's a lot like you."

We had both been feeling it. Tiffany and Susie were the same age, twenty-eight. Both were introverted, sensitive, and staggeringly kind. They were the same height, they dressed alike. They even looked similar. It was almost spooky.

Now the tears were flowing freely. Drew admitted that he felt a strong connection to Tiffany because of the resemblance. He really wanted the two of them to meet. He was sure they'd be besties.

It was my worst fear. We were bonding, hard. It felt stronger than it had with Kristen, but maybe that was just setting us up for an even bigger heartbreak. Drew practically had Susie on a plane out here to meet this couple. What if this was the last time we ever saw them? What if Monday morning brought a call from Andrea saying, "I'm sorry, they said no, but we'll keep trying"?

It was time to end this, now. I asked for the check. Before it even showed up, Eric was reaching for his wallet. It was totally unnecessary, of course, but it was a nice change from Kristen and Paco. Was Eric just being nice, or did he feel guilty because he knew this wasn't going to work out?

We walked together to our cars. Despite living all their lives in southern California, neither Tiffany nor Eric had spent much time in L.A. We made sure they knew how to get back to the freeway, and we said our good-byes with a hug. Then this beautiful young couple climbed into a shiny new Mercedes. Their luxury car confirmed something we'd already guessed: They really weren't doing this for the money.

When Drew and I got into our Honda, we couldn't wait to rehash everything that had just gone down. We loved Tiffany and Eric, but that frightened us. "I don't know what I'll do if she says no," I confessed.

It was Friday afternoon, and since the agency's Alabama office was already closed for the day, we knew it would be Monday before we heard Tiffany's verdict. The weekend ahead was going to be agony.

We followed the Mercedes to the exit and waited behind them at the cashier. As their car pulled ahead, the attendant waved us through. Eric had paid for our parking.

We waited for the Mercedes to turn and speed away from us, perhaps forever. Then a strange thing happened. They stopped.

We figured they needed us to go over the directions again or that they wanted us to point them toward a Starbucks. We watched through the window as the two of them talked for a moment. Then their passenger door flew open, and Tiffany jogged back to our car.

I rolled down my window, ready to make a joke about how they'd managed to get lost already. Then I noticed that Tiffany was crying.

"I didn't want to wait all weekend," she said. "I wanted you to know I'm going to say yes."

11

INTO THEIR BODIES, OUT OF OUR HANDS

By THE TIME I RETURNED FROM ICELAND, Susie was bracing for hot flashes. She had begun taking a medication called Lupron, which drained her estrogen levels to those of a prepubescent girl. The goal was to keep her from ovulating until Tiffany's body was ready to accept her eggs. But in effect, she also got a sneak preview of menopause.

Tiffany's meds did just the opposite. She was pumped full of hormones, a signal to her uterus to gear up, because it was baby-making time. Both women were placed on active birth control pills in order to synch up their cycles. The only way an embryo transfer would work is if Tiffany's reproductive system was primed to take over right where Susie's left off.

It was during all this that I realized Drew and I were pretty much done. My sperm were banked, the trust was funded. We may have been pursuing a nontraditional means of having a baby, but even our way, it was women who got stuck doing all the hard work.

After a couple of weeks of Lupron, Susie started taking two more drugs, Menopur and Follistim, which signaled her ovaries to go into overdrive. And like popcorn exploding in hot oil, eggs would suddenly start ricocheting around her belly.

She only needed to come to L.A. for two days—one day for the egg extraction, the next for her body to sort out what the hell just happened. (The doctor called it "rest.") But she decided to stay with us for two full weeks. That way she would still be around when we transferred the embryos to Tiffany. She wasn't needed for that, but it would be nice to have her there.

I can only imagine what it was like for Susie asking her boss for all that time off.

"So, yeah, I'm going to L.A. for two weeks to help my brothers make a baby, and you have two choices as to what you want to do about it. You can either just give me the time off with no hassle, or you can fire me. And I know you have every right to fire me, because that's a lot of time off, and this isn't much notice and you probably need somebody to fill in for me while I'm gone. But either way, I'm going, so here are the dates. Just let me know your decision."

She got the time off.

Susie's favorite TV show at the time was *Jon and Kate Plus 8*, so we filled up our TiVo with episodes for her to watch. I'd never heard of it before, but I sat down with her a few times to check it out. It struck me as strange that, as we were going through this process, Susie's form of escapism was watching a show about the two most horrible people to ever go through fertility treatments. "Do they fight all the time?" I asked. "He's disgusting. She's shrill and insane." "I don't know whose side to take." Susie pretty much agreed with me, but I think she just liked watching the kids.

Drew was coping in his own way, with wildly inappropriate humor. He teased Susie about setting her up with a hot guy from his office, wondering what would happen if she had unprotected sex right now. She could be the first woman ever to deliver centuplets, which is probably the term they would invent for a hundred babies, if all the eggs inside of Drew's little sister were to fertilize at once. We laughed about her being an addict, constantly in need of her next injection. Drew even made up a song about the egg retrieval procedure, which began like this:

"We're gonna stick a wand inside your cooter, and then we'll do a number count!"

The rest of the song consisted merely of us all shouting out our guess as to how many eggs the doctor was going to find in Susie's lady parts. He had told us that, given Susie's age and good health, we should expect to extract around three dozen ova. But that didn't stop us from speculating higher, sometimes up to a million or two.

Finally, it was the day before the Big Day. Egg Extraction Eve. To celebrate, we took Susie out for dinner at our favorite restaurant. Like every other night during a Susie visit, we had friends meet us there so we could show Susie off to them. This time, though, there were two very special guests waiting for us.

"Omigod, hi!" Tiffany squealed as she threw her arms around Susie. All they'd ever seen of each other were a few pictures on Facebook, but they hugged like BFFs from high school, reuniting after their first semester at college. Their bond was one none of us quite anticipated or understood, but it was definitely unique. They were two women from opposite sides of America who had come together to help Drew and me make a baby.

Drew was already tearing up, just from the sight of them side by side. "It's so wild," he told Tiffany. "I see so much of Susie in you."

The waiter must have come four times before we were ready to order. Nobody wanted to look at a menu. There was too much to discuss. The women compared medications and side effects. Drew told embarrassing stories about Susie as a little girl. We talked about Tiffany's upcoming birthday, on September 11.

Tiffany was a different person that night, nothing like the shy, nervous girl she'd been when we first met her at Rainbow Extensions. She was a giddy, gossipy woman, outgoing, inquisitive, and hilarious. Drew was different, too. Quieter. There was no need for him to play talk show host that night. He would have slowed things down if he had.

My one fear about surrogacy was that it would turn having a baby into a business transaction, something cynical and cold, where the baby became nothing but a product to be haggled over. But there was nothing businesslike about moments like this. You could say the night was perfectly ordinary, just an evening out with people whose company we enjoyed. Yet there was something truly special about it, too, something we all felt. This was bigger than us, bigger than the baby, too.

On our way out of the restaurant, Drew ran into an old colleague and friend named SallyAnn. She was there with her elderly mother, who had just arrived from Long Island for a visit.

"Hi, I'm Drew," he said, introducing himself to the polite older woman. Then he turned to the rest of us. "This is my partner Jerry, our surrogate, Tiffany, Tiffany's husband, Eric. And this is my little sister Susie," he beamed proudly, throwing his arm around Susie's shoulders. "She's getting her eggs extracted for us tomorrow."

It was the first time we had all been together and the first time we'd been introduced this way, like a family. I couldn't help but smile.

We might have expected the elderly woman to do a spit take or roll her eyes at her daughter's wacky L.A. lifestyle. But SallyAnn just happened to have created the reality show *Jersey Shore*, so her mother had long since lost her capacity to be shocked.

"Nice to meet you," she said, grinning, and a minute later, we were on our way home.

Even though there was only one line to the song, we sang "Wand Inside Your Cooter" all the way to the doctor's office the next morning. This time, our guesses on the number count took on a more serious tone.

"You're feeling pretty swollen, right, Susie?" I asked. She nodded. "Okay. I'm going to say. . . forty-eight."

"Wow, that's high," Drew said.

"What? You don't think your sister is incredibly fertile?"

Susie shrugged. "He said the average was thirty-six, right? I'll say thirty-six."

We knew Drew would come in low, cautious as ever. We waited while he mulled it over.

"I'll take two dozen," Drew intoned, confidently. "Assorted." On the way to the doctor's office, we stopped at a donut shop to get some goodies for the staff. It was something Drew did virtually everywhere he went—the dentist, the accountant, his shrink. If you did any kind of business with Drew Tappon, he brought you donuts. It was his way of ensuring you'd remember him and treat him well. And it worked. Whether it was because of the donuts or just his charm, Drew got VIP treatment everywhere he went. Even his mechanic never cheated him.

Drew still hadn't given us a number for Susie's egg count, and whenever I asked, he dodged the question. "What's up?" I asked him finally.

Susie was out of earshot. He lowered his voice, and his confident, jokey façade drained out in an instant. "I'm just . . . nervous."

"Nervous? Why?"

"Because she's my sister."

The office was empty when we arrived. We were the first appointment, at 7:00 a.m., and though the doors were open, there didn't seem to be anyone there. Did Dr. Saroyan forget that this was the most important day of our lives? I wondered if it would be rude to open up the donuts before we gave them to the staff. The smell of cinnamon was driving me crazy.

"Gerald, you're here!" we heard finally. I found it a bit odd that the first nurse we saw was looking for me, not my sister-in-law, the one with the eggs.

"Yeah, Susie's here for her appointment."

"I know. Tell me, were you going to be using a fresh sample today?"

"Sample?"

"Yeah, your sperm."

"No, I thought we were just going to use the leftovers."

"Oh, I don't think we knew that, because we didn't save any."

"What?"

I hadn't expected to be called on to perform that day, but it turned out, I had a function there after all.

Two minutes later, I was sitting in the specimen room on the half couch, half bed, holding an empty cup. I had no choice but to use the office's materials this time. It turned out they had plenty of gay porn, an entire plastic bin full of it. Just another thing Rainbow Extensions got wrong. I popped in a DVD of two beefy blond wrestlers tussling on an athletic mat. Their match started off like any other, but it continued long after most wrestling matches would have come to an end, as the intensity heated up and their uniforms got torn in revealing places. It was a well-made film, but I was having a difficult time focusing on it.

It's not like I hadn't done this before—in this very room, no less. It's just that, well, the cavorting Greco-Romans on screen and I were about to create human life. Ever since adolescence, I'd been doing this at a strictly amateur level. Now, without warning, I was thrust into my professional debut. I'd spent my whole life practicing. Now I was in Carnegie Hall.

I thought about how many untold trillions of sperm I'd wasted over the course of my life. Who knows how many potential Einsteins I'd flushed hastily down the toilet, how many Mozarts I'd wiped away with a wash cloth and wrung out in the sink, how many Ghandis I'd wadded up in a ball of tissues and dumped down the trash chute of my senior dorm with a spritz of Lysol to mask the odor. This time would be different. These sperm were actually going to do the thing that sperm were created to do. Much like the wrestlers on screen, they would continue on where so many before them would have stopped.

I could only hope they were up to the task. My future kid might be floating around inside my body at this very moment, waiting for his big chance. I prayed my wad wasn't full of Saddam Husseins or Snookis. This time, I was even more careful not to spill.

As I rejoined Drew and Susie in the waiting room, Dr. Saroyan was just coming out to greet them, wearing scrubs and ready to begin.

"Hello, guys! How are you feeling?" he asked.

"I'm so nervous," Drew confessed.

Dr. Saroyan rolled his eyes. "Why are you nervous? You don't have to do anything! You know who should be nervous? Me. This is a very complicated procedure!"

Drew cackled, instantly relaxing. I'd never been more grateful for Dr. Saroyan's sick sense of humor.

"I'm just joking, of course," he continued. "This is very routine. Susie will be given some mild anesthesia, and we'll be done in about ten minutes."

As Susie stood up, we hugged like she was shipping off to Baghdad. We told her we loved her as many times as we could before she disappeared down the hall out of sight.

Then, while we waited, our thoughts turned to politics.

It was August 29, 2008, three days before the start of the Republican National Convention. A TV in the waiting room of Westside Fertility was tuned to CNN, which was just about to announce whom John McCain had picked as his running mate. As two gay men in the midst of reproducing, Drew and I were particularly concerned about this decision and what it might do for the tenor of the campaign. I was having uncomfortable flashbacks to 2004.

In his first term, George W. Bush had failed at just about everything—the economy, the war on terror, basic human diction. But he and Karl Rove cooked up a scheme that would get him reelected anyway. Who were the only people in America more hated and feared than Bush himself? The gays. So they made sure everyone knew those child-raping AIDS spreaders from San Francisco were looking to invade their homes, their workplaces, and their classrooms and that Democrats were standing there holding the door open for them. And it worked. The most disliked president in history was swept back into office on a tide of homophobia. (Historians will probably cite other reasons as well, including the suckiness of John Kerry, but that's the way I saw it.)

Bush's second term was equally disastrous, so I was bracing myself for a repeat of those same scare tactics from the Republicans. McCain's choice for V.P. would be the first indication of what we were in for. Would he pick Mitt Romney, the anti-gay governor of Massachusetts? Maybe Mike Huckabee, the even more anti-gay governor of Arkansas? Or perhaps Charlie Crist, the super-anti-gay (allegedly) gay man who ran the state of Florida? I held out for someone like Minnesota Governor Tim Pawlenty, who'd once voted to ban discrimination based on sexual orientation—before admitting nine years later that he regretted that vote. In the Republican Party, that qualified him as a moderate on gay rights. Go Pawlenty!

It was the groundhog poking out of his burrow. Would we have four more years of gay baiting? Or were we on the brink of a welcome thaw?

And the nominee is—Governor—who?

I studied the strange face on CNN. A woman with glasses and her hair pulled back into a tight bun. She looked sweet and studious, like a librarian. CNN shared everything they knew about her, but I couldn't wait for them to get to what mattered. I dug out my iPhone and googled "Sarah Palin gay rights."

Nothing.

There was very little public record of her at all, but when it came to her stance on gay marriage or Don't Ask, Don't Tell, it seemed like she had never before been asked to take one. I could only assume that, in Alaska, gay rights doesn't come up much.

I didn't find the word "gay" attached to Sarah Palin, but I did find a more telling word. "Sarah Palin to Broaden McCain's Appeal to Evangelicals," one article already proclaimed. "Evangelicals Applaud Palin Nomination." "Palin Bid Seen as McCain's Gift to Evangelicals."

Shit, I thought. She's one of them.

I looked up and saw Dr. Saroyan striding down the hallway toward us. He had just left the exam room and was still pulling off his face mask. Was it over? Had he even started?

Drew put down his Blackberry, but the doctor wasn't stopping to talk to us. He was heading with purpose toward his office, on the opposite side of the waiting room.

"How's it going?" we called out to him.

He shook his head. "She doesn't have a lot of eggs, guys."

And just as quickly, he was gone.

"Did he say . . . ?"

Drew cut me off. "Yeah." He buried his face in his hands.

"What does that mean? He did the ultrasound. Her follicles were so healthy. She could feel her ovaries swelling. How many eggs do you think he means? Like twenty-five?"

Drew didn't want to play my guessing games. "I don't know!" he snapped.

A minute later, Dr. Saroyan appeared again, walking just as purposefully back toward the operating room. Once again, he wasn't stopping.

"How many eggs does she have?" I called out.

"We'll have to see," he said, in passing. "Looks like seven."

Seven? Seven eggs? I didn't think that was possible. What did it mean? Could we still have seven babies?

The look of concern on Dr. Saroyan's face was nothing compared to the one he had when he returned a few minutes later. This time, he stopped. He sat down next to us and sighed. "We need to talk, guys."

The expression he wore wasn't one of concern or empathy. It was something I never would have expected: guilt.

"I said something I shouldn't have said," he confided.

"What?"

"Didn't you tell me she had kids of her own?"

"No. She's not even married."

Dr. S buried his face in his own hands now. "I was just trying to make a joke. She was waking up from the anesthesia, and I . . . I said it's a good thing you have your own kids already, because your ovaries are a mess."

We stared blankly at the doctor, hoping the joke was on us. But he wasn't faking. He was devastated.

"Her eggs are just . . . it's not good."

Drew didn't want to hear any more. He just wanted to see his sister.

Susie's smile might have been more convincing if she'd wiped away her tears first. She was lying in a recovery room underneath a TV that was tuned to CNN on low volume. She looked over as we entered, trying to put on a brave face. "So I guess he told you?"

"He told us he made a bad joke," Drew said.

"It's fine. He didn't know. He thought I had kids already."

"You okay, Suz?" Drew asked, stroking her arm gently. He was trying so hard not to cry. It was almost too much to bear, knowing that half an hour ago, Susie had walked into an operating room to do the most selfless thing she had ever done, only to be blindsided by the worst medical news she'd ever received.

"I'm fine," Susie assured us.

We could see she was anything but fine. Her lip started to quiver, and Drew couldn't hold back his tears anymore. I could see him searching his mind for an inappropriate joke to make, but for probably the first time ever, he was coming up empty.

Now Susie was comforting him. "I'm sorry," she said.

Drew caught his breath. "What on Earth are you sorry about?"

"I feel like I let you guys down."

Both Drew and I were speechless for a second. It was so typical of Susie, at a time like this, to be concerned with everyone but herself. Or, as I chose to put it at that moment, "You're insane, Susie. Shut up."

"I just want you guys to have a baby."

"We'll have a baby, one way or another. I mean . . ." I didn't want Susie to think I had already written her off as an egg donor.

A nurse came to check on our patient. She asked her if she was ready to get dressed. Susie nodded, and as the nurse pulled the curtain, Susie glanced at the TV above her bed. On it, Sarah Palin was waving eagerly to reporters.

"Who the hell is that?" we heard Susie say.

From the look on Dr. Saroyan's face, it was clear that he wasn't about to launch into his comedy routine. Susie's low yield had caught him off guard. Nothing in the tests indicated she was anything less than freakishly fertile. He turned toward Susie, and his first question was not encouraging. "Are you dating anyone?"

Susie laughed. "Nah."

Dr. S turned to Drew and me. "You guys need to find her some-body." He was only partly joking. "I can't say for sure you won't be able to conceive, but I'd highly recommend you try as soon as possible. Your ovaries right now are the best they're ever going to be."

Drew groaned. "I feel so bad that we put her through this."

"Don't," Dr. S scolded. "If not for this, we wouldn't have known she had any fertility issues. She would've waited to have kids, and it would've been too late. At least now we can plan."

I had an idea. "Should we forget about our transfer and freeze these eggs for Susie to use instead?"

"No!" Susie blurted out. "These are yours!"

Dr. Saroyan shrugged. "We could do that, Gerald, but I'll learn a lot from seeing how many of these eggs fertilize. If everyone's okay, I think we should proceed as planned."

"Yes." Susie decided to answer for everyone. Drew and I nod-ded along.

"When will we know if they fertilized?"

"In three days." Dr. S sighed. "Guys, I want to be very clear about where we stand. If we don't get at least two or, better yet, three quality embryos, I'm going to call off the transfer. I don't want to waste your time."

Susie had refused to accept any compensation for her eggs. We offered her the standard $8,000 fee, we offered to buy her a car or to rent her an apartment so she could move away from home. She was changing our lives, as we saw it, and we wanted to do some-thing potentially life changing for her as well. But she wouldn't take a penny, wouldn't even let Drew buy her an iPhone for her birthday. I understood perfectly why she was so reluctant. Any reward might have cheapened the gesture.

Now I had a new idea. What if, when this was all done, we paid for Susie to freeze some of her eggs for her own use? Then, years later, if she had any trouble conceiving, she would have a safety net. It was perfect. We would pay Susie back for her eggs— with her eggs. Finally, something made sense.

Three days later, Drew, Susie, and I huddled around the phone to call the doctor's office. Aida, the nurse, answered.

"We're calling to see if our embryos fertilized?"

"Can you hold a minute?"

It didn't sound good. It sounded like Aida was putting us on hold so she could find the person whose job it was to crush people's dreams.

"You have three embryos," she said, a minute later and a bit more chipper. "The doctor would like to do the transfer this Friday."

"Wait, Dr. Saroyan said he might cancel the transfer. Have you checked with him? Are you sure this is happening?" I was suddenly skeptical. I wasn't anticipating good news.

"Oh, for sure it's happening."

In an instant, all our attention shifted to Tiffany. We were determined to make the next few days as smooth and comfortable for her as we could. Dr. Saroyan liked to do transfers first thing in the morning, at 7:00 a.m. So rather than have Tiffany leave home at 5:00 a.m. and fight Orange County traffic, we booked her a room in a hotel near the fertility clinic.

We put together a care package full of magazines, fresh cookies, and other assorted treats, then dropped it off at the front desk of the hotel. As we walked out, Drew muttered, "Kristen Lander doesn't know how good she would've had it! Her IPs probably didn't even say thank you."

When we arrived at Dr. Saroyan's office for the transfer, he presented us with a picture. Against a faint gray background were three translucent blobs, almost perfect circles. These were our embryos. I'm very progressive about women's reproductive rights, and I agree that life begins at birth, not at conception blah blah blah, but I have to admit a strange feeling overcame me as I stared at that picture. They had no defining characteristics whatsoever and I knew they might never be more than blobs on a sheet of paper, but as I stared at them, I saw my children. I would have taken a bullet for those blobs.

I wasn't the only one who felt that way, obviously, because both Drew and Susie were weeping like they were watching the end of *Shawshank Redemption*.

"Wow, Susie," I said, looking at the embryos. "It's like you and I 'did it'!"

When Tiffany arrived, the doctor took us all into an exam room. I'd heard that embryos were graded for their quality, much like schoolchildren, and I couldn't wait to see if we had any A students on our hands. Dr. S told me he didn't normally give letter grades, but that we had "three gorgeous, gorgeous embryos."

"C'mon," I said. "Can you rank them?"

"One is a nine out of ten," he said. "The other two are ten out of ten."

The mood in the room was electric. "So Susie delivered quality over quantity then?" I asked.

"Yeah, who knew?" Dr. S said. "Maybe we shouldn't write you off just yet."

Susie had never looked prouder or more relieved. The same could be said of Drew.

"So we could really be dads?" I asked.

"I mean, there are no guarantees, but I'm a lot more optimistic now than I was after the retrieval."

"Then how many are we transferring?" Drew asked.

"Given the circumstances, I think we should be aggressive," Dr. S informed us. "I recommend you transfer all three."

Drew clutched my hand anxiously. "Three?"

"I just want to increase your odds, but it does mean there's an outside chance you could have triplets."

"Let's do it," Drew said. He turned to me. "Right?"

I wanted to say no. Triplets terrified me, and so did the thought of reducing three fetuses to two once they'd taken hold in Tiffany's uterus. Then again, what if we transferred one or two embryos and ended up with no baby at all?

"Okay," I said. "Let's do all three."

12

BREEDERS

INFERTILITY ISN'T THE KIND OF SUBJECT people tend to talk about at work. "Hey, Frank. How was your weekend?"

"Pretty good. Saw the new Batman movie, tried that new Italian restaurant downtown, found out my sperm count is zero."

"Oh yeah, how was the food?"

In my case, though, it was a source of endless fascination among my coworkers.

I was in the middle of a six-month freelance gig on a TV show called *Smash Hit Video*. Each weekly episode was a compilation of shocking caught-on-tape clips featuring anything from bull gorings to runaway speedboat crashes. It was like a sizzle reel of human suffering. On a daily basis, producers would swing by my desk to drop off screeners and say, "This driver flips over nine times and smashes through a concrete wall. A-minus."

"Does he survive?" I'd ask.

Shrug. "Make sure you say he does."

If I overlooked my contribution to the decline of humanity, it was a decent job.

The writers' room at a place like this is probably not all that different from that of a network sitcom because in a better life, that's where we all imagined ourselves. At any given time, the staff consisted of me and between three and seven straight guys, along with between zero and one woman. We'd goof off, crack jokes, play darts, anything to take our minds off car crashes for a few minutes.

For months now, no topic had been as fascinating as how two dudes could make a baby without having sex with a woman. Nothing was off limits—the cost, the gory details of the procedures, the sperm. On a daily basis, I provided comic fodder and teachable moments for the *Smash Hit Video* writing staff, and I loved every minute of it.

That all changed once the procedure was finished. Drew and I would have to wait ten days before we'd learn if Tiffany was pregnant, and I wasn't in the mood to share how I was feeling.

We texted with Tiffany regularly, and her responses were encouraging, which is to say, she felt like crap. "tiff thinks its morning sickness," Eric wrote once. "she had it real bad when she was preg w gavin."

I didn't share these messages with the writer's room, but I did have one friend I confided in privately: Bernie. He and I had a complicated relationship. We'd known each other forever, which meant since I first moved to L.A. We were classmates in the USC screenwriting program, and we'd kept in touch through a series of weird jobs like this ever since. He was a good guy, so good that he could tell for sure that I was going to hell. I know this because he told me so. "Yes, Jerry," he said. "You're going to hell."

To be fair, this followed about five minutes of me badgering him with, "Just tell me if I'm going to hell! C'mon, just tell me!" Of course, I knew what his answer would be because Bernie believed you only got into Heaven if you accepted Jesus as your savior. Still, I wanted to hear him say it out loud.

Bernie's very religious, but incredibly, that's never gotten in the way of him being my friend. We hung out often, and he laughed more than most people at my jokes, which made me like him even more. He even made me a groomsman in his wedding. It always surprised me how he could look past what his religion said about me and be my buddy. Maybe he was just trying to maximize his time with me on Earth because he knew that in the next life, we'd be long-distance pen pals at best. I guess he's what the nicer Christian people call "a true Christian" in that he tries to love everyone and not judge—unless, of course, some little snot like me really puts him on the spot.

Bernie had always been uncharacteristically quiet when we talked about surrogacy in the office. For a while, I assumed it was because the idea of two men reproducing made the crucifix around his neck quiver and emit smoke. Then, one day, he spoke up.

I'd just informed the room that the success rate for in vitro, as Rainbow Extensions quoted us, was approximately 98 percent.

I've never seen anyone do an actual spit take in my life, but that moment was the closest I ever came. Bernie was just sitting down at his desk, and he nearly fell out of his chair. "What? I hope you don't believe that!"

"Well, it might be a little inflated . . ."

"You think 98 percent of couples who try in vitro get pregnant? It's more like thirty, forty percent. Tops."

"Well maybe. If you mean straight couples. But our situation is different. A straight couple going through in vitro has already had problems conceiving naturally. For us, everyone's healthy. Our surrogate's already had a baby of her own, our egg donor is young and fertile, and if either of them fall short, they can be replaced with someone else. Gay couples even have two potential sperm donors." Bernie had been an engineering major in undergrad, so I knew I could make my point using math lingo. "Straight couples are locked into who's providing the egg and the sperm. In our equation, everyone's a variable."

Bernie got quiet. This was one argument he didn't want to pursue further, although clearly I had hit a nerve. I could tell this was more than just a hypothetical area for him, that he'd pulled his 30 to 40 percent statistic from personal experience.

That's the good news about breaking through the "you're going to hell" barrier in a friendship. After that, nothing's off the table anymore. The next time I was alone with Bernie, I asked him what was going on.

It turned out he and his wife were on their third in vitro attempt. They'd sunk tens of thousands of dollars into procedures, with no luck. This would be their last try.

I told him about Susie's egg yield and how nervous we were. In a weird way, I guess I was hoping to cheer him up, but he didn't take any comfort in my story. "Making eggs was never our problem," he confided. In fact, his wife produced dozens of them. The resulting embryos, though, just weren't making the cut. Where we got nines and tens, Bernie and his wife were getting twos and threes.

We both wished each other the best of luck and made a silent pact not to bring it up again. It was good to have someone to commiserate with, but I knew the odds of both of us getting pregnant were extremely slim. This was bound to end in heartbreak, at least for one of us.

Finally, the waiting was over. Ten days had gone by, and Aida at the fertility office told me to keep my phone close by because there was no telling when they'd hear back from the lab. The test results wouldn't come in the form of a "yes" or "no," just a number that corresponded to the hormone level in Tiffany's bloodstream. If the number was over one hundred, Tiffany was definitely pregnant.

If it was under one hundred, it was a "maybe," and in that case, there would be a second test, three days later.

Some friends of ours knew a couple who had taken this same test and scored somewhere around two thousand. They ended up with twins. "Multiples make your numbers go through the roof," they said. I imagined what number we might get if we were having triplets. Three thousand? Thirty thousand? Three million?

"Tiffany scored an eighteen," Aida told me, late that afternoon.

I didn't want all the other writers to hear my conversation, so I stepped outside onto the patio, where the smokers congregated. I could barely breathe, which didn't help me contain my emotions. "So she's not pregnant?" *Cough, cough.*

"We can't say for sure. I've seen lower numbers than that where the woman ended up being pregnant. We just don't know."

"But it's not twins, is it?" *Sniffle, exhale.* "Or triplets?"

"We don't know. You just have to sit tight for three days. If she's pregnant, the number will at least double."

Three days was better than ten days, but on the flip side, it was three more days. I started my daily count over. "Two days left." "One day left." Ugh.

The morning of Tiffany's retest, my hopes were skyrocketing again. Tiffany said she could feel something growing inside her. I imagined what number Aida would give me this time. Two hundred and twenty? Four hundred? No, one hundred and eleven. I didn't want to get my hopes up.

Finally, my cell phone rang.

"Gerald?"

"Yes?"

Aida sighed. "I'm sorry."

I braced myself against the wall. I was once again standing outside, with the smokers, once more on the brink of tears. "So it's bad news?" *Cough.*

"I can't get through to anyone at the lab. They usually call us by now, but I think they went home."

"Wait. You don't have the results?"

"I'm sorry. We won't know until Monday."

Oh, Jesus. Three more days!

I was tense and furious all weekend. Those lab workers were so unprofessional! What's the equivalent of the Better Business Bureau for medical labs? Was there a Yelp for fertility clinics where I could write a one-star review? Ooh, I was burning up.

Shockingly, Drew stayed calm through the whole thing. I didn't get it. He was supposed to be the panicker. I was the sane one. How had we suddenly reversed roles? "We've been waiting thirteen days, and now it's going to be three more!" I shouted. "How are you not losing your shit?"

Drew just shook his head. "Because I already know the answer."

"What do you mean?"

"Jer, we're not pregnant."

"Why would you say that?"

"Because the odds are one in a million."

"And where did you find that statistic? On Drew Makes Shit Up dot com?"

"Just let it go. You're only going to be disappointed."

"But Aida said lots of people get pregnant when they have a number lower than eighteen. It's all about the next number, and if it's at least double what it was, then there's a good chance . . ."

"Okay. If you want to keep your hopes up, go ahead."

"Yes!" I shouted. "I want to keep my hopes up!"

That was the last I talked to Drew about the pregnancy test. After that, I hid my anxiety. I quietly called Aida on Monday morning while Drew was in the shower. "When will you have an answer? When? When?"

"The lab opens at nine."

It was 7:30. I couldn't believe it. In a mere ninety minutes, I'd know.

I drove to work with my headset in so I wouldn't miss the call. Just as I was pulling up to the Sunset-Gower studio lot, I felt my phone vibrate.

"Hello? Hello?"

"Gerald? Tiffany got an eleven."

"I'm sorry, wait. She got what?" I was hoping we had a bad connection. Maybe she said two hundred and eleven. Or eleven million. Maybe it was eleven-uplets. I refused to give up until I knew for sure.

"She's definitely not pregnant. I'm sorry, Gerald."

"Oh."

"I just spoke to Tiffany and we scheduled a D & C, which is standard procedure . . ."

Everything else she said floated past me. I listened as long as I had to, thanked her, and hung up.

I stayed in my car for ten minutes. The first five, I was doing a mixture of trying not to cry and crying. The next five, I was on the phone.

Drew and I conferenced Susie in to give her the bad news. She didn't even hesitate. "So when do we try again?" she asked.

"Sweetie . . ." Drew began. But I cut him off.

"Whenever you're ready," I told her. "We'll talk to Dr. Saroyan. I think we need to wait a few months. But if you really want to go through this again . . ."

"Well, I'm not gonna stop until you guys have a baby," she said.

"We'll talk about it," was all Drew would say. But I didn't want to talk about it, not with him. I was terrified he might tell me that he'd already given up hope.

The only one less enthusiastic than Drew was Dr. Saroyan. He called me that afternoon to see how I was doing. All I wanted to know was when we could try again.

"Three months," he said. "The question is, are you willing to look for a new egg donor?"

"No! We're not replacing Susie."

Dr. S sighed. "It's going to decrease your odds of having a baby significantly."

"Why? I thought the embryos were perfect. Two tens and a nine. This wasn't her fault. Are you sure it's not Tiffany we should be replacing?" Just that easily, I was ready to throw our surrogate under the bus. I would have hated the idea of losing Tiffany, but the thought of having to dump Susie was unbearable, both for what it meant for us and for what it meant for her.

"I see no reason to replace the surrogate, but if Susan were anyone other your sister-in-law, I would tell you to find a new egg donor. I wouldn't even agree to do the procedure again for you."

"It's that bad?"

Dr. S thought it over for a moment. "Well . . ." he said, pausing cautiously. "There's one hope."

"Tell me! We really want to keep Susie."

"Because she was Drew's sister and not an anonymous donor and because she seemed so healthy, I gave her a relatively low dose of the meds. If we were going to try again—if—I would double her doses, raise her to the absolute maximum. It could be a lot more uncomfortable for her. She'd have to be okay with that, because otherwise, there would be no point in trying."

I didn't even call Susie to check. I knew what her answer would be. "Go ahead and make the calendars then. We'll try again in three months."

"Okay, Gerald," Dr. S sighed. "But listen. If this doesn't work, I won't put her through it a third time. This is your last chance with Susan."

13

PUPPY-KICKING DOODYHEADS

IT'S A GOOD THING Drew and I were only trying to have a baby, not do something as radical as get married. In that case, we really would have been screwed. A few months earlier, the California Supreme Court ruled that gay marriage should be legal, which naturally meant that the gay marriage grinches were going to ensure it wouldn't stay that way for long. Their plot to steal Christmas came in the form of Proposition 8, a ballot measure that, if passed, would end any bride-on-bride/groom-on-groom happily ever afters, effective immediately following Election Day.

I firmly believe in the American ideal of respecting other people's political views, even when they differ greatly from my own. Still, as a gay man seeking happiness, it was hard not to see Proposition 8 supporters as a bunch of puppy-kicking doodyheads. They were pouring millions of dollars into their efforts and airing commercials claiming that, if Proposition 8 failed to pass, school-teachers would be required to teach kids about gay sex in kindergarten and churches would be forced to perform gay marriages or risk losing their tax-exempt status. They were lies, but they won votes, and to the bullies who were trying to take our rights away, that was all that mattered.

The most shocking thing of all was that polls showed the measure in a dead heat. My home state was exactly one-half homophobe. Funding for the measure was coming largely from out of state. The Mormon Church was orchestrating a huge push to pass Proposition 8, urging their followers to donate whatever they could. The *Sacramento Bee* ran an article about a middle-class Utah family who drained their bank account and gave everything they had, a full $50,000, to the Yes-on-8 campaign. Stopping me and Drew—and millions like us—from marrying was more important to them than their own financial security, their kids' college funds, or any other charitable effort they might have directed that cash toward. Puppy-kicking doodyheads.

It seemed like only a matter of time before the haters came for gay parents. We were thumbing our noses at their last remaining argument against gay unions—that gays can't have kids of their own and that therefore what we have is not equal to a marriage. And talk about going against nature. We were making heterosexuality completely irrelevant to creating life. Drew and I were gay breeders—two dudes making a baby with our own DNA. The state of California would even let us put both our names on the birth certificate. Think of all the signatures the angry mobs could get against that. Think of the commercials they'd air.

"Do you know what goes on in [voice lowered for dramatic effect] *California*? The gays can't have babies the normal way, so they *genetically engineer them in labs*. At this very moment, they're creating monster gay super-babies—and marrying them! Do you want your child sitting next to this in a classroom? [Insert picture of a limp-wristed five-year-old in a tank top, earrings, and knee-high kinky boots.] It's time to tell them enough is enough! Do it for our children!"

Between Proposition 8 and the discouraging results of our in vitro attempt, it was a pretty bleak autumn. I needed something to take my mind off all the awfulness.

"Susie got laid!"

Drew shouted across our condo from the bedroom, where he was on the phone with his sister. Finally, some good news.

Now that Susie was off the meds, she was no longer bound by all the restrictions that came with them. She could drink again, lift more than ten pounds again. She could be young again. And yes, she could get laid.

It was as though a clarion call went out to the universe that Susie's lady parts were now accepting guests, and the universe responded, as it often does, with a friend's wedding. Susie was a bridesmaid, and as the night wore on and the dance floor cleared, she found herself cozying up to a super-hot guy she knew next to nothing about. Her friends had warned her that he was trouble, which was perfect. After all she'd been through, she'd earned herself a little trouble. She got bombed, and the next thing she knew, Trouble was in her hotel room taking a number count of his own.

I sat next to Drew as he got the details from his kid sister, and I listened in as best I could, like a dog licking up crumbs that fell from the dinner table. For too long, I'd been starving for some good junk food like this.

Mostly, I was just enjoying the sound of Susie laughing.

Once again, gays were the topic of conversation at work. "Who gives a shit if two dudes get married?" The hetero horn dogs were fuming.

"What bullshit!"

"It'll never pass! It's so fucking stupid!"

They'd all been convinced Proposition 8 would be shot down by somewhere around 90 percent of the electorate. They were stunned when I told them about the poll numbers and the family from Utah who forked over fifty grand. It made me feel really good knowing that a bunch of straight guys could have my back like this.

At least, most of them did. Bernie started at his computer, pretending to be engrossed in whatever construction crane accident script he was writing. His silence on the current hot topic was quite noticeable for a guy whose two cents usually ran about a dollar and a half.

"That fucking prick! He's totally voting for it!"

Our second most popular topic of conversation in the writer's room was Bernie himself—but only when he was somewhere else.

"Haven't you guys been friends for like ten years?"

"More like fifteen."

"Does he really think God gives a shit if gay people get married?"

"Weren't you in his wedding?"

"Yeah, I was."

"Well at least he believes gays can *attend* weddings. That's very open-minded of him."

Then Bernie would walk back in, and the conversation would continue via instant message. *Bing*! I'd look down at my screen, and one of the other guys would have written, "When do we get to vote on *his* marriage?"

No one ever addressed Bernie directly, but occasionally, we'd try to bait him with our comments.

"Why would anyone vote for Prop 8?"

"Simple," I'd say. "They're motivated by hatred. Solely by hatred."

I admit, I felt just a smidge guilty. Here I was, angry about something I found unnecessarily divisive, and yet I was actively turning the staff against somebody I considered a friend. Then again, he was doing it to himself. If he was voting for Prop 8, fuck him.

Drew didn't have time to worry about the election. He was more concerned with Susie. They talked on the phone every night, often for so long that I couldn't imagine they still had things left to talk about. Sometimes they'd be laughing, sometimes crying. One day, after he hung up the phone, he walked into the living room and asked me to shut off the TV. In our home, that was a red alert.

"She's late," he said.

"What's late?"

"Her period. She's three days late."

"How late is that? That doesn't sound too late."

"I guess it's pretty late."

"Is she pregnant?"

Drew sighed. "She's concerned."

"The guy at the wedding?"

"Yup."

"But Dr. S said . . ."

"I know."

I felt like I should laugh, but nothing came out. It seemed so absurd. One minute, Susie was infertile; the next, she was too fertile. Then guilt took hold. Maybe this was our fault.

"Was she so convinced she couldn't get pregnant that she didn't use birth control?"

Drew shook his head. "She says he wore a condom. But it turns out that guy has a nickname. Mr. Fertile."

"Shut up."

"He has a kid from some other one-night stand."

"Stop it!"

"He claims he used a condom then, too. His friends have a joke that he has some kind of super-sperm which can't be stopped by latex."

I let it sink in for a moment. I still couldn't bring myself to laugh. "That's it," I said finally. "If she ends up having a baby, she's giving it to us!"

Election Night brought the promise of relief just because, one way or another, my political anxiety would finally be over. As the results came in, most of my Facebook friends were euphoric. They had their eyes on the big race, and at the moment Obama swept to victory, they began pouring their tears of joy into their status updates. It's history! It's magic! It's the end of bigotry! The handful of Republicans I knew were crankily posting that everyone else should shut the hell up, which made it even better. I wanted to celebrate, but polls showed Prop 8 was too close to call.

I had at least ten windows open in my browser. The *L.A. Times*, the *New York Times*, MSNBC, Talking Points Memo. I clicked refresh over and over. I scoured for any details I could find. Which counties were still uncounted? How did they lean? Had they tallied San Francisco yet or Palm Springs? Hours after the election had been called for Obama, Drew stumbled out of the bedroom, rubbing his eyes.

"C'mon," he said. "Why are you still up?"

"Prop 8's going to pass."

"Shit."

I finally decided it was better to go to bed while there was still a shred of ambiguity. The race hadn't been called yet, not officially. At least for one more day, I could wake up a tiny bit hopeful.

By morning, there was no more doubt. My fellow Californians hated me. They spat on my happiness. Gay marriage was illegal—again. I checked the map for the county-by-county results. Even in Los Angeles, Proposition 8 had received more "yes" votes than "no."

That quickly, the mood on my Facebook timeline shifted. Even my friends who'd never shown much interest in politics were outraged. They went to marches in support of marriage equality, posted angry rants against bigotry. One guy I know kindly invited everyone in his network to unfriend him if they voted for Prop 8 and to avoid him in real life, meanwhile fucking themselves as thoroughly as possible. I strongly considered posting a similar message.

Instead, I decided to get on with life and move on to an old pastime, bashing George W. Bush. Now that he was a lame duck, there was a video going around of him appearing to get snubbed by other world leaders at a gathering. I shared it on my Facebook wall, and most of my friends wrote to say it made them laugh.

There was one dissenter, who made himself known via email.

"Could it be argued that your Facebook post about Bush is motivated solely by hatred?" It was Bernie.

"I hate Bush," I wrote back. "Does that answer your question?"

Later that afternoon, Bernie sent me a response that was roughly the length and earnestness of the Gettysburg Address. He attacked me mercilessly, accused me of revealing my true colors as a vicious, spiteful person. It was not only the angriest I'd ever known him to be, but it was also his best writing, full of big words and complicated reasoning. It was like a PhD thesis on why I sucked. Clearly, I'd touched a nerve, but how? It wasn't the politics. For someone so religious, he was surprisingly apolitical and certainly no Bush apologist. Then I realized there was something familiar about the language he'd used. "Motivated solely by hatred." Wasn't that exactly how I'd described Prop 8 supporters?

It was time Bernie and I had a talk.

"You voted for it, didn't you?"

Bernie sighed. He knew this had been coming. "I don't want to talk about it. It's a private vote."

"You do realize I'm going to take that as a yes?"

"I don't want to say anything that's going to damage our friendship."

"Then maybe you shouldn't have sent that email."

"Okay. Just promise you'll hear me out and have an open mind."

"I'll hear you out," I said. "But if you think you're going to convince me I don't deserve equal rights, I highly doubt it."

We met for lunch near the office. I imagine Bernie spent all morning rehearsing his speech in his head, like a lawyer preparing for trial. I'd barely sat down when he hit me with his opening statement.

"Do you think a man should be able to marry his sister?" he asked.

I groaned. Is that where this was headed?

"I don't want to marry my sister."

"What if somebody wants to marry two women or two men?"

"I don't want to marry two women or two men."

"Just answer me. Hypothetically."

"I really don't care if someone marries twelve women or two hundred men. If they're all consenting adults and it works for them, great."

"But what about the brother and sister? What if they want to have kids together?"

"Well, that's not healthy for the kids."

"Aha!" he shouted. I realized it was too late. I had taken his bait.

"So you do think there should be restrictions placed on marriage? You admit it!"

"That's not what I said."

"But if you think marriage should include you then how do you tell the brother and sister it can't include them?"

I shrugged. "That's their problem. Let them get their own lawyers."

Bernie refused to state his position on gay marriage specifically, but he was boldly going on record as being anti-incest. And he feared that redefining marriage would inevitably give some horny siblings somewhere the legal grounds to get the government blessing for their union. It was clear he'd put a lot of thought into the matter, but it also felt like he was rationalizing a viewpoint he had against gay marriage to begin with. He already told me I was going to hell. Why the sudden evasiveness?

By the end of lunch, I was willing to concede that Bernie wasn't motivated by hate. Self-delusion maybe, but not hate. Still, I wasn't sure where this left us. As we walked back to the office, he tried to wrap things up on a positive note.

"I know the way the tide is turning," he admitted. "I have no doubt that sooner or later gay marriage will be legal, and I'm fine with that. I'm ready for it. And when you and Drew get married, I'll be the first one to dance at your wedding."

I didn't say it out loud, but the only thing going through my mind at that moment was, "Why would I invite you to my wedding?"

I arrived home that night exhausted, physically and intellectually. Drew was already there, talking to Susie on the phone. He was laughing and joking, a complete change from the last time they'd spoken.

"Hold on, Jerry's home," he said, cupping his hand over the receiver. "You ready for some big news?"

"What's up?"

"Susie had her period today."

"Yahoo," I said. "I'm going to bed."

14

SUSIE AND THE BEAST

ONCE THE ELECTION DAY LUNACY had died down, it was time for another November tradition: Christmas. Sure, the holiday itself wouldn't arrive for over a month, but thanks to the eagerness of retail stores to tape cardboard reindeer cutouts in their windows, what was once a celebration of Jesus' birth now covered pretty much the Virgin Mary's entire third trimester. This time of year set the perfect tone for Susie's second egg harvest since we were going for a kind of immaculate conception of our own.

Nobody told Susie what Dr. S had said—that, succeed or fail, this would be the last time we could use her as an egg donor. Knowing her, she was mentally preparing herself to go through this for the next several years—the mood swings, the constant trips back and forth to L.A.—if that's what it took. We wouldn't put her through that, though. As Dr. S told me over the phone, there wouldn't be much point anyway.

She got on a plane, just after Thanksgiving, and we received a warning that her dark side was making an ugly appearance.

"She is being such a little pill!" Mrs. Tappon cautioned us over the phone. "She's cranky, she doesn't want to talk to me, she just mopes around. She's not herself." To all of us, this was fantastic news.

None of us wanted Susie to suffer, but secretly, it was hard not to find her discomfort encouraging. Clearly, the double dose of medication was having an effect. Both her foul mood and the pregnancy scare had given us a renewed sense of optimism going into our second in vitro attempt. She could produce viable eggs. We could have this baby. It was all possible. Of course, her disrupted cycle turned out to be a false alarm, but somehow, that didn't matter. For a moment, we believed in her reproductive system again.

I went with Drew to pick Susie up at the airport, fully prepared to encounter a fearsome, feral version of the sweet, loving girl I'd come to consider like a sister myself. She certainly didn't look any different. She bopped up to us, full of energy and hugs.

"How was the flight?" I asked, because that's what everyone asks when they pick someone up at an airport.

"It was good."

"Are you hungry?"

"I'm okay."

"Did you check any bags?"

"Yeah, just one."

Enough airport talk. It was time for the Big Question. "So . . . how are you feeling?"

"Eh," she said, shrugging, "a little crampy."

Drew and I turned toward each other, jaws unhinged. "A little crampy?" This was worse than we thought. I'd never heard Susie complain before, certainly not about herself. For her to confess even the tiniest sliver of discomfort, she must have felt like absolute shit.

Huzzah!

The Christmas season provided the perfect distraction from the ominous business of baby making, mostly because it wasn't really all that Christmassy. It was Christmas in L.A., a surreal spectacle all its own.

Christmas in Los Angeles is how I imagine St. Patrick's Day to be at the Betty Ford Center. They can't really do it the way it's supposed to be done, but you have to give them credit for at least stapling up a few shamrocks and saying "Erin Go Bragh." Everything to do with Christmas is so antithetical to L.A.—snow, pine trees, the spirit of giving—that it's a little jarring every year to see twinkling lights once again ringed around palm trunks and plastic Santas propped merrily on chimneyless roofs.

The night Susie arrived, we took her out to dinner at the Grove, the same glitzy outdoor mall where Drew and I had our first date. We ate on the second floor of a steakhouse, just inside a huge picture window that overlooked the moonlit fountain outside. As we talked about everything but eggs, we looked out and saw snow fluttering softly around the square. The flakes were actually tiny soap shavings, shot out of blowers on the roof, but it added to the feeling that magic was in the air, that with the right technology, the impossible could happen.

Early the following morning, we walked nervously through the doors of Westside Fertility. By now, we'd come to know virtually everyone in the office. It was our Cheers, where everyone knew our name, but they were always just a little sad we came. They were friendly people and they'd become invested in our situation—the young woman giving eggs to her gay brother and his partner—only to have our story become an unexpected downer. Now we were the two gay guys with the infertile sister, a family doubly cursed when it came to reproduction. The Westside employees were almost as nervous as we were about what would happen when Dr. S brought Susie into the exam room today.

"Susie!" a woman shouted, sprinting across the waiting room with her arms outstretched.

"Hi Debra!" Susie squealed, as the two embraced warmly.

"You look so good!"

"You, too!"

Debra was the liaison to egg donors. She and Susie had been talking regularly on the phone and had grown really close.

"I have some news," Debra said. "I'm pregnant!"

She seemed almost apologetic, a little hesitant to say it, knowing the circumstances that had brought us there. If she thought her announcement might upset Susie, she didn't know her that well after all. Susie gave her a second, even bigger, hug. "I'm so happy for you!" she said.

They exchanged emails so they could keep in touch during Debra's maternity leave. "And don't worry," Debra said. "When I'm gone, you'll be in good hands. I want you to meet our new donor coordinator. Maxwell!"

Drew and I couldn't believe it at first, until we saw his face emerge through a doorway. It was Maxwell from Rainbow Extensions, our old caseworker, who'd left when the agency relocated to Alabama.

"You're alive!" Drew shouted. We'd kind of suspected after all the mysterious caseworker disappearances that when people left Rainbow Extensions, they were fed into a meat grinder in the alley. It was nice to see Maxwell in one piece and not as a series of sausage links.

"I'm fine," Maxwell said, cordial but a bit dismissive. He clearly wasn't as excited to see us as Drew was to see him.

"You work here now?" I asked.

"Yeah, I got to know the folks at Westside pretty well when I was at Rainbow, so it was a good move for me."

Drew wasn't interested in Maxwell's personal story. "You have to tell us what the fuck is going on at that place," he said. "It's such a disaster."

Maxwell just smiled nervously and shrugged. "They're great."

"They're the most disorganized bunch of idiots I've ever met in my life."

Maxwell smiled blankly. He clearly wasn't in the mood to say anything bad about his previous employer, at least not to Drew. "Nice seeing you guys," he said, then he returned to his office.

"Moron," Drew muttered under his breath.

Other than Maxwell's unexpected reappearance, everything about this visit was fairly routine. I was summoned to make a deposit, and by now I didn't even need to read the instructions taped inside the door of the specimen room. "Wash hands and penis, open cup . . ." Yeah, yeah. Start wrestling, boys.

By the time I returned to the waiting room, Susie was already in with Dr. Saroyan. There was no big news on the TV monitors today. The only sound was Drew typing feverishly on his Blackberry.

Taptaptaptaptaptaptaptaptap.

Drew is a compulsive emailer, especially when he's nervous. He's the Michael Phelps of mini keyboards, his thumbs tapping out sentences at world-record speed. He types faster than most people talk. Smart phones are his cardio.

I studied the photos on the Wall of Babies. Next year, we might be up there. Me and Drew, leaning over a bassinet with a little girl in pink booties or a little boy who has my nose and Drew's eyes. I could see it, our condo's living room as a backdrop, Drew in his favorite green checked button-down, me in the red and blue striped polo I always wore on casual Fridays. We'd be smiling, of course—not fake junior high yearbook smiles but real smiles, big ones, because we would always be smiling, the three of us, our family.

Taptaptaptaptaptaptaptaptap.

It was when the tapping stopped that I knew it was time to look up. I smiled, but this one was far from sincere. I was terrified. There, in the doorway, stood Dr. S, in the same spot he'd appeared after the last egg harvest. He saw us glance up at him, and he stopped walking. This was it. We were about to find out what a difference an extra 75 IUs of Menopur made.

We waited for Dr. S to speak, but instead, he just sighed and dropped his gaze to the ground.

It was not good news.

Susie wasn't crying in the recovery room this time. She was just as disappointed as she'd been after our first attempt but a lot less shocked. Deep in our hearts, we'd all feared this outcome.

There were seven eggs, the same as last time. The extra medication had no impact. Susie was a seven-egger, and there was nothing we could do about it.

At least Dr. S hadn't made a bad joke. Susie awoke from the anesthesia to find him leaning over her, a concerned look on his face. "Susan," he said. "Sit up. We need to talk."

He helped Susie pull herself into position so that they sat eye to eye. As he spoke, he took on the tone of a concerned parent. He showed more empathy than you'd usually get from a doctor, but his voice was firm because his message was serious. "I'm very concerned about your ability to get pregnant," he began.

Susie said nothing, just nodded and listened. She'd been hoping for a bonanza of eggs, for a post-op high five rather than this.

"Do you have any idea how much medication I had you on?" Dr. S intoned, gravely. "You're a young girl. You should've . . . look, you want to have a baby of your own, right?"

Susie nodded vaguely. She was determined not to break down this time.

"I'm going to be blunt. You can't afford to wait. Not five years, not two years. You need to do it now."

Susie's voice shook, half from the medication she was on and half from weariness. "I don't even have a boyfriend."

Dr. S stood up, sighing. He clutched his forehead in his palm and began pacing. "We need to figure something out!" In frustration, he bolted out the door.

Twenty minutes later, we sat down in Dr. Saroyan's office. A morbid distress hung in the air, like we were attending a funeral for our dreams of parenthood. Dr. S was nodding quietly. His lips were pursed, and he had a determined look on his face. He leaned forward in his chair, his palms face down on his desk. "Okay," he said. "Here's what we're going to do."

"We need to give Susie the eggs," I interrupted.

"No!" she shouted.

"Yes, Susie! You need them more than we do. We'll freeze them for you."

"I don't want them! I gave them to you!"

"Drew, tell her she needs to do this."

Drew just shrugged. He didn't want to hear from me or Susie at that moment. He was looking at Dr. S.

"I'm sorry," I said. "What were you going to say?"

Dr. S shook his head. "Gerald, we're not going to freeze these eggs for Susan. That's stupid."

"Stupid?" I'd expected my offer to be called "brilliant" or at least "magnanimous." "Stupid" stung a little.

"We've come all this way, and we're going to keep moving forward. I want to see if Tiffany can get pregnant with Susan's eggs."

"But she couldn't. We tried that."

"We're going to try again," he insisted. "And Susan, when we're done, we're going to do one more round of hormones."

"What?!" I said. "We don't want to put Susie through this again."

"The next time will be for her. We'll freeze those eggs as a backup plan if she ever needs them."

Susie shook her head. "I don't want to freeze eggs."

"Too bad. You're doing it. Listen, Susan, you are a very special person. I like you very, very much." Susie rolled her eyes, not because she was embarrassed or she doubted his sincerity but at herself because she knew that all the tears she'd been holding back were about to burst out.

"Here!" Dr. S said, pushing a preemptive box of tissues her way. Susie grabbed the first one, and Drew immediately took the second.

"I'm very touched by what you are doing for your brother. It is a beautiful thing, and it's not your fault that you have such terrible, terrible eggs." He picked a perfect time to lighten the mood. Both Drew and Susie laughed from behind their sniffling. "You need to do this. I'm very serious."

"Thank you," Susie said. "But I'm not going to do it."

"Susie, you're doing it!" Drew insisted.

"No, I'm not!"

"Yes, you are," Dr. S shot back, "because I'm going to pay for it."

"He said she was the nicest person he's ever met!" The last thing the world's proudest brother needed was another excuse to brag about Susie, but now he had plenty of new material. "You should've heard him talk about her. I'm telling you, he just adores Susie!" We were on our way home from the clinic, doing our routine check-in call with Mrs. Tappon. Dr. S's offer had given this call a much more upbeat tone than it otherwise would have had.

"That's very nice," Mrs. Tappon said. "But he doesn't need to pay for Susie to freeze her eggs. Your father and I will pay for it."

"No way," Drew said. "Jerry and I are paying for it."

I truly appreciated this family's generosity, but I'd reached my breaking point with their inability to accept anyone else's. "Just let him pay for it!" I shouted.

Susie was quiet. Since the meeting, she'd clearly had a change of heart. The fear of never having a baby was burrowing into her mind. Now she seemed open to the idea of freezing her eggs.

We talked about Susie all day and all night, about her gift to us, the ways in which she'd touched everyone who worked at Westside Fertility and about what she should do moving forward. We barely talked about the more imminent topic—our embryo transfer. There was no question this would be our last opportunity with Susie's eggs. Just like last time, we had only seven to work with, and now they sat in a petri dish somewhere in the offices of Westside Fertility, with my sperm trying diligently to turn them into potential people.

15

THE TEN EXCRUCIATINGLY
LONG DAYS OF CHRISTMAS

No ONE WAS MORE of an afterthought to In Vitro Round 2 than Tiffany. She was the last part of the process, she was no-body's sister, and if she couldn't get pregnant this time, there was a good chance we'd replace her as our surrogate. As coldhearted as it seemed, two strikes is all a surrogate usually gets when there are so many others who could do the job. It was hard not to think that, if we gave Tiffany the ax, we'd probably never see her again. Sure, we'd bonded with her on a deeper level than we expected, but our relationship was still defined by the baby we were supposed to have together. Would we really meet up with her in two years or ten years to show her the child we'd had with someone else? And what if we never had a kid? Would the sight of her just remind us of our shattered dreams? Bleak as it seemed, Tiffany was either going to be a vital part of our extended family—or a footnote. "What was that second surrogate's name again? Tammy? Bethany?" It didn't matter how much we cared about and admired her. Fate could just as easily turn her back into What's-Her-Womb.

We were resigned to keeping our expectations low this time, but Dr. S was no help. "They're perfect!" he shouted. "Perfect!"

We'd just arrived at Westside Fertility, on the morning of the embryo transfer, and Dr. S rushed out to greet us, tripping over his scrubs as he pulled them up to his waist. It was almost as though he'd been keeping an eye on the door so he could tell us at exactly the moment we arrived, like a kid eager to show off his school art project to his parents. In this case, his macaroni and glitter masterpiece was a curled-up ultrasound photo of three bumpy circles on a gray background.

"Three embryos?" I asked, remembering that was exactly as many as we'd had last time.

"Yes! All tens!"

"Great," Drew said.

"Yeah, great," Susie added.

Dr. S seemed disappointed by our lack of enthusiasm. "Guys, this is awesome!"

"We had three embryos last time," I reminded him. "Two of them were tens."

Dr. S shook his head. "Next to these, those were garbage."

"Hey guys," Eric said, as he and Tiffany walked in behind us. "What's up?"

"We have three embryos," I monotoned. "All perfect tens."

"Great," Eric said, exactly as excited as we were.

"Yeah. Great," Tiffany concurred. "So are we transferring all three?"

Drew shrugged. "Why not?"

"You guys," Dr. S said. "There's a very, very high chance of triplets."

"Great," we all seemed to say in unison. Dr. S sighed. A minute later, he was leading Tiffany down the hall to begin the procedure.

We were prepared to wait an hour before we saw Tiffany again, but it was only a few minutes later that Eric came to get us.

"She said you guys can come back."

"Really? Is she decent?"

"She's recovering. She doesn't mind if you see her."

I assumed this meant Tiffany would look pretty much like she always did—fully dressed, fully upright—but when we entered the embryo transfer room, she was neither. Clad only in a hospital gown, she was posed on what appeared to be a backward-tilting luge that might launch from the starting gate at any moment. Her legs were in the air, spread apart, and held up by stirrups. Her body sloped downward to the abdomen before leveling off at the neck. It seemed like a position invented to torture Chinese political prisoners that someone just happened to discover was also helpful in getting embryos to attach to the wall of a woman's uterus.

"Hi!" Tiffany said, cheerfully, as we spread out around the outskirts of the room.

"Are you sure you want us in here?" I asked, guiltily. I half-shielded my eyes, unsure which would be ruder—not making eye contact or gazing directly at a woman in embryo-attachment position.

"It's fine," Tiffany assured me. Clearly, she had overcome whatever modesty she had around us. While we were keeping our emotional distance from her, she was welcoming us freely into a realm of personal privacy that normally included only her husband.

"How are you doing?" Susie asked. She fearlessly sauntered up right beside Tiffany.

"I have to pee," Tiffany confessed. "Like, really badly."

"How long do you have to stay like this?"

"The doctor said an hour," Eric replied.

"How long do I have left?" Tiffany pleaded, shifting her weight back and forth to find a slightly less excruciating spot on her medieval contraption.

Eric checked the clock. "Fifty-two minutes."

Tiffany groaned.

It was all so strange, knowing that three embryos created by my sister-in-law and me were tucked away inside this woman we barely knew, just inches away. In nine months, one or more of them might slide out of her, with a face, a Social Security number, and twenty tiny appendages protruding from its extremities, more or less. Drew and I might be dads to a person who was, in some form, in this room with us right now.

All Tiffany could think about was her bladder.

"Oh my God! I really have to go!" she whimpered. She shifted some more, clutching the sides of her torture luge, struggling to hold in her pee.

"You can't even go to the bathroom?"

"No! She's not allowed!" Eric insisted. "The doctor was very clear!"

"How long now?" Tiffany asked.

"Fifty-one minutes."

I really wasn't sure what my role was at that point. On the one hand, I've never felt within my rights to tell a woman she couldn't relieve herself. On the other, I didn't want Tiffany peeing out my baby.

In any other circumstance, Drew and I would have done anything to ease her pain, screaming at the doctor to just let her go to the bathroom, dammit. Instead, we just played dumb.

"We can check with Dr. S, but you know what he's going to say . . ."

"I'm sure he's with other patients. Do we really want to bother him?"

Tiffany squirmed and danced, even though she was in no position to do either. I couldn't decide: Were Drew and I the world's biggest assholes, or were we just being good parents?

Tiffany's bladder was wrung through the Iron Maiden for forty-four minutes, after which we all decided unanimously that it had been an hour. It was the length, without commercials, of an hour-long TV show, so that was good enough for me. We called the doctor in. "She really has to urinate. Is that okay?"

"What?!" He threw his hands up and focused on Tiffany. "These guys won't let you go to the bathroom?"

Susie flew home, and a few days later, Drew and I joined her. The entertainment industry traditionally shuts down for the holidays, so we regularly spend the last two weeks of the year visiting our families on the East Coast.

With the possible exception of the Clauses, no family takes Christmas as seriously as the Tappons. It's the one time of year all four kids can get together, and they always arrive loaded with gifts. Their ceiling-scraping Christmas tree is buried in them— neatly wrapped boxes with bows and tags that feature everyone's names in every possible combination in the "To:" and "From:" fields. Packages for more distant relatives and friends are dispersed throughout the house underneath one of the half dozen other trees.

Rochester is a perfect place to spend the holidays because there's almost always snow, and it's so freaking cold that no one wants to go outside. It's like a Norman Rockwell Christmas, where people sit around all day, swapping stories by the fireplace. Drew and his siblings still wrote a note to "Santa" every Christmas Eve, though their notes took on a snarkier tone as they entered their twenties and thirties. "Susie's been a good little girl this year. Please bring her some new ovaries."

The afternoon of the twenty-second, a car pulled up in the driveway.

"He's here!" Drew shouted, and he sprinted outside in shorts, barefoot, to give his brother Peter a hug.

Since declaring our arrangement "fucked up," Peter had done a complete 180. All he wanted to know as he lugged his shopping bags full of gifts over the threshold was if we'd heard from Dr. S's office yet.

I shook my head. "Any minute now."

Two hours went by, with no call. I wondered if the lab would screw up again and forget to give us the results. This time, we'd have to wait until after Christmas. That would ruin everything— or maybe save the holiday from gloom. I couldn't be sure.

As usual in a family that size, there were half a dozen conversations going on simultaneously when we were all called to dinner. We gradually assembled in the dining room as Mrs. Tappon put a platoon-sized meal on the table. Ham, turkey, fresh-baked rolls, side dish, side dish, side dish. Nine chairs were squeezed in around the table, gathered from every room in the downstairs.

"Where should I sit?" each of us seemed to ask at the same time. As we negotiated our positions near our favorite foodstuffs, I felt a vibration in my pocket.

It was a private number, but I knew who was calling.

"Hello?"

In an instant, the entire room fell totally silent. Everyone stopped scrambling for seats, put down whatever food they were holding, and turned toward me, tense with anticipation.

"Hello, Gerald?" I heard Aida say. It was only two words, but I got the sense from her tone that she knew the results.

"Yes?"

"I have some good news!" she continued. I looked around the room, just then realizing that no one else had heard what I'd heard. They were all still waiting, searching my expression for clues.

"Hold on," I said. "I'm going to put you on speaker."

Mrs. Tappon was stone-faced. She thought I was being foolish to broadcast the call to the room. She was sure it was another letdown. She didn't know I'd already figured out what Aida was going to say.

Everyone leaned in. "Tiffany's blood test came back," Aida said. "She scored a 142. You're definitely pregnant!"

The cheers shook the room. Drew, Susie, and I shared a tight hug that seemed to last for hours. All around us, the rest of the family paired off in every possible combination and hugged everyone else. But the three of us never let go.

"Congratulations!" the nurse shouted, trying to be heard over the rest of us. I'd almost forgotten she was on the phone.

"Thank you so much! You made our Christmas!"

I had to walk into the other room to finish the call. Keeping the ebullient Tappons quiet would have been impossible at this point, but the nurse had much more to tell me. She had already scheduled Tiffany's first ultrasound for Tuesday, January 6. She even gave me the baby's due date: September 1. Our baby. This wasn't just a hypothetical kid anymore.

I was just about to hang up when I realized I'd forgotten to ask one very important question.

"Is there any chance we're having triplets?"

Aida chuckled. "With a 142, it's probably a singleton."

I couldn't believe it. A baby. I was going to be a dad.

16

IPS IN THE CLOSET

WE HAD BEEN OFFICIALLY PREGNANT for about ten days when I concluded that we'd already reached the best stage of parenthood. When your kid is just a batch of rapidly dividing cells clinging to a uterine wall, he's still perfect. He hasn't Nerf-gunned your boss at a dinner party yet. She hasn't joined a doomsday cult that worships a flying boot. And they definitely haven't shouted "I hate you!" and then locked themselves in their bedroom for three days. Better still, it's only prenatally that you get to play all those wonderful prospective parent games like "What's the Most Ludicrous Name We'd Willingly Give Our Child?" and "How the Hell Are We Going to Fit a Crib in This Space?"

Two dads have it even better. Yes, your fetus is igniting furious mood swings, morning sickness, and bizarre food cravings but not to either of you. At most, you get a grumpy text about it once in a while. You're not even the guy who has to run out at 3:00 a.m. to buy peanut butter and pickles. (Sorry, Eric!)

I wanted to take full advantage of the golden days while they lasted, but there was only one early pregnancy game Drew was interested in playing:

"Don't Tell Anyone We're Pregnant!"

"Don't Tell Anyone" was as natural as pregnancy itself. It was probably played by every species in the animal kingdom. Nervous hummingbirds would hum out their own name for it, which was "What? Can't I Just Build a Nest and Sit in It for a Few Weeks? Don't Be So Nosy!"

The reason for the radio silence was obvious: Everyone wants to make those initial "We're Pregnant!" phone calls, but no one wants to make that awful second round of phone calls less than nine months later, the ones that undo the first round of calls and invite all kinds of references to things Oprah once said. Still, I hated the idea of holding back such a huge piece of information from the people I cared about. Hadn't I sworn off keeping Major Life Secrets after all those years in the closet?

Besides, this wasn't some ordinary pregnancy. Tiffany had been carefully screened and tested for Jerry/Drew fetus preparedness. Those thousands of baby photos on the wall of Westside Fertility attested to that. I hated to think we were sitting on the best news of our lives for no reason, but Drew insisted on sticking to the straight people's playbook on pregnancy. He had another rule, too: "No shopping."

I was dying to browse for baby goods—shrunken dining utensils, inflatable bathtubs shaped like turtles, and footie pajamas with bunnies on them.

"Jerry, you can't buy anything until you know this is real!" Drew insisted.

"I'm not talking about buying a crib or a swing set or something that'll haunt us forever if the baby doesn't make it. Maybe just a onesie. One onesie!"

"No onesies!"

I was stunned by how fast this had gone from a playful bicker into a full-on fight—our first official argument as parents.

"Fine, I'll go without you," I said.

"You're not going!"

I was furious. It was the happiest time of my life, and the person who made me the happiest was trying to squash it.

"What are you afraid of? You think if we lose the baby, all we're going to worry about is the drawer full of onesies we need to get rid of? Or if we don't have any baby stuff, that'll make it easy? 'Well, so much for that. Let's move on!' Because that's bullshit. It's going to be unbearable with or without the onesies. But at least we will have had a little while to enjoy it first."

"Jerry," Drew warned. "Don't go!"

I went. Alone. I walked the aisles of Babies R Us and imagined the future. Pushing a stroller. Tucking a human the size of my forearm under an Elmo blanket. Comparing diaper disposal pails to determine which one held the stink in the best. I saw a talking potty and thought, "Wow, someday we'll need one of those." From across our condo, a robotic voice would say something like, "Nice poopin', dude!" and a tiny person who lived with us would fill up with pride. I didn't buy anything, but I got exactly what I needed out of the experience.

On the way out of the store, my cell phone buzzed. It was an email from a friend of ours, someone we'd agreed not to share our news with just yet. "OMG!" she wrote. "drew told me!!! so excited for you both xoxoxoxoxo!!!!!"

Maybe he was willing to relax just a little.

There's no day all year when it's harder to go to work than the first Monday in January. I'm so used to having two weeks off for Christmas that I always resent a return to the grind after so much freedom. This year, it should have been harder than ever, knowing how much work must have backed up on my desk while I was away, how fast I'd need to resume the manic pace of producing a manically paced TV show. And yet, I didn't mind a bit.

I was still in baby bliss. Yes, I'd no doubt be walking into a shit storm, but so what? I was doing it all for my baby. My boss could keep me there all night, and it wouldn't phase me. I was looking much farther into the future, to September 1.

I made it about an hour before I started telling people my news.

No one was more ecstatic than my boss. He never struck me as a hugger before then, but he practically leapt across his desk to embrace me.

"I want to go to all the medical appointments," I told him. "I'm going to miss a bit of work, but I'll stay late to make up for it, or I'll come in early, or you can dock my pay, or . . ."

"Don't worry about it," he said. "This is bigger than work. It's your family."

"Great," I said. "My first ultrasound is tomorrow morning. I'll be in at eleven."

I'd only planned to tell a couple of people, but I was on such a roll, I couldn't stop. Once I told Marcello, I had to tell Steffen. Once Steffen knew, Travis was bound to catch wind of it, so I might as well tell him.

It felt like I was coming out all over again, except this time I wasn't worried how people would react. Just about the only person I didn't tell was Bernie. I was still bitter about our Prop 8 spat. He voted against my happiness, so why should he get to share in it? Midday, an email popped up in my inbox. "So I never found out," he wrote. "Are you starting the new year with a successful pregnancy?" Instead of replying, I hit "delete."

At three in the afternoon, I was in a meeting with a few segment producers in my office. A "private" call came in on my cell phone.

I'd been expecting the doctor's office to confirm our ultrasound in the morning, and here they were, right on schedule. I figured it would be quick, so I answered it. "Just a sec, guys," I said.

"Gerald, hi it's Aida from Dr. S's office. I'm afraid I have some bad news."

I did my best to keep smiling, but already I felt queasy. Bad news? Shit. This was it. Drew was right. None of the people in my office knew the good news yet. A second ago, good news was all there was. Why did I have to pick up the call? "I need to take this. Can we finish later?"

The second they were gone and the door was closed, I sat back in my chair and sighed. "How bad is it?"

"Tiffany's been bleeding and cramping a lot," she said. "She just spoke to Dr. S. He told her that if she soaks through a whole pad, she needs to go right to the emergency room because that means she's having a miscarriage."

Ugh. She was being so casual yet so graphic. It was the worst sentence I'd ever heard.

"Are we still having our ultrasound tomorrow?"

"If Tiffany makes it through the night, then yes."

And just that quickly, I had a new worst sentence I'd ever heard. "If Tiffany makes it through the night, then yes." I couldn't bear to think about the flip side of that statement, the one that resulted in "then no."

"I knew it!" Drew shouted.

Because I was the one who got the call, I had to break the news to Drew. I repeated what the nurse said, then I tried my best to cheer him up.

"It might be nothing. Lots of women bleed and cramp when they're pregnant." I wasn't sure I believed it myself as I said it, so I quickly did a Google search at my desk. Yes, indeed, lots of women bled and cramped when they were pregnant. Whew!

"This is why you don't tell people. We shouldn't have said anything!"

"I'm really scared, Drew."

"I knew it!" Drew repeated.

"Are you going to tell Susie what's going on?"

"No!" Drew shot back. "We're not telling anyone. Let's see what happens tomorrow." Now we had two levels of secrecy— people who didn't know we were pregnant and people who didn't know we might be losing the baby.

There was a knock on my door. I had been secluded in my office for ten minutes, an eternity. A coworker poked her head in. "Everything okay, Jerry?"

"Yeah," I said, forcing a smile. "Just fine."

Work made the day go by faster than it had any right to. I spent every moment in fear of feeling my cell phone vibrate again. That night, I turned my ringer on and left my phone at my bedside, just in case an urgent call or text came while I was asleep. It was a relief when the sound that woke me up was my alarm clock the next morning.

As Drew and I arrived at Westside Fertility, I half expected the receptionist to stare at us sadly, shaking her head and saying, "Sorry, I was about to call you." Instead, we were greeted like we always were and told to have a seat until Tiffany arrived. A few minutes later, she did. She looked miserable and sick, like she hadn't slept all night. I'd never felt so relieved.

A few minutes later, Tiffany was lying on an exam bed, and Drew and I were pelting Dr. S with questions.

"How common is this?"

"Is it going to go away?"

"Is our baby okay?"

Dr. S had Tiffany lift up her shirt, exposing her belly. For the first time, I realized she had her navel pierced. I wasn't sure I should know that. I made a halfhearted effort to look away, but Tiffany just rolled her eyes and groaned. "Oh, please . . ."

Dr. S rubbed a wand over Tiffany's midriff, and a big gray blob appeared on a monitor across from her. Inside the gray blob was another blob, a white one. I had no idea which of these blobs, if either, represented our baby. Was it some composite of both blobs, or was it just a tiny speck amid all the noise, still too small to be distinguishable?

Drew held my hand as we waited silently for Dr. S to speak, but for a long time, he said nothing. He repositioned the wand over and over, shook his head repeatedly, sighed more than once, and typed a few times on a dull tan keyboard.

"Well, guys," he said finally, "there's a lot of blood in there."

Drew squeezed my hand harder. I could feel his bones pressing against mine, as if there were no skin between us, just two skeletons clinging as tightly as they could.

"I have no idea what we're looking at," I confessed.

Dr. S used a pen to point at the monitor. He waved it around the gray blob, which took up about 80 percent of the screen. "All of this is blood," he said.

"That's a lot of blood," I replied.

Dr. S nodded. "It's a lot of blood. That's not good. We implanted three embryos, right?"

"Yeah."

"There's a chance Tiffany is just rejecting the third embryo, after which the blood will clear out. I can't tell for sure."

"So that could happen, and the other embryo could still survive, right?"

"Yes, they could."

They? I realized Dr. S was leaving out possibly the most crucial detail of all.

"You said the third embryo is being rejected. Does that mean there are two left?"

"Oh yes," he said. "Didn't you know? It's twins."

For the first time, Tiffany smiled. "You guys couldn't tell?" she said, pointing at the screen. "Those are the embryos." I never could have found them on my own, but now they seemed perfectly obvious. Two tiny peanut shapes, each inside its own little clearing amid the blobs. They had oversized heads, translucent skin, and barely discernible limbs, but they were unmistakably fetal, just like out of a health class textbook.

I gasped, turning to Drew. I was ready to throw my arms around him, but he was shaking his head. "We only got a 142. We thought that meant a singleton."

"Oh no, it's definitely twins," Dr. S said. "Count them!"

"We're having twins!" I beamed. I squeezed Drew's hand again, but at the same time, I felt him let go. He looked as if he might pass out.

"Want to hear their heartbeats? " Dr. S asked.

He moved his wand some more, and soon we heard the rapid throbbing of each baby's heart, one at a time. I never expected to experience so much from a first ultrasound. Dr. S explained that because they were conceived in vitro, these fetuses were six weeks old already. I still couldn't believe there were two of them. Two babies—my kids. I felt an instant attachment. Even though they lacked faces, I fell in love.

I was also paralyzed with fear.

"Are they going to make it?"

"I really don't know, guys." Dr. S showed us how the sacs containing the fetuses were barely making contact with the uterine wall. "The blood is keeping them from fully attaching."

"Is there anything we can do?"

He shook his head. "Just wait."

I felt impotent. I'd been quietly gloating about not having to deal with morning sickness and the other inconveniences of pregnancy, but now I would have done anything for the comfort of knowing my babies were inside me, that their fate was in my hands.

"What's going to happen? I know you can't predict, but . . ."

I was hoping he'd say something to cheer us up, but if there was a silver lining, it was too cloudy right now to see it. "If we're lucky," Dr. S said, "one will survive."

Just to be safe, he ordered Tiffany to go on immediate bed rest. He set up another ultrasound for the following Tuesday because these babies would need to be monitored closely. "Call my office immediately if you have any more bleeding or cramping," he instructed.

He tore off his surgical gloves and switched off the monitor. "Here," he said, tearing a crinkled paper out of the machine. He handed it to me, a still image of our two fetuses, the thin wall of their egg sacs separating them from a sea of blood.

"I know it's hard to say," I started, "but what are the odds of them making it for the next nine months?"

"I'd say the chances of Tiffany carrying either one to term are about fifty-fifty."

17

THE SAD HAPPY FACE

I DON'T UNDERSTAND GOD. I'm not saying I don't believe in him—or Him or her/Her, it/It or them/Them—just that I don't understand. Sure, maybe there is some unseen big shot on another plane of existence who's secretly micromanaging our lives, but I don't get how anyone finds comfort in that. I mean, what kind of person (or faceless entity, for that matter) takes that much interest in whether some shady contractor is telling the truth when he's sworn in on *Judge Judy*? No disrespect intended, but the type of God so many people claim to believe in sounds like a loser. If anyone needs to get a life, it's the guy who has all the power and knowledge in the universe but who spends his time helping pro bowlers take out 7-10 splits.

At the same time this loving, omnipotent gajillion-year-old whatever-it-is is helping Jay-Z clean up at the Grammys, he sits by while people carpet bomb and date-rape each other into oblivion. Sure, some people believe they can explain all the bad things away. Cancer? That's God's way of making you appreciate life. Tsunamis? God's way of making us respect nature. YouTube videos of people dancing with their dogs? God's revenge for all that cyber porn. I'm not saying any of these explanations are wrong, because they make as much sense as any other justification for human existence. But if that's the way God does business, why bother praying? If God shrugged off the Holocaust because it made some point about faith or brought some nice people up to Heaven to live with him sooner, then my babies and I were fucked.

Tough times have been known to drive heathens to prayer, but if you ask me, the worst time to pray to a god like this is when you actually need help. I wasn't going to ask a favor of some guy who got off on jerking people around. Better to fly under the radar than alert you-know-who to the fact that my fetuses could be a tool in teaching me some kind of bat-shit spiritual lesson.

At the same time, I couldn't accept the notion that I was completely powerless. There had to be somewhere I could turn to help me save those kids. I know it's impossible to write the following sentence without it being political, but I'm going to try anyway: Those six-week-old fetuses I saw on the sonogram monitor were people—real people, and I loved them like a father already.

I'm pro-choice and pro-women's rights, and I don't want to give any fuel to the people who aren't, but to be honest, I was already mentally preparing myself for the day those two hovering blobs moved out to go to college. I could picture me dressing the blobs as ketchup and mustard for Halloween, me and the blobs riding the teacups at Disneyland, and me breaking my back in a bounce house at the blobs' fifth birthday party.

"Blob 2, call an ambulance!" Blob 1 would say.

"On it!" Blob 2 would reply.

They were real people, capable both of injuring me and of summoning medical assistance. If they didn't make it, I would cry real people tears.

Maybe I didn't see any point in addressing some cloud-floating cruise ship blesser, but there was still someone I could turn to.

Someone I fully believed in, who was directly involved in this situation. I decided to take this matter straight to them:

January 11, 2009

Dear Babies:

That's right. Babies. There are two of you. We saw you in the doctor's office last week. Two little blobs came up on a screen, and Dr. S said, "It's twins!" and Daddy Drew almost fell over. (He claims I'm the one who almost fell over, but suffice it to say we were both pretty shocked.)

So that's the good news. You may not have a fully formed brain yet, or any fingers or toes. But you've got a buddy.

When you're gay dads having a baby with a surrogate, it's easy to put the baby out of your head. We're not living with Tiffany, so we're not taking care of her when she gets morning sickness or waiting on her when she's resting in bed to make sure you're okay.

But although we may not be living under the same roof with you yet, seeing those tiny little beams of light on the doctor's low-tech screen, well, it was like meeting you for the first time. I'm sure what I'm feeling now is only a tiny fraction of what I'll feel when I'm holding you in my arms in a few months, but all I want to do is take care of you and protect you and let you know that you're loved.

And, really, I can't.

That's the scary part. Okay, so I'm kind of avoiding the bad news, but that's because I know it won't amount to anything and I can't let myself focus on it. But we did have a bit of a scare last week. Tiffany's body wasn't expecting twins either, and if it doesn't figure out how to handle you, there's a chance you won't be born.

Dr. S said there's nothing any of us—even Tiffany—can do to make sure you hang in there. So we all feel kind of powerless and are just hoping for the best.

That's why I'm glad there are two of you. I know down the road, you'll have all kinds of sibling rivalry. You'll fight over toys, then you'll fight over girlfriends or boyfriends or who gets to borrow the car. But for the next 7 1/2 months, I hope you'll get along. Share that womb, kids. Take care of one another. Grow together, tiny unformed hand in tiny unformed hand.

Until you're born, there isn't much Daddy D and I can do to shield you from danger. But that doesn't mean you're alone.

Until then, you've got each other.

Love,

Daddy J

Going into the next ultrasound, I was cautiously optimistic. Tiffany was still cramping, but the bleeding—which was far scarier—had stopped. There had been no obvious signs of a miscarriage, but given how tiny our fetuses were, I could easily imagine them slipping out of Tiffany's womb undetected.

It was a huge relief when I again saw both of my kids on the monitor. They were slightly bigger and slightly more developed, each tethered to an umbilical cord in its own little sac. Gazing at the image, I imagined that they were sending me a message of their own.

"It looks like a happy face," I observed. I pointed to the fetal sacs, two wide round eyes, then to a crescent-shaped mass below them. I knew from our last visit that this was the blood. While the babies were growing, the blood was shrinking, but it still comprised almost half the volume of Tiffany's uterus. Somehow, it had taken on the upturned crescent shape of a tremendous grin. It did look like a happy face. Everyone agreed—although Tiffany got more specific.

"It looks like Jack Skellington," she countered. It makes sense that, as a Disney freak, she would reference the lead puppet from

The Nightmare before Christmas, but her comparison was spot-on. There was something about us standing there before a gruesome image trying to find something lovable in it, which I think Tim Burton would have appreciated.

The next week, we took a step closer to the Disney of *The Little Mermaid*. The fetuses had developed clear extremities—feet, hands, heads. We could see them squirming in their sacs—alive and kicking, literally. It was quite a thrill.

If there was an upside to being stuck in a high-risk pregnancy, it was this ongoing ultrasound marathon we were treated to. The doctor needed to check and make sure things were progressing reasonably, and that gave us a regular opportunity to check in with our growing offspring. We'd only known we were pregnant for a month, but we'd already had as many ultrasounds as most expectant parents had in their entire pregnancies.

Tiffany's Uterus became my favorite weekly TV show. We tuned in every Tuesday morning to enjoy the ever-developing adventures of our lovable main characters, labeled helpfully by the doctor as Baby A and Baby B. This week on *Tiffany's Uterus*, Baby A sprouts predeveloped nostrils, while Baby B finally loses his vestigial tail. The two main characters had parallel storylines but distinct personalities. Baby A was our squirmer, constantly swiping and pawing with his protruding limb buds. No doubt about it. We were in for some regular shenanigans from Baby A. Baby B was the little one—cute, smooshy, and lovable. That fetus may still have been lacking eyelashes or discernible genitalia, but one thing the kid definitely had was charisma.

It was appointment viewing, like *Lost*, speaking of which, bed rest had turned Tiffany into that show's number one fan. Our gift to her while she minded our growing babies was a complete series box set. She had never seen it before, but we assured her it would keep her busy on those long days when she was confined to the couch. Boy, were we right. She watched the episodes over and over, with and without commentary tracks. She started developing her own theories about the mysterious island and its inhabitants.

Every week we'd ask her where she was in the show. Had she met the survivors from the tail section? Did she reach the flash-forward? Was Kate with Jack or Sawyer or Jack again? It was our dream come true. We'd turned our surrogate into a nerd, like us. There was no more awkwardness or hesitation between us. When we ran out of baby talk, there was always Oceanic Flight 815 to discuss.

Tiffany caught up before long, and we were all on the same page, waiting for season 5 to start airing live. Right around then came the best episode of *Tiffany's Uterus* yet. Tiffany had stopped cramping entirely, and Dr. S announced that the blood in the uterus had been officially written out of the storyline.

He had some other big news for us, too—the introduction of a new supporting character.

"It's time for Tiffany to start seeing her own ob-gyn," he said.

"So this is the last time we'll see you?"

"I'm not delivering these babies!"

Drew got choked up. Reflexively, he launched into a speech. "We're really going to miss you, Dr. S. You've been so helpful through this entire process. Back when we started, we were so scared, but you really guided us through . . ."

"Does he always do this?" Dr. S interrupted.

"Yes."

Drew stopped himself. Dr. S wasn't a big fan of sentiment.

I hadn't been asking any tough questions for a while because I'd been so afraid of what the answers might be, but I had a big one ready to go. "So . . . a few weeks ago, you told us the odds of either of these babies being born were about fifty-fifty. What would you say they are now?"

"Are you serious?" Dr. S asked. I shrugged. I wasn't sure if he was serious either. "You're out of the first trimester. The odds of Tiffany losing one of these babies now is less than 1 percent."

Drew gazed at me and smiled, just as nervous to ask his own question. "So does that mean we can start telling people we're pregnant?"

"What?! You mean you haven't been telling people? Yes, tell the world!"

18

A FAMILY OUTING

"**Y**OU GUYS ARE FUCKED!"

This was not the reaction we were hoping for when we started telling our friends our good news. Sure, most people went for something more traditional, like "Congratulations!" or "(Sniff, sniff) I'm so happy for you!" Not Jessica.

"YOU'RE ALMOST FOUR MONTHS ALONG, AND YOU'VE DONE NOTHING! YOU GUYS NEED TO WAKE THE FUCK UP!"

Throughout his phone call with her, Drew was practically hyperventilating.

"HAVE YOU REGISTERED FOR GIFTS? SIGNED UP FOR BABY CARE CLASSES? WHAT'S THE THEME OF YOUR NURS-ERY GOING TO BE? DO YOU WANT BASSINETS OR CO-SLEEP-ERS? ARE YOU BAPTIZING? CIRCUMCISING? BANKING CORD BLOOD?"

"Well . . . um . . ."

"YOU'RE FUCKED!!!"

Jessica really is a lovely person. Though she's roughly the height of the average fifth grader, her personality is ten feet tall. She's type A-plus-plus-plus. She'd been friends with Drew since his early days at MTV, and it's no wonder she'd been so successful in her career because she's smart, tough, and focused. She had two young kids of her own and was a terrific, caring mother. That's pretty much how she behaved toward Drew, too, like a mother—a very strict one.

"OH SHIT! WHAT ARE YOU GOING TO DO ABOUT THE SHOWER?"

"My friend Dana offered to host a shower. And Lauren did, too."

"Tell her Victoria said she'd throw us one," I added, listening in.

"SO YOU JUST TOLD EVERYBODY YES?!"

Drew sighed. "I don't really even want a shower."

"TOO FUCKING BAD BECAUSE IT SOUNDS LIKE YOU'RE HAVING THREE!"

"I'll tell them I don't want one. Baby showers are for women. It feels weird."

"SHUT UP! YOU'RE HAVING A SHOWER. END OF STORY."

"I don't like parties. I don't need all the attention."

"NOBODY DOES IT FOR THE ATTENTION. THEY DO IT FOR THE SHIT."

"The shit?"

"DUH, BABY SHIT! YOU NEED BABY SHIT!"

"We'll buy our own."

"NOBODY BUYS THEIR OWN, BECAUSE IT COSTS A FOR-TUNE, BECAUSE NOBODY BUYS THEIR OWN. IT'S ALL A BIG SCAM, AND THAT'S WHY PEOPLE HAVE BABY SHOWERS."

"We don't need much."

Jessica laughed. "YOU'RE HAVING FUCKING TWINS, YOU PSYCHOPATH! THAT'S IT. I'M TAKING YOU TO REGISTER. MEET ME AT BABAS & BOOTIES ON SATURDAY AT NOON."

"Where's Babas & Booties?"

"YOU DON'T KNOW WHERE BABAS & BOOTIES IS? JESUS CHRIST, FUCKING GOOGLE IT!"

Jessica was waiting for us when we arrived. "OKAY, RELAX," she said, in a completely unrelaxing tone. "I TALKED TO DANA, LAUREN, BETH, HEATHER, VICTORIA AND DAVID. WE'RE ALL PLANNING YOUR SHOWER TOGETHER."

"Whoa," Drew protested. "I don't want all those people to have to . . ."

Jessica shoved him. "GET IN THE FUCKING STORE!"

Babas & Booties was a charming baby shop in the San Fernando Valley, with the highest concentration of cuteness I'd ever been completely surrounded by. I didn't know where to turn first. Everything was calling out to me, saying, "Buy me! I will make your babies' lives even more adorable!" I picked up a giant white teddy bear and gave it a squeeze. It was soft, precious, perfect. Jessica snatched it out of my hands.

"NOBODY REGISTERS FOR STUFFED ANIMALS!" she said, throwing the bear back on the shelf. "YOU'LL BE DROWNING IN THAT SHIT BEFORE YOU KNOW IT."

She marched up to the cash register and waited patiently to talk to a salesperson—for about two seconds. Then she waited impatiently.

Cough. No response. Louder *cough.* "HELLO? WE'RE HERE TO OPEN A REGISTRY!"

Finally, a salesman peered up at us. "Mm-hmm," he muttered quietly. He slid a form into a clipboard, then slowly sauntered toward us. He was tall and well dressed, wearing a crisp white button-down shirt and freshly pressed slacks. He had impossibly perfect posture and square shoulders, like the product of a breeding program for snooty salespeople at high-end shops. His hair was carefully slicked back, his lips pursed as he looked us up and down.

"I'm Edmond," he said. "Who's the lucky dad?"

Drew and I looked at each other. He was assuming Jessica was the mother. We hadn't had to explain our family to a stranger before, and we weren't sure how to go about it.

"Um, actually, she's just a friend of ours and . . ."

"THEY'RE BOTH THE DADS," Jessica replied, matter-of-factly. It didn't seem to me like the kind of thing you said matter-of-factly since to most people it was apt to be quite a surprising fact. Drew apparently felt the same way because he jumped in to explain.

"We have a surrogate," he said, and when Edmond stared back stonily, he elaborated. "My sister was the egg donor. We're having twins."

"YEAH, SO SHOW US YOUR DOUBLE STROLLERS!"

Jessica stomped past Edmond, and he lowered his clipboard, sneering at us. I turned to Drew, who clearly noticed it, too. This douchebag sneered at the two dads. Apparently, we didn't fit the profile of the preferred Babas & Booties customer.

I realized this was our first real outing as a gay family, and it was an outing in both senses of the word. Most of the time, Drew and I probably "pass" as straight in public. Two guys, hanging out, joking and laughing, like a couple of frat brothers or a beach volleyball tandem. But when two men are shopping for a double stroller together, it's pretty clear they're more than just drinking buddies. I'd never been introduced to a stranger and outed in one breath like that. I realized this is what I was in for the rest of my life. When you have a baby with your boyfriend, you're not going to pass for straight anymore, and sometimes, as a result, homophobia will stare right down its stuck-up nose at you.

I looked back and forth between two strollers. These were the only two-seaters Babas & Booties sold, which should have made this decision easy.

"What are the advantages of one over the other?" I asked Edmond.

"Well, you could get this one," he said, shrugging, "or you could get that one." He rolled his eyes and waited impatiently. That was his comparison of the two models, in full. Again, Drew and I turned toward each other, both feeling slighted.

"THEY WANT THIS ONE!" Jessica announced. "YOU GUYS PICK THE COLOR."

Drew and I flipped through the swatches for about thirty seconds, before Jessica became annoyed. "JUST PICK ONE, GOD DAMN IT! ORANGE! WHO GIVES A SHIT?"

Edmond uncapped his pen and made a note on his clipboard. "Orange, then?"

Other than Edmond's attitude, registering for baby supplies was a blast. We could point at anything we wanted, and one day soon, *bam!* A UPS truck would deliver it to our door. It was like getting a one-time pass into the magical world where straight people live. Procreating was the key to a fantasyland full of free stuff most gay men would never know, and all of it was delightful. Puppy-faced blankies, crinkly crib toys, musical monkeys that lit up whenever a tiny hand swatted at them.

The only thing more fun was the way Jessica beat Edmond down at every turn.

"Will you be registering for a crib?" he asked at one point.

"THEY ALREADY HAVE CRIBS!" Jessica waved him off, then leaned in toward us for what she considered a whisper. "GET YOUR CRIBS AT BABIES 'R' US. THE FURNITURE HERE IS A RIP-OFF!"

It was hard to be irritated at Jessica because her bossiness was extremely helpful. Edmond made a much better target for our anger.

"I guess we can skip this section," Edmond deadpanned when we came to the breast-feeding equipment. He drew a giant "X" through that line on his registry form.

As Jessica led Edmond around the store, I pulled Drew aside. "Is he being rude because we're gay?"

"Why else would it be?"

"Should we leave?"

"I'm thinking about it," Drew said.

"HEY! FROGGY OR MONKEY?" Jessica shouted from a few aisles away.

"What?"

"COME PICK OUT YOUR TUMMY TIME MAT!"

We rejoined her and Edmond, who was now doodling disinterestedly on our registry form. I had officially reached my fed-up point. It was approximately seventy-five minutes, forty-eight sneers, and eighty-two heaving sighs into our visit when I started mentally preparing myself to shout, "I guess there are no fags allowed at Babas & Booties!" and then storm out.

"WHERE ARE YOU GUYS GOING TO HAVE THIS STUFF DELIVERED?"

"I guess they should send it to Warner Bros," Drew said.

Edmond looked up, suddenly interested. "What is it you do for a living?" Of course. He was probably an actor, and after all his condescension he was now going to slip Drew a head shot. Classic. I couldn't wait to see the smackdown Drew gave him.

"I'm a reality TV exec," Drew said. Yup, there's the bait! Here comes the nibble!

"Oh," Edmond replied. "I was on a reality show."

"Really? What show?"

"*America's Got Talent.*"

I struggled to suppress a guffaw. America may have had talent, but I was pretty sure Edmond didn't. I tried to imagine him performing in any manner. Juggling bowling pins while riding a unicycle. Irish step dancing. Eating fire. Nothing quite seemed like him. I was dying to know.

"What was your talent?"

Big shrug and eye-roll. "Drag."

"Drag?"

"Yeah, I was also on *Ru-Paul's Drag Race.*"

Okay, so we called that one wrong.

Finally, Drew had his opening, and he seized on it to start the Drew Tappon Talk Show. Edmond opened up about everything—his drag persona, Moody Garland, his boyfriend, and how we were so much cooler than all the other gay couples who came in to register for baby stuff. We realized that maybe we had been the ones who were too quick to judge. Edmond wasn't a homophobic prick. He was just a prick.

I knew we'd encounter actual homophobes at some point, and there'd be Edmonds, too, who'd surprise us. This was our life now, and hiding wasn't an option. We were a nontraditional family, and we couldn't control how other people would react to us. All we could do was be ourselves and be proud.

Across the store, Jessica hadn't noticed any of this. She was still running through Edmond's checklist to make sure we had everything we needed. "UGH! I AM NOT LETTING YOU GET A WIPES WARMER! THEY'RE FULL OF FUCKING GERMS!"

19

BYE BYE, BUBBLE

BABAS & BOOTIES was the perfect preparation for the next stop on our parade to parenthood: Orange County. As any good L.A. homosexual knows, Orange County is where they hunt gays for sport. It's also where Tiffany's ob-gyn was located.

"Oh, he's very nice," she assured us. "He delivered Gavin."

"But is he gay-friendly?"

Tiffany shrugged. Of course. How would she know that? It's not something straight people think about when they meet other straight people. Hmm, I wonder if he'll throw a rock through my window if he finds out who I sleep with? That's purely a gay person concern. It's pretty much the first thought that goes through my mind anytime I meet anyone, ever. The ability to spot enemies is the one thing more important to the modern homosexual than gaydar. It's homophobe-dar, and it can save your life—or at least spare you a few moments of awkward conversation with an asshole.

It turns out I didn't have to get very far into the doctor's office to get my first hint of the man's inclination.

"Oh my God, do you see that?"

Drew stopped short. He was just about to open the door to the ob-gyn's office. "What? The nameplate?"

"Yes, the nameplate. I can't believe I didn't notice it before." Drew looked back at me blankly. "Tiffany's doctor's name? See?"

"Dr. Robertson?"

"Patrick Robertson. Drew, our babies are going to be brought into the world by Pat Robertson!"

Drew sighed and pushed me into the waiting room.

By now we'd come to anticipate a certain kind of reception when we first met new people and shared our arrangement with them. "Oh my God, that's incredible! I'm so happy for you all! What an amazing story!"

I believe when Tiffany introduced us to her doctor, the conversation went something like this:

"This is Drew and Jerry. They're the dads of the babies."

"Hello."

The "hello" came with a half nod, but no handshake. Homophobic? Who knows? The man made his living inspecting vaginas. Maybe we just weren't properly equipped to get his attention.

He was nice to Tiffany, and that was more important. He asked her how she was feeling, what she was eating, and how often she was puking. While his hands kneaded her belly like a lump of bread dough, he made gynecological small talk. "You've never had a C-section, right?" "You getting enough folic acid?" And finally, the big one. "Are you going to learn the sex?"

Tiffany shrugged. "Ask them. These are their babies."

Dr. Robertson chuckled, as if she'd made a joke. *Their babies! Ha ha! Good one, pregnant lady!*

Quick to defuse any awkwardness, Drew jumped in. "Yes, we want to find out. We can't wait!"

"Make an appointment for the eighteen-week ultrasound," Dr. Robertson said, again addressing Tiffany. "They'll be able to tell you."

"He hates us," I said to Drew, once we left the office. Tiffany was at the receptionist's desk, making the ultrasound appointment. It was the first time we had a minute to talk.

"What? He was totally nice," Drew said.

"Are you kidding? He didn't even look at us."

"Well, he's her doctor."

"He's a homophobe!"

"What are you guys talking about?" Tiffany asked, rejoining us.

"Nothing!" I said, instantly. "When's the appointment?"

Finding out our babies' sex was a no-brainer for us. We'd had enough surprises already, and the delivery would be incredible enough without the added zing of Dr. Pat Robertson deadpanning, "It's a . . . !"

More than that, we felt the need to mentally prepare ourselves for whatever was coming. We hated to admit it, but the time had come to face our fears: We were terrified of having a daughter.

Drew and I aren't "girly" gays. We have no interest in makeup or hairdressing. We don't know how to tie pigtails or throw tea parties for stuffed animals. We don't know Sleeping Beauty from Cinderella, and we groan when we see those little girls traipsing around Disneyland in their Snow White ball gowns. We couldn't even imagine how we'd deal with puberty. Sure, we could swap notes with our daughter about which boys we thought were cute, but we feared all her questions about getting her period would send us running to Wikipedia or trying to find whichever *iCarly* episode covered the topic. No, she deserved better than that. There was no way we could have a girl. We'd be such a crushing disappointment to her.

The only thing worse than having a girl would be having a boy. Drew and I aren't "manly" gays either, not the kind of Schwarzenegger-slash-Schwarzkopf tough guys a little boy wants to write his "My Dad Is My Hero" essay for school about. We've never owned baseball cards or G.I. Joes. We wouldn't know how to hold a gun upright, let alone sideways the way Keanu Reeves does in *The Matrix*. We don't like monster trucks or mud. And no matter how hard I've tried, I've never been able to get a football to do that cool twirly thing real dudes can do so effortlessly. What would we say when our teenage son came to us with girl troubles? "Eh, sorry kid. Not our forte!"

The ultrasound room was down the hall from Dr. Robertson's office, with an entirely new staff to gawk at us. Tiffany giggled excitedly the moment she saw us. "Well . . . ," she said, "what do you think they're going to be?"

"It really doesn't matter," I replied, though in the back of my head, the rest of that sentence was, "because either way, we're screwed."

As nervous as I was, it was calming to see Tiffany so at ease with the pregnancy at last. The cramps and nausea had subsided, and she could feel the distinct presence of two tiny people inside her. She looked rested and happy. She was as excited as we were, eager to show us her ever-evolving baby bump.

"Tiffany Ireland!" the nurse called. Eric stood up instantly to accompany his wife. Drew and I hung back. We never knew how naked Tiffany was going to have to get at the appointments, so we always waited for the okay to join her.

"Come on!" she smiled, waving us in. We stood up, collected ourselves, and strode confidently to the doorway. This was it. The big moment. The unveiling of our unborn children's genitalia.

"Uh-uh!" a nurse scolded, blocking the doorway. "Only the husband can come!"

Never ones to defy authority, Drew and I stammered. We could see everyone looking at us, the receptionists and patients, wondering who these two other men were. We felt like intruders, exposed and ashamed.

"But they're the dads," Tiffany explained. It was so casual, as if the situation needed no further explanation. Yes, I'm carrying two babies, and this is my husband, but those two men will be raising them. Why are you looking at me like that?

I could feel the pain of a half dozen tongues being bitten simultaneously, but the nurse stepped aside and let us through. "No talking," she warned, as if to get in a parting shot.

As we entered the ultrasound room, a technician was busily preparing the machine. Tiffany lay on the table, with Eric at her side. Finally, the heavyset woman looked up, staring uncomfortably at me and Drew.

"Hi!" Drew beamed, extending his hand. "We're the dads!"

The tech sneered at him. "Ugh, I can't have all these people in here!" She stomped across the room and threw open the door, as if looking around for someone to complain to. "Ugh!" It was like she suddenly remembered some sensitivity training the staff had been forced to endure for our benefit. She slammed the door.

"Stand against the wall, and don't say a word!" she barked.

She didn't introduce herself, but the ultrasound screen identified her by her license number, R423A. She squirted Tiffany's torso with goo from what looked like an old mustard container and began the procedure.

There they were. Our kids. Baby A and Baby B. It had been weeks since we'd seen them, and I just now realized that I actually missed them. I knew almost nothing about them, but I'd grown so attached. They were so much bigger now, so much more human-looking. I could almost picture the day Drew and I would bring them home.

R423A was examining Baby A very closely, nodding and grunting occasionally. She took a still photo, then leaned over the keyboard to type something on the screen.

"B-" she typed.

I squeezed Drew's hand, misting up. It was a boy!

"L-A-D-D-E-R."

Huh? I looked at the whole word. "Hmm . . . bladder looks good," R423A grunted. Then she rubbed her wand over another part of Tiffany's belly.

A minute later, she stopped and took another snapshot. "L-I-V-E-R," she wrote.

It went on like this for ten minutes. "One kidney," she counted, then, five seconds later, "Two kidneys." She went through the entire digestive, circulatory, and respiratory systems, then she started over with Baby B.

R423A sure knew how to keep us in suspense. We'd been in her office for twenty minutes, during which she'd subjected us to the world's longest sonographic striptease.

"Can you tell us the sex?" I asked, finally.

Drew glared at me. How dare I anger R423A? It didn't matter, though, because she ignored me completely.

Finally, I noticed the distinct butt crack of Baby A. This was it. The tech hovered over the crotch, nodding and making notes but saying nothing. I had no idea what I was looking at. I didn't see anything that looked like a penis, but I didn't see anything that looked like a bladder or a liver either, and the kid apparently had those.

"You wanna know the sex?" R423A asked.

Drew and I clutched each other's hands. "Yes! Please!"

She drew a circle on the screen around something that was supposed to be a giveaway. She looked at me to see if I'd figured it out, but all I could do was shrug. She bent down over the keyboard and typed in, excruciatingly slowly, "I-T-apostrophe-S, space bar, A, space bar . . ." Yes? Yes?

The instant the letter "B" popped up on screen, I gasped. "A boy!" I cheered. "Ah, so that's a penis!"

"O-Y," R423A typed. Then she printed out another snapshot.

Drew and I smiled at each other. A boy! It was amazing. With every detail we learned about Baby A, he became more real. He was a boy, with lungs and a stomach and a spleen! In that moment, there was no fear about having to coach his little league team or help him pick a prom date. That could come later. For now, we were just happy to learn a little bit about our kid.

R423A spent a few minutes checking out Baby A's junk and making notes before she switched over to Baby B. She once again paused over the fetus's groin before asking, "Any guesses?"

From where I was standing, this crotch looked exactly the same as the last one. Apparently, though, I was missing something.

"It's a girl!" Tiffany squealed.

The technician confirmed her guess by typing "IT'S A GIRL" on the screen. The second I saw Drew's tears, my own came pouring out, too. Tiffany was crying. Eric slapped us on the backs triumphantly. A boy and a girl. A boy and a girl! It was the biggest shock since we found out we were having twins, but this time, there was no blood in the uterus to dampen our enthusiasm. It was the kind of thing life gives us far too seldom—pure, solid, perfect, completely unspoiled good news. This was a moment to savor.

It took a few moments before we realized R423A had switched off her ultrasound machine and wiped the goo off Tiffany's skin. She lowered her glasses down the bridge of her nose and glared at us, as if wondering why we were still standing there.

"We're done," she said. "Go."

As quickly as we could scramble out the door, we moved our celebration to the hall.

20

THE WEDDING WE'D NEVER HAD

N O ONE WAS MORE AWARE of our impending parenthood than the UPS man. Every day, he arrived with between one and five squijillion packages full of adorable crap for our twins. It seemed like the entire inventory of Babas & Booties was shifting from their San Fernando Valley location to our West Hollywood condo, one cardboard box at a time. Drew's generosity toward his friends had been one of the things that made me fall for him in the first place. I felt doubly lucky that I got to be there when he finally cashed in.

Of course, Drew's good-heartedness had its downside in that everyone who expressed the slightest goodwill toward us was scoring a shower invite. Waitresses, yoga instructors, book club acquaintances. They would all be among our well-wishers.

"Didn't Jessica tell us to keep the guest list to fifty?" I asked Drew, knowing it had ballooned to almost three times that number.

"I'll deal with Jessica," he insisted.

I'd always been under the impression that a baby shower was something you only went to grudgingly. Getting that pastel blue or pink invitation in the mail meant a pregnant friend was shamelessly groveling for gifts, and you'd feel like a jerk if you didn't show up with a steamer trunk full of crib toys. Nobody seemed to see our shower that way, though. People we barely knew were calling us to ask if they could come. "I won't eat anything or take up much space," they pleaded. "I just want to be there!"

"Of course you can come!" Drew would say, and I'd quietly cringe in anticipation of Jessica's inevitable meltdown.

For me, excluding people was much easier, especially when it came to one guest in particular. Things were still tense between me and Bernie, so when the guest list began to swell, he was the first name I crossed off. He'd asked me to be a groomsman in his wedding. Now I was declaring him unwelcome to bestow me with a baby gift at a party someone else was paying for. It felt harsh but also satisfying. This is what you get for voting against my rights, jerk!

It would have been easy to get away with—if not for Drew. "I wish he were coming," Drew sighed more than once when Bernie's name came up. It was two weeks before the event, and fate had nudged my number one frenemy to the forefront of my boyfriend's conscience. By a frustrating coincidence, they'd just spent a week together on jury duty.

For days, they sat next to each other, ate lunch together, watched each other's stuff during bathroom breaks. They were forbidden from discussing their case and forced to talk about absolutely everything else. Inevitably, Bernie opened up about his and his wife's struggle to have a baby. As I'd suspected, they'd given up on in vitro.

"Did you know they're adopting?" Drew asked me.

"No. Really?"

"They're pretty far along in the process, actually. They might be parents before we are."

The shower was only days away, and suddenly, I was having second thoughts about snubbing Bernie. I thought I'd put the decision firmly behind me. I'd weighed all the arguments of whether to invite him and come down firmly with a verdict of "fuck him." There was a strong case indeed to be made for "fuck him," so why did I feel so guilty? I wondered if there was an even stronger case to be made for "enlighten him." He had a good heart. Maybe he'd appreciate our gay family more if he saw it at its most celebratory.

Drew finally broke me down. I decided to rise above the vindictiveness, to be the bigger man. I sent Bernie a lying email telling him his invitation had been returned to me because Jessica had mistakenly put the wrong address on it. Damn Jessica! "I'm so embarrassed, and I'm sorry for the short notice, but of course, I'd love it if you and your wife could join us."

Now I'd have Jessica to deal with myself.

When the big day finally arrived, we rolled up to the shower in style—in a sleek, shiny new minivan. For most people my age, minivans are the great evil, a sign of youth dying, of admitting that you're satisfied to be identified as a parent rather than as a human being with good taste. For me, that stretched-out super-car with the sliding doors was a symbol of triumph. Drew and I had spent two years and a veritable fortune trying to make babies, and we did it. Yes, my youth had died—and hooray for that. Youth sucked. Bring on middle age! This gay's got kids, everyone! Climb aboard, there's room for eight!

The only thing slicker than our new ride was our friend Lauren's house, where the party was held. Her home was a stunner, a masterpiece of modern architecture you could hardly believe was real as you were walking through it, all bold angles, high ceilings, and sunshine. It wasn't the design that made it the perfect place to celebrate, though. It was its hard-partying pedigree. One of the home's previous owners had been the movie producer Don Simpson, known for his raging cocaine keggers in the 1980s. There was no telling how many hookers had turned up dead in the pool in those days. This was a more subdued occasion than wrapping principal photography on *Top Gun*, but it was comforting to know that the ghosts of awesome parties past were smiling down upon us.

We wanted everyone to have a good time, of course, but no one was more important to us than four guests in particular: Tiffany, Eric and their tiny, intrauterine plus-ones. Usually, the person at a baby shower who gets the showering is the one with the baby inside her. At our shower, that woman would be a virtual stranger, and it would be up to us to make her feel welcome.

Before the shower began, we presented Tiffany with a few gifts of her own. Maternity clothes, flowers, a gift certificate for a pregnancy massage. That way, she wouldn't have to go home empty-handed. She was also the first to hear our big announcement, the babies' names. Drew and I, like so many annoying straight couples, had been brainstorming baby names pretty much since our first date. Sometimes, in the middle of a conversation about something completely different, I'd interject with a name that had just popped into my head—"Buster?"—and he'd know just what I meant. "No!" he'd reply.

After eight years of dating, we had exactly seven boy's names to choose from and four girl's names. From those lists, we made our selections.

Our son would be Bennett, our daughter, Sutton.

We tested them out to see how they sounded. "I'm so proud of you, Bennett." "Nice diorama, Sutton!" "Bennett and Sutton, stop smearing pudding on the wall!"

They were perfect—to us, at least.

"Sutton?!" Tiffany said. "Where did you come up with that?"

"We just liked it."

"Did you make it up?" Eric asked.

"No, it's a real name. Ever heard of Sutton Foster?"

"Who?"

"What about Bennett? Are you going to call him Ben?"

"No. We're going to call him Bennett. Why?"

"Nothing."

"Drew!" I needed help, desperately. I was doubting my own children's names. I waved my boyfriend over and pleaded for him to do the explaining. "Tell them about the names."

"Bennett and Sutton?" he said. "They sound rich!"

Tiffany and Eric laughed. "Now that's a good reason!" I knew instantly I'd be using that line for the rest of my life.

Despite being the last guests invited, Bernie and his wife were among the first to arrive. They brought with them an enormous gift basket full of children's books. Like everyone else, they were beaming, so happy for me and Drew.

"Bennett and Sutton," Bernie said. "Love those names!"

In that instant, all was forgiven. We talked about how perfect it would be if the twins could have playdates with their kid someday, and they let me in on a secret they hadn't told anyone else yet.

"There's a birth mother who liked our application. Nothing official yet. She apparently thought it was cool that I worked in Hollywood."

"Does she know you write voice-overs for car crashes?"

"Hey," Bernie said. "We have glamorous jobs."

I'd been worried that seeing them at the shower would be awkward. They'd struggled so hard to have a baby, and now I was rubbing their noses in the fact that my boyfriend and I were having two. Instead, it was the best talk I'd had with Bernie since before Proposition 8. We had more in common than either of us ever expected, and each of us was genuinely happy for the other.

I only spoke to them for a few minutes because there were so many other guests to greet. All of Drew's siblings had flown out, as had his mother, who hated to travel and hadn't visited L.A. in fifteen years. Just about everyone I cared about in the world was in Lauren's house, and I was determined to hug them all.

In our eight years together, Drew and I had never thrown a party before, certainly not one that celebrated us personally. Now here we were with an open bar, a five-person catering crew, and a cake the size of Rhode Island. There was a guest book and a gift table sagging under the weight of far, far too many packages tucked inside stork-themed wrapping paper. We hadn't asked people to wear anything fancy, but even our hippiest friends washed their dreadlocks and put on their best puka shell necklaces for the event. As I gazed around the room, I was stunned to see people from different factions of my life—family, friends, coworkers, Drew's and mine—all mingling effortlessly. My mother and sister conversing with Drew's old boss, my guy friends talking baseball with Eric Ireland, Tiffany bonding with the women from my old writing group.

I suddenly realized that this had become far more than a baby shower. No one even knew these babies yet. That wasn't who brought them here. They had come to celebrate us, me and Drew, in high spirits and business casual attire. At some point, this little party grew into the wedding we'd never had.

"EVERYBODY IN THE KITCHEN! MOVE IT!" Though a hundred fifty people were chattering at once, no one had any problem hearing Jessica.

As the guests shifted en masse, Jessica became impatient. "WHERE'S JERRY? WHERE'S JERRY!!!"

There was no point trying to avoid her. I struggled to slink through the crush of people to get to where she could see me. Jessica was by far the shortest person at the party, and I was fairly well dwarfed by my tall friends, too, so it wouldn't be easy.

Somehow, I found my way next to Drew, who was standing over the cake with Susie, Tiffany, Eric, and most of our immediate families. Jessica was choked up, struggling to contain herself so that she could begin. It was speech time. Jessica took a deep breath and actually talked in a normal voice.

"I'm not going to cry, but I want to say something."

She gazed around the room, which resembled a Mumbai subway car at rush hour. "There are TOO MANY FUCKING PEOPLE HERE!" Everyone laughed, except me and Drew. We knew she was only half kidding.

"You know, it really says something that so many of you came here to celebrate the fact that Drew and Jerry are having kids. It says that DREW AND JERRY CAN'T FUCKING FOLLOW DIRECTIONS! I TOLD THEM TO INVITE FIFTY PEOPLE!"

"It's my fault!" Drew confessed.

"SHUT UP!" Jessica snapped. "It says a lot about Drew that he invited ten thousand people to his baby shower, but it says even more that you all said yes. And I know it's because you care as much about these guys as I do, and the fact that they're having twins just makes you feel like sometimes, life happens the way it should. Good things happen to good people." Jessica shoved Drew, hard. "OH MY GOD, DREW, STOP LOOKING AT ME, OR YOU'RE GOING TO MAKE ME CRY!"

Drew stared at her, all but daring her to break into tears. It worked.

"FUCK IT. I'M DONE!" Jessica waved her hand and disappeared back into the crowd.

All eyes in the room were on Drew and me. One of us had to say something. "Go ahead," Drew said. "You're the writer."

"But I didn't write anything. You're the talker."

That was all the prodding Drew needed. He thanked Jessica and the rest of the Shower Planning Supercommittee for everything they'd done to make this day so perfect. He thanked everyone for coming. He thanked the bartender and the kitchen staff and, though they weren't present, the bakers who'd made the cake. As he was talking, I realized I did have something I wanted to say after all. I tapped Drew on the shoulder, and he gave me the floor.

"When Drew and I started thinking about having kids, it was because we really wanted to make a family, and nothing went exactly the way we planned. Most of you know the story by now. Susie offered us her eggs, and the surrogacy agency matched us up with this amazing woman, Tiffany, and her amazing husband, Eric. For a long time, it didn't look like we were really going to have a baby at all, but somehow now we're having twins. And our lives have already changed so much. We're closer to Susie than ever, and we're so grateful to know Tiffany and Eric. I'd been worried about having a baby with a surrogate because I didn't know what to expect, but when I look at these people now, I realize we've already made a family, and it's one I can't wait to share with my kids."

By now, everyone was sobbing—not just the easy targets like Drew, Susie, and Tiffany but Eric and me, too. Our families and friends—and somewhere in the crowd, Jessica.

Packing up the car with all the gifts took almost as long as the party itself. We filled the entire minivan and had to ask Tiffany and Eric to follow us home in their car with the spillover. With Gavin at home with a babysitter, the Irelands stayed the rest of the day at our condo, helping us open packages. They even bought us a few gifts of their own: some baby clothes and our very first case of diapers and wipes.

The whole day had been so overwhelming—such a constantly shifting kaleidoscope of emotions—that it was a bit of a relief the next day just to bask in the aftermath. By then, all of Drew's family had left, and among the out-of-towners, the only ones who remained were my mother and my sister, Kathy. While Drew caught up on work, I took them to a restaurant down the street for dinner.

"That baby shower was nuts!" Kathy said, as we sat down. A day later, the party was still the only thing we could talk about. "That was bigger than my wedding. C'mon, how many people were there?"

"I think . . . a hundred?"

"That was more than a hundred. It was one-fifty, easy."

"Kathy," my mother elaborated, "they're like the king and king here. They know half the world."

The two of them had visited me many times in the past, but this was their first trip where they met most of my friends. It struck me that they still thought of me as the sheltered, lonely teenager I used to be. This new Jerry came as a bit of a shock to them.

"I'm really glad you're here in California," my mom said. "It's good for the kids."

"How's that?"

"You would have a lot of trouble with a family like this in the Midwest. Here, people actually think this is normal."

Kathy cut her off. "I think what she means is it's nice to see you have so much support."

I knew what she meant. "You're worried about your grandkids, Mom. It's okay. I am, too. Most kids have moms, even here in L.A. We're kind of in uncharted waters. But Drew and I wouldn't be having kids if we didn't think we could give them everything they needed. You saw it yesterday. These kids aren't even born yet, and already, they're so loved."

"Jerry," she replied. "They're gonna be fine."

We started talking about parenthood. My sister, a mom of three, was full of anecdotes and advice. My mom was happy to remind both of us of all the headaches we gave her when we were growing up. We all tried to imagine how I'd handle the challenges ahead. We laughed, worried, and wondered. It was one of the best conversations we'd ever had.

Just as our food arrived, my cell phone began to vibrate. I almost didn't answer, but I decided I should at least see who was calling. The ID came up "Eric Ireland," so I picked up. He wasn't a chatty man, so whatever he wanted, it would be quick.

"Hi, Eric."

The connection was terrible, and the street noise didn't help. I caught a few words here and there. "Tiffany . . . strong . . . drove . . ." I couldn't make sense of it.

"Hold on, Eric. I can barely hear you. Where are you?"

His next sentence came through loud and clear:

"The emergency room."

21

TIFFANY'S REPLACEMENT

ERIC SPOKE IN A CALM, reassuring manner. Nothing in his tone suggested cause for alarm. He urged me not to panic.

Tiffany had gone into labor, that was all.

"They gave her some medication to stop the contractions," Eric explained. "They're doing a test now that will determine if she's going to deliver in the next two weeks."

"Um . . . what? How do they know when she'll deliver?"

"They can't tell exactly. But somehow, they can tell if it'll be in the next two weeks. We'll know the results in two hours."

"Should Drew and I come down there?"

"No," Eric insisted. "I mean, not unless it comes back positive. Then . . . yeah."

I raced home to be with Drew, googling "contractions 25 weeks" on my iPhone all the way. As I suspected, the results weren't encouraging. I found a few articles about preemies who'd survived at this stage, but—there was always a "but."

The more encouraging stories were the ones of women who went into labor at twenty-five weeks but scored negative on this test. Many of them went on to carry their babies full term. That was a much, much better outcome to hope for.

Meanwhile, we had two hours to wait. To wait—and to curse the very notion of surrogacy. This was supposed to be the easy way for us to have a baby, the one that put us in the driver's seat. Instead, it felt more like we were banging around in the trunk, bound and gagged. First we found out Susie's eggs were no good, now Tiffany's womb was suspect—again. Our babies, who weren't even born yet, had already lived through more adversity than I had in my entire life. This was hardly the ideal way to make a family.

I felt like a fool for believing I could be a dad, for naming two little bundles of cells who might never even take their first breath, for throwing a fucking party to celebrate my good fortune. We should have held off longer before announcing the pregnancy, like until the kids were in preschool. I wondered if this was a sign God existed because he'd found a way to jerk me around after all.

To say it was the longest two hours of my life would be inaccurate because it was exactly as long as two hours were supposed to be. I know because I was staring at my cell phone the whole time, eyes transfixed on the clock, watching each minute tick away exactly sixty seconds after the last one. It was two hours of my life, the same as it was for people who spent that time waiting in line for Space Mountain, or watching the extended season finale of *The Amazing Race*, or pushing out their own little miracle just a few floors up from Tiffany in Labor and Delivery. Two hours— hardly any amount of time at all and yet forever.

Kathy and my mom went back to their hotel so Drew and I could be alone. We didn't say anything as we sat on the couch, waiting for my cell phone to vibrate. Every conversation we would have for the next few months would be predicated on the call we were about to get, on a simple yes or no that determined the fate of two babies and all the people they'd already touched just by attaching to a stranger's uterine wall. The silence was broken at last by a gentle buzz. In front of us on the coffee table, my iPhone was quivering.

"Hello?"

"It's negative."

I doubled over onto Drew's chest, wrapped my arms around him, and squeezed as tightly as I could. It was exactly what I would have done if Eric had given the other answer instead.

If the baby shower had been like our wedding, then the honeymoon had just been abruptly canceled. Dr. Robertson ordered Tiffany on full bed rest. No work, no walking, not even any standing if she could avoid it. She filed for a leave of absence from her job, and Drew and I didn't need to reread our surrogate contract to figure out what this meant. We were on the hook for everything— not just her lost wages but housecleaning and child care, too. For the remaining trimester, Tiffany's entire function in life would be to incubate our fetuses. As a result, she was going to have to hire someone else to be Tiffany for a while.

She deserved every penny, of course. She'd endured so much more than she signed on for, without ever complaining. We just weren't sure exactly where the money would come from. After all the other expenses of surrogacy, we were broke.

As it turned out, the solution to all our problems came from an entirely predictable source.

"I'll do it."

Drew was on the phone with Susie. "Do what?"

"I'll be the person. The one who lives with Tiffany and takes care of her."

"Susie, she lives here, in California."

"So I'll fly out."

"For three months?"

"Why not?"

"What are you going to do about your job?"

"Quit."

"Susie!"

"It's just a job."

"No. You don't have to do this."

"This is family. Family's more important."

Before Drew could convince his sister not to throw her life away for our benefit, Susie was on a plane to L.A. No one was more excited than Tiffany. She had already logged what felt like ten thousand hours on her living room couch, and now she'd imagined having to open her home to some crotchety old woman who barked at her to lie completely still at all times. Susie would be more like a roomie, a chatty girlfriend who'd keep her morale up.

We picked Susie up at LAX and drove her to the Irelands' house. Only as we lugged Susie's suitcase over the threshold did the surrealism of the situation hit me. These were two women from different walks of life, brought together by fate to live together so that they could bring two babies into the world and hand them over to a pair of gay men to raise. Forget *Tiffany's Uterus*. This was our sitcom, *Wombmates*.

The Irelands' home was perfect for a family of exactly three. Susie would need to be squeezed in, but she didn't mind sleeping in Eric's home office, underneath the shelves of trophies from his pro ball days. In many ways, it was preferable to living at home with her parents. This would be an adventure.

For Drew and me, it felt a little like we were dropping our daughter off at college. I had to assure Drew that his little sister would be all right. "How well do we know these people?" he asked.

"Well enough to let them give birth to our children."

Around this time, I was highly tuned into the news of anyone else's pregnancy. I stopped being one of those people who groaned at all the ultrasound photos expectant parents would post on Facebook and instead began commenting on every single one. "Aw, look at his unfused cranial cortex!" "That's a good healthy placenta there! Way to go!"

One night, Drew told me the story of his friends Doug and Peggy, who'd just had their first child. Peggy had such a rough C-section that afterward she couldn't even hold her own baby, much less feed her or sing her lullabies. Stories like that always broke my heart, though quietly I sighed in relief that these kinds of scenarios didn't apply to Drew and me. No matter how difficult Tiffany's delivery ended up being, Drew and I would come into our kids' lives well rested and raring to go.

With Peggy out of commission, Doug was forced to snap into action. When his daughter screamed her head off, Doug tried everything he could think of to calm her. He changed her, fed her, cradled her, but she was inconsolable. What finally did the trick was *Goodnight Moon.*

All throughout his wife's pregnancy, Doug had been reading the book to her belly. As soon as his newborn daughter heard the sweet, calming poetry, in her daddy's familiar voice, she felt safe. She stopped crying, and she looked up at Daddy with big, loving eyes. In an instant, Doug bonded with his daughter. Drew could barely finish the story, he was so choked up. It was a gorgeous anecdote—touching and hopeful. It was the tale of a dad, without any help from a mom, saving the day. No sooner was Drew finished than I flew into a raging panic.

"Why would you tell me that!" I shouted.

"What do you mean? It's the most beautiful story ever!"

"Yeah, and it'll never happen to us! We've never said a word to those kids!"

Drew's story resonated with me for all the wrong reasons. It wasn't our voices the babies would recognize. It was Tiffany's and Susie's. Let's face it. Eric wasn't very chatty, so his voice was unlikely to make a big impression. Our kids, destined to be raised by two men, would be used to hearing only the voices of women. Oh my God. The first time we spoke to them, they'd be terrified!

A nightmare scenario leapt into my head. We're in the delivery room. It's the happiest moment of our lives. But when the doctors hand us the babies, the two of them treat us like strangers. They won't stop crying. Then they hear Tiffany's voice, and finally, they calm down. It's only when she holds them that they're at ease. Instantly, all the biology in the world becomes irrelevant. They welcome Tiffany like a mother and come to regard us as the jerks who took them away from her.

Then I pictured an even more alarming scenario. What if the voice they were drawn to wasn't Tiffany's but Susie's? She had the biological connection, and now she had the proximity, too. They would know her much better than they would know us.

I'd heard so many stories about the agony that comes with adoption. Birth mothers crying for hours or days. Adoptive parents wracked with guilt and torn apart by a swell of sympathy, even as they're celebrating the arrival of their child.

Surrogacy wasn't going to spare us that kind of pain. It would only shift it into different forms, onto different people. I finally realized that we weren't going to get through this without crying some sad tears as well.

"I don't want Susie in the delivery room," I said to Drew. The topic had never come up, but it seemed obvious now that it would. Susie was living with Tiffany, so she was sure to be around when the babies arrived. She'd want to witness their birth—who wouldn't? Drew would want her there, and Tiffany probably would, too. To me, though, it just didn't seem right. Susie was quickly becoming more important to our babies than we were. All the boundaries we swore we'd draw were quickly disappearing. It may have been the cruelest thing I'd ever done—it certainly felt like it—but it also felt necessary. At that moment, I probably would have kept Tiffany out of the delivery room if it were possible.

"Okay," Drew said. That easily, he gave in. I was stunned that he didn't fight me. He'd always been so protective of Susie, such a compassionate big brother. Now, though, he had an even bigger concern—in fact, two of them.

I felt guilty, conflicted, and yet pettily validated. It was a new emotion to me. Fatherhood, I figured. That's probably what it was.

22

FOURTH OF JULY WITH THE FAMILY

WHAT DO YOU SAY TO SOMEONE you've never met, who doesn't speak English, and whose brain is approximately the size and consistency of a lump of personal pizza dough? Add to that the fact that you won't be speaking to them directly but rather through the protruding belly skin of a woman you've known for less than a year. And go!

I had decided to record a message for Tiffany to play to my kids so they would know my voice. Suddenly, though, I'd found myself with a severe case of Daddy's block. I couldn't steal the *Goodnight Moon* thing. I'd feel like a fraud to my own kids. What else was there? *Green Eggs and Ham*? The libretto to *Miss Saigon*? At least I knew that one by heart. How about that paper I wrote for my college Shakespeare class on the notion of nothingness in *King Lear*? That was a solid A-minus, if I remembered correctly. It's not like it mattered what I said anyway. The kids wouldn't understand the words. The idea was that they would find comfort in the sound of my voice. My squealy, whimpering nerd voice. I tried to forget how much I hated the sound of it on tape and just hit "Record."

"Well, hewwo there, everyone! It's your Daddy! How're my wittle fwiends today?"

Stop. Ugh, did I just do that? Baby talk? Erase! Time for a new take.

"This is a message for the two best babies in the whole wide world!"

Stop. Yuck. Pandering. These fetuses are going to walk all over me if they hear me talking like that. I needed to sound more natural.

"Yo! Daddy here!"

Stop. Just stop. I didn't need to talk down to my kids just because they were roughly the size of gerbils. Even their precognizant mush brains deserved a little respect.

Nothing I said sounded right. I didn't want to force my kids to listen to me rambling nonsense night after night, much less my sister-in-law and my surrogate. They'd think it was sweet at first, but after a few weeks, it'd be a regular nuisance. Ugh, time to play the tape again. Susie and Tiffany would probably work up an impression of my baby tape and crack each other up by doing it. "Yeah, Tiff, you really nailed his awkward pause that time!" Together, they'd swipe my heartfelt sentiments and turn them into catchphrases to use behind my back. Why not? It's what I would do.

My baby tape would be only one of dozens of things bonding Tiffany and Susie. From the sound of things, they were getting along famously. When Drew called his sister to check in, she always had a ton of stories to share, usually with Tiffany guffawing in the background.

For years, Tiffany had been making Eric a thermos full of coffee to keep him awake during his night shifts. When they were out of cream, she grabbed the closest thing she could find—Bailey's Irish Cream. She didn't realize until Susie pointed it out that her dairy substitute was 17 percent alcohol. Of course, Eric never complained.

Tiffany would tease Susie constantly about finding her a boy-friend. "You'll make a great wife someday," she assured her. "You're so homely." She had meant to say "homey," of course, but by mis-speaking, she provided them with one of their favorite running jokes. They'd also discovered the computer game Plants vs. Zom-bies and would kill hours together by killing the walking dead.

"Did you get to the ones who ride dolphins yet?" Tiffany would ask.

"No, I'm stuck on the pole vaulters."

"Block them with the giant nuts!"

Nothing was more entertaining to the stars of *Wombmates* than their wacky neighbor, Mrs.—well, nobody actually knew her name. Nobody knew much about her at all. She was ghostly and rail-thin—or maybe she was morbidly obese. She was in her late seventies or eighties, or perhaps she was only thirty-five. It was hard to tell much about her when all anyone ever saw was the faint glow of her irises peeking out from behind her curtains. All anyone knew for sure was that she was obsessed with the Irelands. Though she never spoke to them, she watched them the way other recluses watch QVC. Instead of ordering herself a lot of cheap crap, she sent the cheap crap to her neighbors.

Every few days, she'd drop off some bizarre gift on the Irelands' doorstep. A plate of donuts, a can of off-brand cola, a dying pot-ted plant. When Tiffany's belly started to show, the goodies took on a prenatal tone. One day, it would be a trial-size can of Similac, the next a handful of newborn diapers or a set of feeding spoons rubber-banded together. She left a coloring book, presumably for Gavin, about being a big brother. Who knows what she thought of Susie. The gifts were unwrapped, save for a plastic Target bag. There was never a note or card. She didn't ring the doorbell. Her packages would appear when the Irelands were away or in the backyard, as if by magic.

When we first met Tiffany, she reminded us deeply of Susie. Now the few differences they'd had seemed to be melting away. As Susie grew closer to our surrogate, so did we. Tiffany told us about her frustrations with work and how she was dreading turning thirty. To qualify for surrogacy, a woman has to agree that she's not planning to have any more kids of her own, but Tiffany confessed to us that she really wanted another baby. Eric didn't. If we'd known that before we chose her, it might have given us pause. At this stage, though, we trusted her fully with our kids.

Three weeks into Susie's stay, we all decided that she'd earned a weekend off. Drew and I arrived on Saturday morning to pick her up. She would be gone only a day and a half, but from the way she hugged Tiffany good-bye, it was as if one of them were being deployed overseas. They were verging on inseparable.

I hopped in the back of the minivan, and we waved to the Irelands as we drove off.

"Woohoo! Weekend off! Let's party!" I shouted, but nobody shared my enthusiasm. In the front seat, Susie had her head in her hands, trying to keep from sobbing.

"What's wrong?" I asked.

Drew rested his hand on her shoulder. "You're miserable, aren't you?" It was then that whatever tears Susie had been holding back came out in a flood. "Oh, honey . . . ," Drew said.

Was it possible I'd misread the entire situation? Clearly, Drew knew his sister better than I did. He'd seen through her brave face when I hadn't. She was a champion at masking her pain, just like her brother. No wonder he knew she was faking it.

"Is she mean to you?" I asked.

"No!" Susie insisted. "Tiffany's great."

"Are you homesick?" She shook her head. Susie took a moment to collect herself, then she told us the part of the story she never felt comfortable sharing in Tiffany's presence.

Many of her complaints were typical new job gripes. She was feeling overworked and underappreciated. With Tiffany always on the couch, Susie never had a moment to put her feet up. She was constantly mopping, scrubbing, changing diapers, playing board games, and, most exhausting of all, trying to stay upbeat. One night, Tiffany and Eric teased her about a lackluster dinner she'd prepared, and afterward, she closed the door to her room and bawled. Susie was also struggling with standard roommate issues—a lack of privacy, differing schedules and interests. Even Plants vs. Zombies had become a trial. It turned out Tiffany was hypercompetitive, turning each Flash-powered game into a showdown on the scale of Ali vs. Frazier. All Susie wanted to do was to slaughter zombies. Tiffany wanted to slaughter her new houseguest—and rub her face in it.

But the real problem wasn't her—it was him.

"He hates me," Susie confessed through her sobs. "He doesn't like anything I do. He barely talks to me. I know he doesn't want me there."

Susie had a new nemesis, and he was only three feet tall. She may have been a hero to us, but to Gavin, she was Lex Luthor, a devious villain intent on taking over his world and destroying his hero, Mommy. Susie made scrambled eggs for him, changed his diapers, and played trains with him—all the things Mommy was supposed to do. She put him in time-out when he misbehaved, told him when to go to bed, and she made his peanut butter sandwiches all wrong. Mommy no longer did much of anything for him. When Gavin wanted something, Mommy's response was, "Ask Susie."

Our unique plan for making a baby had confused a lot of people, but none more than the little man whose life had changed the most of all. He could point at Mommy's belly and say, "Drew and Jerry's babies!" But when he pointed at Susie, he'd shout, "Go home!" To his two-year-old mind, Susie had been brought in to replace Mommy, and he was going to fight her with every weapon in his arsenal—tantrums, tantrums, and super-tantrums.

Gavin was at the age where he'd perfected that ear-piercing squeal only toddlers, teakettles, and suffocating dolphins make, the one that makes grown-ups give in instantly just so they'll stop. That excruciating sound was just about the only thing Susie ever heard from him. That and "I don't want you here!" More than once, he dragged her suitcase with all his might to the front door and demanded she leave his house, now. "Bye!" he'd shout.

"Gavin, I'm not . . ."

"Bye! Bye, Susie!" Then he'd shove her so hard she'd almost fall over.

The hardest part for Susie was that Tiffany did very little to stop Gavin's defiance. It wasn't just that she was bedridden and unable to chase after her kid. On some level, Tiffany must have appreciated the attention. With all the bed rest restrictions, she wasn't even allowed to pick her son up or get down on the floor and play with him. The two fetuses she was carrying came between her and her favorite job, being a mother. Gavin's fierce loyalty to her was one of the few things she was still able to enjoy. She never noticed how much it was hurting Susie.

Susie's status among our friends had now eclipsed sainthood. She had taken on the aura of a mythical superhuman-like creature and was revered with goddess-like devotion by everyone we knew. Everyone except Rainbow Extensions.

"Well, good for her, but I would never do anything like that for my brother." Our caseworkers may have changed, but their cluelessness was one constant we could count on.

I called them to make sure they were taking care of Tiffany financially. I knew how unreliable their accounting department was and how reluctant Tiffany was to complain. It seemed wise to step in.

"We haven't paid her anything," caseworker number 4283 told me. Not surprising, but what did shock me was the reason. "She hasn't asked. In fact, I was going to ask you if you'd heard from her. She won't return our calls."

Tiffany had confessed to us before that she couldn't stand Rainbow Extensions. They phoned her regularly to check in, but the calls were awkward and forced. They never knew what to say to her, and she never knew how to respond. When she saw Rainbow Extensions' number pop up on her caller ID, she sent the call to voicemail, then deleted the message without listening to it.

We'd always been slightly amused by her attitude toward them, mostly because we wished we could do the same thing. Now, though, we were worried. She was losing a huge amount of money on bed rest. The Irelands may not have been destitute, but they weren't rich either. Losing Tiffany's salary was a big blow to them. How were they getting by?

We realized we were going to have to have a very uncomfortable talk with Tiffany, about the one subject surrogates and intended parents were never supposed to discuss: money. I knew why it was off limits. It devalued the whole arrangement to acknowledge the price tag. On some level, Drew and I were consumers purchasing a service from Tiffany, but it was better to talk about the other levels—the sacrifice, the goal, the gift of life. Pregnancy inspired happiness. Money inspired cynicism.

"Are you doing okay?" we asked Tiffany in her kitchen one day. "You know, financially?"

"Oh yeah. I'm fine, thanks for asking."

"It's just that Rainbow Extensions told us you never asked for your lost wages compensation."

"Oh, I don't want you guys to have to pay that."

"But we want to!" Drew insisted. "You're making babies for us. We want to take care of you."

"You deserve it," I added.

"If you don't like dealing with the agency," Drew said, "we can pay you directly. I'll write you a check right now."

Tiffany smiled and waved him off with her hand. "I don't need it. I filed for disability."

"You can get disability? How come Rainbow Extensions never told us that?"

Tiffany shrugged. "Because they're idiots."

Not wanting to deal with the agency, Tiffany had found her own solution to the problem, one that paid her 100 percent of her lost wages and saved us thousands of dollars. After all our worrying, it turned out she was the one taking care of us.

I realized that by sidestepping the subject of money, we had only been allowing the cynicism to flourish, to suppress our discomfort at the thought that when Tiffany looked at us, she saw dollar signs. It didn't feel that way any longer. Now I knew for sure that we were on the same side.

We spent Fourth of July weekend with the Irelands, doing all the things people do on the Fourth of July. We cooked hamburgers on the backyard grill. We sat on lawn chairs and waved tiny American flags. We watched from a safe distance while Eric set off fireworks at the bottom of the driveway.

For weeks, Tiffany had been talking about how much the babies kicked. One time, Bennett wailed on her so hard she expected to see his foot poking through her skin. They just never seemed very mobile when I was around. Somewhere amid all the revelry and the crackling of M-80s, Tiffany reached out and nearly yanked my hand off my arm. "Now!" she shouted. "Here they go!"

She pressed my palm hard against her belly. I waited and waited but felt nothing.

I started to pull my hand away, convinced I had missed the tossing and turning once again, but Tiffany wouldn't allow me to let go. "Wait!" she commanded. She laid back and relaxed, like she was trying to will the babies to move with her mind. A moment later, there was a rumble, like a tiny earthquake with an epicenter at her belly button. Then I felt it—a forceful thump rippling beneath my palm. Thump. Thump. The baby seemed to appreciate the resistance my hand created, because the first kick was followed by two more.

"Did you feel that?" Tiffany shouted.

"Holy crap, yes!"

Tiffany laughed. "That's Bennett."

"You can tell which one is which?"

"Yeah, he's the kicker. He wakes me up at night."

"Wow, that was Bennett! I can't believe I just felt Bennett kick."

"What are you waiting for?" Tiffany asked. "Talk to him!"

She was right. This was my chance—not to lay down some overly thought-out, rehearsed-sounding diatribe but just to chat with my kids. They were definitely paying attention. I leaned over Tiffany's midriff.

"Hi, Bennett. Hi, Sutton. This is Daddy. Well, one of your daddies. The other daddy thinks it's dumb to talk to a belly. Maybe you'll think so, too, but too bad. You're stuck in there, so you're going to listen. I really can't wait to meet you guys. I promise I'm going to love you no matter who you turn out to be, and I'm going to let you figure that out all on your own. Personally, it took me a while. Hopefully, you'll get to it a little quicker.

"Just hang tight in there. You've been doing a great job these last few months, and I know it hasn't been easy, but it's all going to be worth it. Just keep taking care of each other, because that's what a brother and sister should do. Oh, and Bennett, I know it's fun to kick, but take it easy on Tiffany."

I looked at Tiffany, and she smiled back at me in a way that affirmed exactly why she'd chosen to become a surrogate in the first place. I turned back toward her belly, correcting myself.

"Aunt Tiffany," I said. "That's what you guys should call her."

23

ONE LAST PEACEFUL SLEEP

THERE'S NO PERFECT TIME to have a baby, but if there is an absolute worst time, it has to be during summer movie season. No matter how old Drew and I got, the deluge of heavily promoted blockbusters that arrived on a screen near us between Memorial Day and Labor Day could always turn us back into giddy, Sno Cap–addicted kids. As we approached our due date, we started marking time not by how many weeks our children had been incubating but by what box office smashes we'd managed to cross off our must-see lists. As much as we were dying to see Bennett and Sutton, we were really hoping they didn't mess up our plans to see the new *Harry Potter*.

With every film that we caught on the big screen, we relaxed a bit more. By the time we saw *The Hangover*, the nursery was set up. Sacha Baron Cohen's *Bruno* took us past the point of viability. The only thing arriving with the same regularity as the big-studio releases were Tiffany's false alarms. Just as often as we headed out to the multiplex, we found ourselves rushing down to Orange County to meet Tiffany in Labor and Delivery, only to get a call halfway there that she'd been sent home. We spent a couple of nights sleeping on the Irelands' couch because Tiffany was convinced she'd be checking into the hospital by sunrise.

We never actually made it as far as the admission desk, but eventually, Rainbow Extensions decided it was time we visited the place where our babies would be born. They set up a tour right around the time Judd Apatow's *Funny People* came out. Drew and I thought it was unnecessary. We'd been in hospitals before. It's not like we would notice if this particular Labor and Delivery unit was missing some crucial piece of equipment we wanted them to have. "They call that a speculum? We're outta here!" We certainly weren't requesting anything out of the ordinary, like Tiffany giving birth into a vat of butter or a hollowed-out tree trunk or something. Drew didn't even bother to come with me. There seemed like no point in both of us taking time off from work.

As I entered the hospital, it was just as I expected, perfectly hospital-like. People in white coats, people in wheelchairs, Purell dispensers aplenty. I stepped off the elevator and was greeted by Ann, the woman who conducted these tours. "Hi," she said. "I'm Ann." So far, this was totally skippable.

Ann showed me the waiting area. Age-old magazines, check. She took me to the nurse's station. Politely smiling ladies, check. She allowed me to peek into the delivery room. A bunch of equipment I knew nothing about, check.

Then she explained the security band procedure. After a baby is slapped on the butt, sponged of goo, and has its umbilical cord tied off, he or she is fitted with a high-tech bracelet that lists their name, their parents' names and a UPC code that can be scanned by hospital personnel. Any time a parent goes to visit an infant in the nursery, parent and baby both get scanned to make sure they match up. It was all a means of preventing baby theft, but it seemed funny to me that for their first forty-eight hours, my kids would essentially be treated like boxes of Cocoa Puffs at Shop Rite.

"You'll need to decide whether you or your partner is going to wear the band," Ann said.

"We'd each like to have one, actually."

Ann shook her head. "Nuh-uh. Can't do that."

"What do you mean? I thought each of the parents got one."

"We only have two bands, and the mom has to wear one."

"Actually, there are two dads and a surrogate. There is no mom!" Over the last few months I'd come to sound like Wes, the president of Rainbow Extensions, when someone brought up the M-word.

"She's giving birth, so for our purposes, she's the mom."

"You can call her what you want. She's not a legal parent and she's not allowed to take the kids home, so she doesn't need a band. Drew and I should have the bands."

"The babies come out of her, so she needs to wear the band that matches them. It's a security procedure. And that leaves us one band for either you or your partner."

"So if she's wearing a band, that means she'll be able to visit them in the nursery?"

"Is that a problem?"

"No, but it's a problem that my partner won't be able to visit them because there aren't enough bands for him."

"We only have two bands."

"We're having twins. Do the babies split one band?"

"No, we'll make two."

"Well, if you can make an extra band for the kids, why can't you make an extra band for the parents, too?"

Ann and I had reached a turning point in our relationship. I'd thrown an unwanted curveball into her well-rehearsed routine. She stared at me, wearily. "We can give your partner a visitor band," she sighed. "He can visit the babies as long as he's with you."

She meant to placate me, but it only made me feel worse. On the night our kids were born, they would have one dad—and one visitor. It might only be a matter of procedure, but one of us would start off as a second-class father.

Things only got worse when Ann showed me the patient recovery rooms, where new moms would enjoy precious bonding time with their infants.

"Great," I said. "Ideally, we'd like our room to be in the same wing as Tiffany's, but not right next door, so she doesn't have to hear our kids crying or anything. She'll probably want to get some sleep."

Ann gave me that look again. "You want two rooms?"

"Well, of course. Tiffany needs a room to recover."

"Tiffany will have a room. That's what Labor and Delivery is for—recovering mothers."

"Right, but she's not the mother."

"For our purposes, your surrogate is the mother."

"So Drew and I can't have a room?"

"I assure you, it's just an issue of space. One baby, one room."

"But we're having two babies."

"You know what I mean."

"I'm not suggesting you throw a pregnant lady out on the street, but my partner and I would like an opportunity to bond with our kids when they're born."

"And you'll have that. You'll be able to visit them in the nursery."

"Of course," I said. "We'll have wristbands."

I could see the logic from both sides. Ann had a hospital to run, and rooms were for people who needed medical attention. Then there was my side of the argument, which was that it broke my heart to think of spending our children's first night on Earth in a motel down the street. After all we'd been through, hadn't we earned the right to be awoken every fifteen minutes by our crying twins? Wasn't that one of the reasons we chose surrogacy in the first place, because we wanted to be present for all our kids' crucial moments, such as their first pee, poop, and late-night feeding?

Finally, I understood the point of the hospital tour. It wasn't so I could check out the hospital. It was so they could check me out. This was very possibly their first-ever surrogate birth, and they were in no way prepared for us. I thought back to our first conversation with Wes, when he called us pioneers. In twenty-first-century America, this was what being a pioneer meant. It meant dealing with a world that has no procedures in place for a family like yours, that has yet to understand and respect your situation, where no one has yet fought for and won your equal rights.

I knew Rainbow Extensions would be no help. If Drew and I wanted what we felt we deserved, we were going to have to win it for it ourselves—and fast.

At exactly thirty-five weeks, or roughly around when Drew saw the Sandra Bullock-Ryan Reynolds romcom *The Proposal* for the second time in theaters, Dr. Robertson called an official end to Tiffany's bed rest. She was allowed to stop taking the medication that suppressed her contractions and could roam around her own home freely. If she went into labor, no one would try to stop it. That meant two things for Drew and me: one, that we could be dads any day, and two, that Susie was now relieved of her Tiffany-minding duties. We headed down to the Irelands' house to pick her up. Drew was ecstatic his little sister would be staying with us for the remainder of the pregnancy. Not only could she help us decorate the nursery, but he was dying to have someone new to see *The Proposal* with.

What none of us expected is that we'd have to fight to get Susie back. As we lugged her suitcase to the front door, Gavin came screaming across the house. "NOOOOOOOOOO!"

He lunged for her bag and held on with all his might. "Susie, stay!" he demanded.

Drew got down to reason with him. "Aw, Gavin. It's okay. Mommy can take care of you again. We need Susie to come with us."

"Nope!" Gavin yelled. "Sorry!" He refused to budge, his tiny hands clawing the canvas of Susie's luggage.

None of us had realized until that moment how attached Gavin had grown to Susie. I looked at Susie to see if she had any ideas of how to calm him down, but she was hiding her face. Crying. The separation, it seemed, was hitting her just as hard.

"Just go," Tiffany urged. She crouched down on Gavin's level and pried his hands from the bag. "Trust me."

So we did, hurrying out the door to the sounds of a little boy sobbing and his mommy trying to comfort him.

By Tiffany's next doctor's appointment, she was fully embracing her newfound freedom. I'd never heard anyone so excited to describe a trip to the supermarket or Quizno's. Emboldened, she was setting her sights even higher. "Does this mean I can . . . go?" she asked Dr. Robertson.

We all knew where she meant. This had been the longest period of Disneyland withdrawal of Tiffany's adult life.

"I'd wait another week before you do that," the doctor said.

Five days later, Tiffany drove to Anaheim, advising us to wait by the phone. It was time to realize her dream of giving birth in Mickey's homeland. She could practically taste the golden lifetime passes Sutton and Bennett would be granted, the early welcome they'd receive into the realm of Disney elite.

The irony of bed rest ending was that it did nothing to speed the delivery along. Now off her anticontraction medication, Tiffany was actually having fewer contractions. Even a day spent waddling across Tomorrowland did nothing to jolt her uterus into action. All it did was exhaust her so much that she spent the next day mostly in bed, though at least this time it was by choice.

It was disappointing to me, too, because if nothing else, a Disneyland birth would have meant not having to deal with Ann and her procedures. Surely, Drew and I would have full visitation over Bennett and Sutton if they arrived on Mr. Toad's Wild Ride. Would Cinderella kick us out of her castle the night our kids were born? I think not.

It was a fun dream, but it wasn't going to happen, not for us. Damn it, our kids would be born in a hospital after all.

At thirty-seven weeks, Dr. Robertson brought up a previously un-thinkable idea, that we might actually have to induce labor. Drew and I waved off the notion. We would have preferred to leave the kids in as long as possible, both for their sake and so we could squeeze in a screening of *Inglourious Basterds* before they were born. At the first mention of the word "induction," though, Tiffany was ready to check into the hospital. "Can we do it today?" she asked.

We settled for an appointment at the thirty-eight-week mark. That was generally considered full-term for twins, and seven more days was about all Tiffany felt she could last.

The day before Tiffany's induction, Drew's mother flew out from Rochester for the second time in three months. Together with her and Susie, we checked into a motel five minutes from the hospital.

It was here that Drew and I would spend our last night of child-lessness, within ten feet of an ice bucket and eighty of the River-side freeway. We'd probably be up all night, or so I thought, until Drew pulled out a Xanax a friend had given him. It was supposed to help him sleep. Instead, the thought of taking a nonprescribed medication was just adding to his anxiety. "I don't know how I'll react to it! What if I can't wake up tomorrow morning?"

He rolled the little pink pill over and over in his palm. "Do you want half?"

"No way. I'm not taking pills I don't have a prescription for! Besides, I don't think I'll have any trouble falling asleep. I'm exhausted."

ZzzzzzzsnAAAAAAARRRRFFFF!   ZzzzzzzsnAAAAAAARRR-RFFFF!

Twenty minutes later, it was Drew's snoring that was keeping me awake, along with a surge of anxiety. It didn't seem fair, so I jabbed him in the ribs.

Zzzz—"HUH?"

"Hey," I whispered gently. "You up?"

Drew growled. He had decided not to take the pill, but he was still in too deep a slumber to respond.

"Drew! Drew!" Yes, I felt like a jerk for waking him, but this was a mental health emergency. I was officially freaking out.

"Oh my God," Drew grumbled. "It's happened."

"What's happened?"

"You've become the crazy one."

"I'm not crazy. I'm just worried."

"Why?"

I looked around the room. "I'm scared of spending our kids' birthday in this motel."

"That's it?" Drew laughed.

"Yeah. What? Don't you care?"

"Dude," Drew said. He only called people "dude" when he was at his most relaxed and confident. "I've got it covered."

Then he rolled over, and a few seconds later, he was snoring again.

24

PIONEERS AGAIN

D REW'S PLAN BEGAN, as his plans often do, with breakfast. When we arrived at the hospital on induction morning, the staff got to know us not as "the gay dads" or "those cranks who want to rewrite the rules and hog up all our beds" but as "those guys who brought us a shitload of bagels, bless their hearts." Not just bagels but lox, schmears, muffins, a veggie platter, giant carafes of coffee. Drew had basically walked into the bagel shop and said, "Give me twelve of everything." We dropped it all off at the nurses' station and let everyone know that today's daily grind would be generously catered by the family in room 303. If they weren't already talking about the two dads and the surrogate carrying twins, they would be now.

Drew made sure to learn every nurse's name and to tell them he worked on *The Bachelor*. By the third time I heard someone say, "I can't believe Jason dumped Melissa!," I knew he was working his magic.

He also paraded his sister around like a celebrity. "She was our egg donor!" he bragged, and anyone who showed any interest got to hear the ten-minute version of our baby story.

No one responded better to our narrative than the head nurse, Karyn. She was cheery but officious, with a warm smile and a bubbly laugh. She had Bugs Bunny and Daffy Duck on her hospital scrubs. Drew asked if it would be okay to give her a hug, and she let him walk behind the counter to do so. "Anyone who feeds my whole staff earns a hug from me!" she giggled.

Once again, I was in awe of my boyfriend's superpowers. Already, I felt confident asking the big question. "Do you think there'll be a room for us to stay in after Tiffany delivers?"

Karyn's bright smile shrunk away. She bowed her head at me and sighed. "It all depends on how crowded it is. We've been pretty full lately."

I decided to appeal to her sympathy. "We're just really hoping we can spend time with our children on the night they're . . ."

"We understand," Drew interrupted. "You do what you can do." He gently motioned for me to hush my mouth, pronto. I had clearly jumped the gun.

Karyn came in personally to make sure Tiffany was as comfortable as a woman surrounded by beeping, chattering medical appliances could be. "Just let me know if I can getcha anything," she said.

"Yeah, an epidural!" Tiffany shot back.

We all laughed—except Tiffany. "I'm serious," she said. "I want an epidural."

Karyn giggled. "When the time comes, Honey."

Tiffany had mentioned the epidural to us before—about five thousand times, in fact. She wanted one when she gave birth to Gavin, but the nurses kept telling her it wasn't time yet. As she was being shoved into the delivery room, she asked again, only to be told it was too late. As a result, she learned firsthand how excruciating an undrugged labor can be, and if that meant she had to ask twice as often this time, that's what she was going to do.

I don't know what I expected to happen after the hospital induced labor, but what actually happened was nothing. Inducing labor isn't like inducing vomiting. It takes a while.

In the waning days of bed rest, Tiffany and Susie had taken up an interest in Rummy 500, so to pass the time, we bought a deck of cards from the gift shop. This gave us our first glimpse of the hypercompetitive side of Tiffany that Susie had been lamenting for months. "You guys better watch out," our sweet little surrogate warned as she shuffled the deck. "'Cause I'm takin' you all down!"

All I knew about the process of labor came from TV sitcoms, where the joke was that the pain turned some sweet, subservient housewife into a screeching, sailor-mouthed psychopath who shouted all the worst obscenities the censors would let her get away with. "Shoot damn hell! Get this monkey-flipping baby out of me, Dr. Huxtable!" Now I realized the reality was much worse. Our mild-mannered surrogate had fully morphed into Kanye West.

From that point, Tiffany turned a simple, civilized game into an ultimate fighting smackdown. I hadn't played rummy in ages, but the strategy came back to me immediately. I won the first round, and Tiffany was not happy about it. She didn't pout or say a word. She just glared. It was a vile, hungry glare, the kind that was usually followed by a live gazelle being ripped to shreds, its organs sprayed hundreds of feet across the savannah. And I was the gazelle.

I just happened to be a gazelle who was very good at Rummy. Once I took round 2, Tiffany accused me of cheating. "I need to check this deck," she said. By the time I won the third round, she wasn't joking. She grabbed the deck and sorted through every card, checking for dupes. She made me remove my sweatshirt to ensure I didn't have anything stashed up my sleeve. "Where did you say you bought these cards again?" She held them up to the light, checking for hidden marks.

I realized that it didn't serve me well to anger the woman who was about to give birth to my son and daughter, so I decided to throw round 4. As Tiffany slammed down her hand and yelled, "Gin!," it was as if she'd just been crowned champion of Wimbledon. "Oh yeah! You suck! You suck! You suck!" Well, if she was a Wimbledon champ, she was John McEnroe.

Every round she won ratcheted her cockiness upward by a thousand degrees. Susie shot me periodic glances, as if to say, "See what I was talking about?" I constantly checked the scores because I was counting the moments until she hit 500 and this torment could end. Periodically, a nurse would enter, take some readings off the machines, and scribble down a few notes before leaving.

"Don't forget my epidural!" Tiffany would demand with increasing confidence.

Finally, we played the hand that gave Tiffany her 500th point. I was nervous how she might top off her poor sportsmanship at this moment of ultimate triumph. All we got, though, was a polite nod. "Good game, everyone," she offered, pleasantly. It almost made it worse, as if she actually believed herself to be a gracious winner. I hoped my kids weren't paying attention.

Still, I shook her hand, relieved to be done. Instead of packing away the deck, Tiffany shuffled again. "Let's play to one thousand!" Sure, why not go into a second round with her already up 200 points on the rest of us? Somehow, though, we all agreed. It's not like we had anything better to do.

Before I knew it, Rummy 1,000 had stretched out to Rummy 1,500, then Rummy 2,000. The entire morning disappeared with no sign of our twins. I was a little suspicious that maybe Tiffany was squeezing them in so she could trounce us further at cards. Every once in a while, she would close her eyes, grimace slightly, then announce, "Another contraction!" Other than that and the fact that we were using her belly as a discard pile, we might as well have been hanging out at a bar on a Friday night.

Friends were emailing us constantly, begging for updates. By now they were sharing the kind of horror stories you would never disclose directly to a pregnant woman. "You know I was in labor for sixty hours, right?" one friend wrote. "It was hell."

I started to wonder if this might go that long—or worse. Maybe the labor would never end. What if our kids just grew up inside Tiffany? They'd lose their baby teeth, learn their alphabet, go through puberty—all within the confines of our surrogate's uterus. Once a year we'd shove some birthday cake up there, and they'd make a wish. Then, seventeen years from now, Tiffany would poop out two college applications, and Sutton and Bennett would become the only fetuses in the Harvard class of 2032. A couple of uterus-bound IV twins raised by gay dads? Talk about ideal diversity bait.

The Pitocin may not have been producing any noticeable results, but at least Drew's schmoozing was bearing fruit. At one point, Karyn came bursting through the door, breathless. "Oh my God!" she shouted, collapsing against the wall. We wondered what could have happened in the maternity ward to provoke this reaction from a nurse. An immaculate birth? Alien baby? Nope—apple muffin.

"You have to tell me where you got them!" she exclaimed. "That was the best muffin I've ever had! I hid the others from the other nurses. I'm keeping them all for myself! Hahaha!"

"Excuse me, Karyn?" Tiffany said.

"Yes, Tiffany. Your epidural."

By roughly Tiffany's four hundredth request, a nurse came in with the biggest needle I'd ever seen. It looked more like a shish kabob that could pierce straight through this tiny woman and come out the other end. "Yay!" Tiffany cheered.

While the nurse prepared to dull Tiffany's pain with the surgical equivalent of a samurai sword, Drew and I quietly excused ourselves. "Hold on," Tiffany said. "I want to talk to you before I get all doped up and you just think it's the drugs talking."

"Okay."

"I just want to say thank you." She turned her head and wiped her eye. "I don't want to cry!"

"Why would you thank us?"

"Because I had no idea what I was getting into when I started this, and I couldn't have asked for better IPs than you guys. You've been so good to me, and I'm so excited to see you become dads."

"We feel the same way," Drew gushed. "I can't imagine what it'd be like if we'd gone with that first surrogate. You mean so much to us."

"I just have one more request," Tiffany said. "You know I can't wait to meet these babies, but when they're born, I don't want the doctor to hand them to me. When they gave me Gavin in the delivery room and I held him for the first time, that's when I bonded with him. Make sure they hand the babies to you. Then later on when I'm in my recovery room, you can present them to me, as Aunt Tiffany."

There seemed to be so much more to say, but there was a woman standing next to us with a very large needle, waiting very patiently. We pulled back Tiffany's curtain and excused ourselves from the room.

Drew and I used the break to buy about $200 worth of dinners from a Panera Bread across the street. Once again, we were greeted like heroes at the nurse's station. This time, Karyn gave us both hugs.

"I've been working on getting you guys your own room," she said. "I'm gonna try."

Just then, Eric stepped into the hallway. We asked how Tiffany was feeling, and he hung his head.

"Not good."

"The epidural didn't help?"

"It made her worse. She wants someone to come check on her."

Karyn jogged into Tiffany's room. We wondered if this was a sign that things were progressing, but when she came back out, it was clear that it wasn't.

"Those babies of yours are very stubborn," she told us. "I don't think they're coming tonight."

"How's Tiffany?"

"Nothing out of the ordinary. I think she just needs to rest."

Drew put his arm around Eric, and I smiled a devious little grin. "So she probably shouldn't play cards then, right?"

As we sat at Tiffany's bedside, nurses kept stopping by to thank us for dinner and to wish us well. It was clear Drew had done exactly what he set out to. We were like celebrities to the hospital staff, and they were all rooting for us. It was only around the fifth thank you that I noticed something strange. Everybody who stopped in to see us was back in their street clothes.

Even Karyn was changed out of her Looney Toons scrubs the next time we saw her. "Just wanted to say good luck tonight!" she peeped.

"Are you leaving?" I asked.

"Yeah. Shift change."

I don't know why we hadn't anticipated this, but the nurses we'd spent all day wooing were on their way home. They were being replaced by a new batch, with nothing left in the break room to greet them but the end stubs of bread loaves and a bunch of trash. We were going to have to start all over again.

"Any idea who our new nurse is going to be?" I asked.

Karyn shook her head, consolingly. "Yeah, you've got Betty."

"What's wrong with Betty?"

Karyn patted me on the shoulder. "She's a wonderful nurse. You'll get great care." Something in her tone wasn't at all reassuring. She looked over her shoulder, as if Betty might be stalking up behind her. Then she whispered, "She's not the friendliest."

As usual, Karyn was overly polite. I tracked Betty down in the hallway half an hour later, while she was reading another patient's chart. A short, thin African American woman with thick glasses, she was all business.

"Betty? Hi, I'm Jerry in room 303."

"I'll get there when I get there," she rasped, never taking her eyes off her clipboard.

Before my brain could respond, my body had instinctively taken five steps backward. Betty was smaller than I was, but I'd never met anyone so intimidating. "Oh, okay," I muttered, then I crept quietly back to Tiffany's room.

Before Betty came in, Dr. Robertson swung by to check on Tiffany. "Still nothing, huh?" Tiffany told him how the epidural had only increased her pain. After a brief exam, he determined the shot hadn't been administered properly, and he ordered her another epidural, stat. Tiffany smiled. I was starting to like him at last.

After the next injection, we saw a noticeable difference in our surrogate. She was calm and relaxed, with a doped-up expression on her face. I had no idea how strong the shot actually was, but whatever its effect, she was definitely grateful. I thought of challenging her to a rematch of Rummy 500 now, to see if she played nicer.

Then a voice rang out behind me. "WHAT ARE ALL THESE PEOPLE DOING IN HERE?"

I whipped around to see Betty, finally making an appearance. Drew smiled and extended his hand.

"Hi, I'm Drew. This is my partner, Jerry, my mom, and my sister Susie. She was our egg donor!"

Betty looked right past him, focused only on Tiffany. "I don't care who you are!" Betty shouted. "This woman needs her rest. Everyone but the husband needs to leave. Now!"

I turned to Tiffany, but she was no help. She was still reclining in bed, blissing out on her epidural. I waited for Drew to work his charm, but he said nothing. When I looked around, I realized why. He had already fled the room. So had Susie and Mrs. Tappon. Other than Eric, I was the only one standing there, and Betty was boring through me with her eyes. "Okay, bye," I whispered.

By the time I reached the waiting room, Drew was freaking out. He had left Tiffany's room so fast that he forgot his Blackberry. It had only been a minute or so, but this was already the longest he had ever gone without it.

"I have to go back," he announced.

Susie and I pled with him not to go or at least to wait until Betty had moved on to another patient. We were terrified of what she might do to him if he showed his face again. With all the surgical equipment at hand, she would have plenty of options.

"I know exactly where I left it," he assured us. "I'm just going to sneak in, not say a word, then duck back out again. She won't even know I'm there."

I took a deep breath and showed Susie my panic face. She gave me hers, too.

As Drew slid through the doorway of room 303, I waited to hear thunder or the sound of two jumbo jets colliding above us. Instead, there was silence. The door closed behind him, and nothing happened. A minute went by, then another minute. What could be taking so long? What had Evil Betty done to him? I wanted to check on him, but there was no way I was going in. Our kids needed at least one dad to make it through childbirth.

When the door finally opened, Drew began sprinting toward us, as if being chased by a bear. It was pretty much how I expected him to emerge, but then I noticed he wasn't holding his Black-berry. "Let's go!" he shouted.

"What?"

"It's time!"

I wasn't sure what he meant, until he grabbed my hand and started dragging me toward the room.

"You're kidding!"

"No, the babies are coming," he insisted. "C'mon! They said to hurry!"

25

ANOTHER COMING-OUT STORY

I LOOK SURPRISINGLY GOOD IN SCRUBS. I was surprised, at least. I mean, who looks good in scrubs? Not most doctors. Hardly any delivery room dads. Only about half the cast of the TV show *Scrubs*. Yet somehow, on me, they worked. As I was checking myself out in the crinkly blue paper garments, I wondered if I had missed my calling. Maybe I should have been an industrial supply fashion model. Or maybe I was just dizzy with the fact that I was moments away from meeting my son and daughter.

"Let's go, dads! Those babies are coming!" Evil Betty poked her head in and was gone in a flash while Eric, Drew, and I were still slipping what looked like tiny shower caps over our shoes.

"C'mon!" Drew said, grabbing me by the arm. There are articles of clothing you can slip on while you're running, but footwear is not among them. I stumbled my way around the corner, trying to remember where the delivery room was.

"Who's going to cut the umbilical cord?" Drew asked. "One each?"

I had a sudden attack of stage fright. "No," I said. "You do both. I'm afraid I'd pass out."

Hospital policy mandated that twins be delivered in an operating room due to the likelihood of the woman needing an emergency C-section. It was a huge space, full of blinking and beeping medical equipment. Except for Bennett and Sutton, Drew and I were probably the last of the key players to arrive.

Eric had agreed to be our official birth photographer so Drew and I could just enjoy the experience. It was a relief because Eric was sure to feel a lot more comfortable than I would pointing the camera at certain key places. Tiffany had a large sheet draped over her lower half, so Drew and I positioned ourselves discreetly behind her head, clear of the viewing area. She told us she didn't mind what we saw in the delivery room, but I minded. As much as the expectant father in me was dying to see my kids, the kid in me was nervous about catching sight of a woman's hoo-hoo.

All around us, people were shouting medical terms. "BMTs!" "Infarction!" "Hemostat!" They were all words that sounded familiar from TV medical shows but that still meant nothing to me. I may as well have been scanning the male faces trying to crown this staff's McDreamy.

We'd only been in the room a few seconds when Dr. Robertson announced it was go time. "Cauterize the arterial phlebotomist!" he announced, or something like that. A ring of nurses sprung up, seemingly from nowhere, and surrounded Tiffany's bedside. There must have been at least six of them. One on each side held one of Tiffany's hands. Two leaned down by her face, and two bent over her feet. All at once, they started directing encouragement toward her head. "Come on, you can do this!" "You're ready. I know you're ready!" "This is it, this is what you've been waiting for!"

Then one of them started counting loudly, so everyone in the room could hear. "Three . . . two . . . one . . ."

And then, all the nurses screamed in unison, "PUSSSSSSSSH-HHH!!!!!"

That's just what Tiffany proceeded to do, as hard as I've ever seen anyone push. She pushed and pushed and pushed some more, and the whole time, the nurses kept repeating, "Pushpushpushpushpushpush!"

When Tiffany relaxed, they went back to their general encouragements. "Good girl!" "Good pushing!" "You're doing great!" The entire process was kind of disturbing, less like I pictured childbirth would be, more like an exorcism.

Everyone calmed down for about twenty seconds, then the encouragement ratcheted back up. The next thing I knew, the lead nurse was counting again. "Three . . . two . . . one . . ."

"PUSSSSSSSSSHHHH!!!!!"

The combined force of the shouting and the pushing practically made the room shake.

"Oh my God," Drew said. "Are you looking?" He motioned toward the part of Tiffany's body I was trying very hard to ignore.

"No!" I said. "I'm not looking."

"I can see his head!"

I nodded nervously. "Great! I'll look soon."

"Look!" Drew demanded. "Look now! Your son is being born!"

And so I looked. I can't say it was the most flattering view of either Tiffany or Bennett, but for the split second I was willing to take a glimpse, I witnessed the miracle of life.

The nurses were now chanting at fever pitch. "This is it!" "One more big push!" "You're doing so well!"

"Three . . . two . . . one . . ."

Then I heard someone crying. It could have been any of us, really.

The next thing I heard was the clicking of Eric's camera shutter, and I realized that just a few feet in front of my face was a tiny person. Dr. Robertson held him up like a fisherman displaying a prized trout, and for all I could tell, this may actually have been a fish. He was so covered in clumps of chalky goo that it was hard to tell what species, genus, class, or phylum he might belong to. He was humanoid, at best. A curled up lump of dough, mushy and underbaked. One thing was for sure, though. This repulsive little mole rat was the most beautiful sight I'd ever seen. This was my son, Bennett.

For that one moment, there was no one on Earth younger than he was. Everything he saw, heard, and felt in that instant was brand new to him. Light, air, cold, confusion. Things most of us barely noticed jolted his tiny brain in a tsunami of stimuli. It was hard to conceive of something so new as this little boy. He had never been hurt or hugged, never seen day turn into night, never felt the soft touch of cotton against his skin, never seen a kangaroo or tasted a Fruity Pebble, never fallen asleep to the sound of crickets or woken up to a dog licking his face. Just for now, he belonged to that .001 percent of living creatures who couldn't recognize Mickey Mouse or Mario. Or me, for that matter. But he would know me before them, and despite what he might say while slamming his door as a teenager, he would love me more. I would be there for millions of my son's little discoveries, things that would shape him into a person all his own. For now, the sum total of his breaths could be counted on one of his tiny, balled-up little hands, but already, my entire world had changed. Bennett had become a person, and I had become a parent.

No one told me what I should do next. Drew and I were the least relevant people in the room—medically, at least. We were spectators, and as such, we were free to focus on whatever we chose.

A couple of people did a couple of hospital-type things to Bennett, then they left him in the warmer to fend for himself, messy and naked. He sputtered and stretched, probably trying to feel the uterine walls or the touch of his sister, all the things that had confined and comforted him for the last nine months. For the first time, he had his own space—more of it than he could handle. I'm not sure if a two-minute-old human is capable of real happiness, but I imagined that's what he was feeling.

I wanted him to know I was there, that this gargantuan life change he'd just gone through wasn't an abandonment. But the doctors had coated his eyes with a thick gel that probably served some important function while also temporarily blinding him. Was I allowed to touch him? No one told me I couldn't. I'd already scrubbed off at least three layers of hand skin before I entered the OR. Besides, Bennett was the one covered in gross stuff, not me. Anyway, he was my kid. If I were a horse or a mongoose, I'd have given him a full tongue bath by now and snarfed down his placenta. I decided to go for it. I stroked the back of his hand gently with my index finger. He made the slightest twitch in response, but he didn't pull away.

I felt like I should say something profound and memorable, a "One small step for man . . ." kind of thing. Surely, this was the closest I would ever come to landing on the moon. If ever a moment in my life called for erudition, it was this one. These would be the first words my son would hear me say.

"Hi Bennett," I whispered, finally. "We're your dads."

It was then that I noticed a tied-off umbilical cord, protruding from his midsection. In the rush of activity, I had completely missed the big moment.

"Did you cut his cord?" I asked Drew.

He shook his head. "I didn't even see them do it."

The unprecedented cocktail of emotions swirling inside me suddenly received a twist of anger. Maybe it was just a matter of expediency that Dr. Robertson decided to cut the cord himself. There was no time for parent involvement, not with twins. He had another baby to deliver. Snip, on to the next one. That was probably all it was. Or maybe he'd never accepted us as dads.

He didn't even ask us if we wanted to cut the cord.

I decided to say something—to make a scene, there in the delivery room, if need be. "Excuse me, Doctor, but we'd like to cut the cord next time." Yes, that's what I'd say. I rehearsed the line in my head as I slowly turned around.

I couldn't even see Tiffany. There were so many doctors and nurses surrounding her. While I'd been busy bonding with Bennett, the mood around me had shifted drastically. The number of people in the room had tripled. The door burst open, and a nurse wheeled a new machine into place with great urgency.

Drew clutched my hand. I searched his face for an explanation. He was always so much better than I was at deciphering situations. His face was starkly white. He stood stone-still, petrified, the only movement in his entire body coming from the frantic quivering of his lower lip. I'd never seen him so frightened before.

"We need to go now!" Dr. Robertson announced.

People began shouting jargon at each other. "Triage!" "Avulsion!" "I need fifty ccs of coagulated antigens, stat!"

Amid all of that, the pushing had begun. "Three . . . two . . . one . . . PUSSSSSSSSHHHH!!!!!"

Then I heard one thing very clearly, from a nurse who was staring at a monitor. "We've lost the baby's heartbeat!" she declared.

26

HEART-STOPPING

"THREE . . . TWO . . . ONE . . . PUSSSSSSSSHHHH!!!!!"

Never before had I wished so strongly that I had spent seven years of my life in medical school. It would have been worth it just to know what was going on in that moment. All I could tell for sure was that something was seriously wrong with our daughter. Once she was mine to hold, I would be able to protect her, to whisper softly in her ear to calm her, to kiss her boo-boos and make her pain go away. For now, I could do nothing but stand at Tiffany's beside and join the chorus of cheerleaders.

"You're doing great!" "We're almost there!" "Attagirl!"

I didn't know what I was saying. I was so nervous.

It was then I felt a nudge. More people were squeezing in to chant, as if the problem were merely one of volume. Six people caterwauling, and the baby's still inside. Let's try ten. My poor daughter. They really expected her to move closer to the sound of these screaming strangers? I sure wouldn't.

At some point, an unwelcome guest had snuck into a prime location. She appeared instantly, as if by witchcraft. It was Evil

Betty, and she'd squeezed her way through the throng right next to Tiffany's head. She had that look on her face again, like it was time to lay some smack down. She bent down, whispering angrily in Tiffany's ear.

How dare she interrupt at this moment! A voice in my head told me to lunge for her, to tackle her to the ground, there in front of everyone, rather than let her upset my surrogate yet again. It's a story I could tell the kids someday. Daddy made a scene in the delivery room. I'd been mild-mannered all my life, but when the need arose, I transformed into a hero and saved the day.

Instead, I did what I always do and glowered quietly at her. I doubt she noticed.

"Three . . . two . . . one . . . PUSSSSSSSSHHHH!!!!!"

On that third push, Sutton emerged—or so I could only assume. A team of doctors surrounded her like a rugby scrum and shuttled her off to the new piece of equipment that had just been wheeled in. I barely caught a glimpse of her, maybe a toe or a shoulder. She went by so fast I couldn't tell which it was.

Again, I didn't see who cut her umbilical cord. It was snipped off and dumped into a biohazard bin before I even noticed. There was no time for ceremony. Our daughter lay under a heat lamp, three deep in medics. Was she even in there? Was she even alive?

The room fell eerily silent, and I realized what was missing: the sound of a baby crying. Sutton had yet to take a breath. Drew and I stood near Bennett, just a few feet away, utterly helpless. Our son twisted and gyrated, feeling around for his sister. This was the farthest he'd ever been away from her. He was probably wondering why he could no longer feel her touch—and if he ever would again.

It all happened in a matter of seconds, seconds that felt like lifetimes—and they were. Two lifetimes, albeit brief ones, yet to take any kind of shape. So far, this tension was all our kids knew.

Then, finally, we heard her. "Eeeaaaaah! Eeeaaaaah! Eee-aaaaah!" It was impossibly high-pitched, like a pterodactyl screech or a dog whistle set off by a teakettle. Loud and urgent. It was the sound of our daughter crying, the most wonderful thing I'd ever heard. A wave of relief washed over the room. Doctors practically high-fived each other.

Drew couldn't hold back anymore. Tears cascaded down his cheeks, and he whimpered like a puppy. His knees gave out, and he fell into my arms. Our children were less than ten minutes old, and we'd already endured one of those heart-stopping moments of anxiety that other parents had warned us about. They were supposed to happen on a jungle gym at the playground years from now, not in the hospital the moment they were born.

As the huddle surrounding Sutton dissipated, I could see her at last. She was tiny, even smaller than Bennett. She was curled up, as if still unaware that she'd been freed from the confines of the womb. She had a tiny cap of dark, matted-down hair. She seemed far too beautiful to have come from my genes.

"Congratulations, guys," Dr. Robertson said as he strode past us. He removed his surgical gloves and headed for the door, a sure sign that the uncertainty had passed.

"Is she all right?" I asked, just to be sure.

He nodded. "She just decided to give us a scare on the way out."

We bent over Sutton, and she stared up at us with her big eyes wide open. Unlike her brother, she was in no hurry to explore. She was studying us, these two dudes hovering over her and blubbering like children. Like I did with Bennett, I stroked the back of her hand gently with a single finger.

"Don't you ever do that again!" I said.

Introducing Bennett and Sutton to Aunt Susie was like watching them be born all over again. Drew and I each took a baby and wheeled them in their warmers back to the room where we'd spent most of the day playing cards. Tiffany and Eric were already there, telling the story of the delivery. Mrs. Tappon, the only other one among us who'd ever given birth, was aghast. Three pushes and out came the first baby. Three more pushes and out came the second. Except for the spine-chilling uncertainty of Sutton's birth, it was an exceptionally smooth endeavor.

As soon as Susie saw us, her face scrunched up, like someone who dared to stare directly at a solar eclipse and was blasted by more light than a human being could handle. The compression of every muscle at once served to wring out a Niagara of tears. Her eyes weren't sure where to look—one baby, the other baby, one daddy, the other daddy. She spoke only with hugs and gasps. I'd watched her cry so much over the last couple of years, it was nice to see her finally shed some tears of joy.

Just a few feet away, Tiffany waited patiently for her turn. This was how she wanted it—Drew and I introducing our kids to her, as if she were just another visitor who came to congratulate us rather than one who was lying in a hospital bed, dilated and physically spent.

"I want to talk to that Bennett!" she said. We laid our swaddled son down on her chest, and she wagged her finger at him. "So you're the one who's been giving me all that trouble! You'd better never kick your sister like you've been kicking me."

As always, I marveled at the way she was able to tell these two babies apart when they were still inside her womb. She always knew who was jabbing her in the ribs and who was lying upside down, and she had developed feelings toward them based on their time together. I admired and envied her for the unique bond she'd already formed with my kids, and knowing she'd stay part of our lives made me feel closer to them.

"Sutton, this is Aunt Tiffany," Drew said, as he laid our little girl across Tiffany's forearm. Tiffany was the first one to hold both infants at once, which seemed fitting.

If I had been worried about maintaining boundaries before, I wasn't anymore. Seeing the three of them together seemed so natural, so familiar, yet not at all maternal. Their relationship was different, unique to the three of them and beautiful in its own way.

When the babies started crying, Tiffany had no trouble handing them off to Drew and me. "Here you go, guys!" she said. "Good luck!"

We couldn't stop talking about what had occurred in the operating room, though we mostly focused on what a pro Tiffany had been.

"I need to thank that nurse," Tiffany said. "She made all the difference."

"Which nurse?" Drew asked. We jogged our memories as to who had been in the room. There were so many.

"The one who kicked you guys out of here," she replied.

"Betty?!"

Drew shook his head, astounded. "I almost punched her when I saw her talking to you. She was so mean."

"She was so mean," Tiffany agreed. "It was just what I needed."

"What did she say to you?"

"Well, she leaned down into my ear." Tiffany sat up a bit to do her impression of Evil Betty. She was really getting into it. "She sounded like a drill sergeant, and she said, 'Girl, they're getting ready to cut you!'"

"No she didn't!"

"Yeah. She said, 'This baby needs to come out of you right now, or they're going to cut you open and take it out. I don't want them to cut you, so the next push better be the hardest push ever!' I didn't want a C-section, so I pushed so hard, and Sutton popped right out!"

I realized I'd judged Betty all wrong. She wasn't power-mad or homophobic. She was a nurse whose job was to take care of women. When she met Tiffany, she saw a woman at the mercy of far too many men—me, Drew, her doctor. We didn't have a stake in what happened to her or her body, and because of that, she would never fully trust us. Betty had been present at countless births. She'd probably seen doctors perform C-sections just for the sake of expediency. None of us men knew what it was like to be the one in the stirrups, the one left with a permanent scar on her belly, so Betty wanted to make sure the pregnant lady was taken care of and that emergency surgery remained a last resort.

Once we'd heard Tiffany's side of the story, we tracked Betty down to thank her. It was clear she didn't receive a lot of gratitude, because her gruff demeanor melted instantly. She even hugged us. Just a few minutes earlier, we would have thought her incapable of affection.

"They come in to move you yet?" she asked.

"Not yet."

She shook her head. "I know her room's ready. What are they waiting for?"

She shot off down the hall, as much to check on the room as to cut the lovefest short. She had a soft side, but her tolerance for sentiment was clearly low.

Whatever she did definitely goosed things along. A few minutes later, a nurse arrived to transfer Tiffany to the recovery wing. Eric grabbed one side of her bed, and the nurse grabbed the other. As they wheeled her toward the hallway, I wondered how she must be feeling.

"You can come back and see them anytime you want," I assured her.

She smiled. "Honestly," she said, "I'm so glad not to have two babies to take care of tonight. Have fun!" With that, she was gone.

We had no idea what would happen next. Would Drew and I be kicked out? Would the babies be ripped from our arms and taken to a nursery to spend the night? Maybe the staff would forget we were in here and we'd just be able to stay until the shifts changed again.

That would have been a great plan, if only the kids had played along.

"These babies are hungry," Mrs. Tappon said, as their wailing built in intensity. Twenty minutes had gone by, and no one had checked on us. Maybe we would be able to stay all night, but only if we starved our children.

I had to step up, to do the fatherly thing. I flung open the door of room 303 and strode confidently to the nurses' station.

"Um, can we get some, like, formula or something?"

It didn't come out with quite the authority I'd hoped, but it did the trick.

"We'll send someone in to show you how to feed them."

"Great. Thanks."

"As soon as your room is ready."

"Our room?"

"You wanted your own room, right?"

"Yes! Yes! Thank you!"

It took a few minutes before they moved us down the hall, but in the meantime, they set us up with our wristbands—one for Drew and one for me. Each one had the word "Father" printed on it and came with full visitation privileges.

After all my fear, we were treated like parents, both of us, with as much respect as any other couple that came through these halls to experience the most important day of their lives. Ultimately, I don't think it was the bagels or our story that won people over. I think most people are just basically good at heart, and when presented with an unfamiliar situation, even if it may be slightly outside their comfort zone, they'll tend to react in the most humane way possible. This was the world I'd chosen to raise children in, and in that moment, I had no regrets and no fears. Sutton, Bennett, and their two dads were going to be just fine.

27

THE LOTTERY

I WAS PERFECTLY CONVINCED that a baby could thrive in a family with two dads until precisely the moment there was no one around to care for our newborns but me and Drew. Tiffany was asleep in her own room, six doors down. Susie and Mrs. Tappon had gone back to the motel for the night. It was just our family now. Two dads, two babies, no mom. What the hell were we thinking?

Drew and I quickly developed a system. We were each responsible for one baby. When your kid woke up crying, it was your job to feed, diaper, swaddle, or panic. Those were pretty much the only four options. Most times we would go through various permutations of all four before we finally got the squirmer back to sleep. Our confidence in ourselves was extremely low, but our determination to succeed couldn't have been higher. We felt like we had something to prove, not to the people who think gays shouldn't have kids. Fuck them. But to ourselves—and more importantly, to Bennett and Sutton. They were stuck with us now. The least we could do was fool them into thinking we knew what we were doing.

We did have one very special woman on our side. "Knock-knock, Daddies!" she would announce, and an instant later, a sliver of light would bisect the room and the door would gently creak open.

Georgia was our night nurse. It was her job to monitor every baby in our wing, though I think she made a few extra stops by our room to check in on Drew and me. Whenever she peeked in on our new little family, inevitably, at least two of the four of us would be crying. She never lost her cool, never puzzled over what to do or which twin to help first. Effortlessly, she'd pick both of them up at once and throw one over each shoulder for simultaneous burping. Those tiny hiccup sounds would be a huge relief to all of us, and within minutes, all was calm again in room 325E.

It was like picking up a tennis racquet for the first time, then having Andre Agassi show up to coach you, or finding yourself in a magical mushroom kingdom, facing down a spiky-shelled reptile fifty times your size who's madly chucking fireballs at you, when you suddenly hear a voice behind you calling, "It's-a me, Mario!" With Georgia, we knew instantly that we all were in good hands.

Her awesome proficiency could easily have made us feel inadequate, convinced us that the only way we'd ever get the hang of this parenting thing was to get nursing degrees and spend a few years working the overnight shift in a delivery ward. But thanks to her nurturing spirit, it was an inspiration. We never got the feeling that caring for our twins would be easy, but as long as we knew it was possible, we'd get it done. We'd probably never be the best at it, but so what? Fred, Velma, and Daphne were the ones with the skills and the self-confidence, but it was usually Scooby and Shaggy who solved the mysteries.

"You guys are doing fantastic," Georgia would assure us, in a voice five octaves above my highest falsetto. She was that kind of person—small, mousy, and impossibly cheerful, like the Good Witch of Orange County. With her tight black curls, Georgia was a dead ringer for Jane Wiedlin of the Go-Gos, though she was probably too young to know who that was. Any voice-over artist would kill to cast her as a kitten or a busty canary.

I wasn't expecting to bond with Sutton and Bennett that first night, but thanks to Georgia, those early hours were filled with countless tiny triumphs. Every suck of every shot glass-sized bottle, every whisper-like belch and every gentle sleeping breath the twins made in my arms felt like a validation of my parenting. These weren't just selfish blobs carrying out the involuntary activities of new life. Every action they made felt like a subtle acknowledgment of trust in Drew and me. They accepted us as their caregivers. Even in those sticky, tar-like meconium poops that filled their size 0 diapers, there was love.

Like any group emerging from a traumatic experience together, be it the siege of Normandy or a 5:00 a.m. spinning class, the four of us were permanently bound together that night. Drew and I made it through the biggest challenge of our lives. We learned to care for our children without once yelling, "Mommy!"

In Los Angeles, asking someone to brave more than half an hour of freeway traffic to see you is like asking for a kidney, so I wasn't expecting a huge influx of visitors for our babies' first full day of life. Somehow, though, our kids always had a warm lap to sit on, a friendly hand to rub their bellies, a camera shutter clicking in their vicinity. I was relieved there were two of them to go around, but there were times that didn't seem like enough. "I haven't held Sutton in a while," I'd announce. "Gimme!"

Some people swore Bennett was my twin. Others thought Sutton was 100 percent the girl version of Drew.

My friend Victoria was the first to mention what was probably on a lot of people's minds. "Is it okay if I point out how much they look like Susie?" she asked.

She was right. Susie's link to the twins was unmistakable. It was there in Sutton's eyes and Bennett's chin. I could understand why people wanted to be sensitive about the subject, but I'd noticed it, too, and it was part of what made these babies so perfect. We chose Susie as our egg donor because we wanted to see her when we looked at the kids. Just laying eyes on them was a constant reminder of her gift and a promise that they themselves might inherit all the many qualities we loved in her.

If anyone was uncomfortable with the comparisons, it was Susie herself. "I think they look like their dads," she insisted, whenever anyone would bring up the resemblance. Then she would lean down and let Sutton or Bennett wrap their hand around one of her fingers. She knew only as much about baby care as Drew and I did, but she had a level of patience we both envied. She loved to feed them, talk to them, and to rock them gently to sleep in her arms. There was something so beautiful about seeing her with our kids—yet, admittedly, so painful.

Susie had already agreed to stay with us for a few weeks while we adjusted to our new life. Still, there would come a day, not far off, when she would return to Rochester. The kids would still be infants, and she'd still be a virtual stranger to them, an aunt to two babies she loved dearly, three thousand miles away from her. It was hard not to feel like she deserved more. If Susie felt the same way, she never let on, but then again, Susie wasn't one to complain.

All day long, no one made as big an impression on us as the visitors who traveled the least.

"Can I see them?" a voice called as the door slowly swung open. It was Karyn, our favorite nurse from the day before, along with another nurse named Jody, who ran a close second. Their arms were loaded with presents wrapped in duckie paper. Staffers in a maternity ward spent their own money to buy baby gifts for our kids. Now they were using their break time to visit them. It was almost more kindness than I could handle.

Drew had now perfected his telling of the delivery story. He knew all the dramatic beats and pauses to hit. The nurses were riveted. Their favorite part was the revelation that Betty had been Tiffany's savior.

"You should write a letter," Karyn suggested.

"Yeah," Jody added. "I don't think she gets a lot of compliments."

"Oh, we're writing a few letters," Drew assured them. "Starting with one for our night nurse."

"We thought you'd like Georgia!" Karyn said. She and Jody looked at each other and shared a conspiratorial giggle.

"We made sure they assigned her to you."

"Isn't she a doll?"

"She was so good with the babies. Does she have kids of her own?"

Karyn sighed and bowed her head. "She's been struggling. She had a couple of miscarriages."

Jody added, "We're really pulling for her around here."

At that moment, I added another woman to my list of personal heroes. I couldn't comprehend the strength it must take Georgia to take care of other people's babies every night, when she wanted so badly to have one of her own.

"Let's give her one of ours," I said finally, to break the tension. "Drew, you pick."

When Karyn and Jody left, it felt like the last day of summer camp. "We'll keep in touch!" we swore. We traded emails and promised to friend each other on Facebook. We opened their baby gifts, but it wasn't until after they left that I peeked inside Karyn's card:

To the Tappon-Mahoney family,

Every once in a while I get to meet someone that just "feels right." You were it. I knew I was going to like all of you from the moment you came in with those muffins (just kidding). You were so nervous, excited and full of love that it reminded me of what life is all about. We all need to be reminded of that sometimes.

I want to thank you for letting me be a tiny part of your day. It was my pleasure to meet you all and I look forward to updates.

Take care of yourselves. Eat, drink lots of fluids and sleep when you can. They will sleep through the night soon, they do stop crying for long periods of time eventually and just about the time you start asking yourself "what were we thinking," they will throw their little arms around you and tell you they love you and you will feel refreshed and renewed.

Love,
Karyn

Once again, I was reduced to tears. We'd started off the day before just hoping to score ourselves a room for the night, but to our surprise, we'd actually made friends.

It was mid-afternoon when Tiffany swung by to visit us. We hadn't expected her to be on her feet so soon, but it was her appearance that truly shocked us. Relaxed, refreshed, vibrant. She was practically as fit as she'd been the day we met her, but with a much bigger smile. Any postpartum adjustment we feared she might suffer had yet to surface. Like Susie, she was full of joy, perfectly at ease with this new family we'd made.

She had some big news for us, too: Less than twenty-four hours after popping out twins, she was headed home. The doctors had given her the option to stay another night, but she turned them down. She'd accomplished her goal, given us our family, and now she wanted to go back to hers. She was eager to lift Gavin up and dance him around the room. It had been far too long since she'd been able to do that.

Once again that night, Drew and I were alone with our children. We didn't say much, not to each other at least. We were too busy talking to our son and daughter, telling them all the amazing things we couldn't wait to share together as a family—bedtime stories, their first day of school, maybe someday a trip to Paris. In one of the rare moments when they were both asleep at the same time, when Drew and I were both awake and off duty, he turned to me. We had so many things we wanted to say to each other, but all Drew could get out at that moment was a simple, "We're so lucky."

He didn't need to spell it out in detail. We both knew what an understatement that was.

I thought about Georgia, how loving and maternal she was and how much she deserved to experience this kind of joy.

I thought about Susie—and Dr. Saroyan's devastating assessment of her fertility.

I thought about Bernie and his wife, all they'd gone through to have a baby and how much hope they still had that their dream would come true.

I thought about all the gay couples who couldn't have kids because they lived somewhere the law didn't allow it, and all the gays and lesbians from previous generations who never even considered the possibility.

I thought about all the scares we'd gone through, about how Tiffany defied everyone's expectations and her own body by carrying our children full-term.

I thought about Rainbow Extensions and how the one thing they'd managed to do right was to bring Tiffany and Eric into our lives.

I thought about the unlikelihood of Drew and me meeting in the first place.

I thought about a teenage boy who was miserable in his own skin and how he could never have imagined a future that looked anything like this.

When we started the process of having kids, I wanted to have a truly remarkable story to share with them about how they came into the world. Now I had that. It was a story full of love and surprises, of fear and of the greatest happiness imaginable. It was uniquely ours—the tale of our family—yet in another way, our journey was just like anyone else's. Isn't that how every baby comes to be, through a million little moments of serendipity, co-incidences of geography, and the completely unforeseeable whims of the human heart? These babies were no more special than any other, and yet they were the most important creatures in the world because they were ours.

The odds of experiencing this moment, of there being a Bennett and Sutton Tappon-Mahoney, seemed so astronomical, but then again, it felt like a forgone conclusion. Of course we had a family. Like Karyn said, it couldn't have felt more right.

I put my arm around Drew and looked down at our two sleeping babies, swaddled so tightly that only a tiny segment of each of their faces was exposed. "I think we won the lottery," I said. "Twice."

As we prepared to leave the hospital the next day, we received our children's birth certificates. On the line marked "Father/Parent," the name "Andrew Tappon" was filled in. Below it, the line "Mother/Parent" read "Gerald Mahoney."

Hospital regulations required new moms to leave in a wheelchair, holding their infant in their arms. No one was quite sure how that applied to us, but eventually, the administration decided that one of us would have to exit in a wheelchair, holding both babies, for liability reasons. Having already accepted my role as the "Mother/Parent," I volunteered.

I settled into the wheelchair, making sure to get myself comfortable because I knew once I held the babies in my arms, I wouldn't move a muscle. Susie handed me Bennett, and Mrs. Tappon handed me Sutton. I cradled one in each arm as Karyn grabbed the handles and pushed me toward the elevator. "Here we go, guys," I said to my kids.

Outside, Drew pulled our minivan up to the patient loading zone. *Pioneers*, I thought. *In a Honda Odyssey!*

Sutton and Bennett squinted, gently taking in the sights of the outside world but bristling from their first exposure to sunlight.

We strapped them very carefully into their car seats, snapped the car seats into the bases, made sure they had pacifiers and blankets and that the seat-back mirrors were aligned so we could see them from up front.

"Do you want to drive?" Drew asked me.

"No way."

"Me neither," he said. "But I will."

At least an hour separated us from our condo, if traffic was kind, but never before had the stakes felt higher for this kind of trip.

Drew took a deep breath and climbed into the driver's seat. He turned off the radio, set the air conditioning to a comfortable level, and buckled his seat belt. The kids were silent, gazing around. Every single thing they focused their eyes on was something they'd never seen before, except for me and Drew. When they saw us, they instantly looked away in search of something more interesting. *Oh, those guys again. They're always here.*

Drew pulled up the GPS menu. He tapped a single button, the one labeled "Go Home," and then we let the robot-voiced lady inside our car guide us back to the freeway.

EPILOGUE

AS WE TURN OFF THE INTERSTATE toward Philadelphia, Drew and I begin to panic about the flower girl dress. For weeks, it's all we've been talking about. The gray sash. The silky fabric. The fact that it's so special you only get to wear it on one very important day. Every time we mention it, Sutton acts like she might spontaneously combust from a surge of little girl glee. If we mistakenly say that the dress is white, she'll quickly correct us. "It's cream-colored." Right now, the dress hangs from a hanger in the back row of our minivan, blocking Sutton's view of the window. She doesn't mind, though. She'd rather stare at the dress than the Jersey Turnpike. The dress is elegant, shimmering, perfect. The problem is that we only have one of them.

"I'm going to be a flower girl, too!" Bennett insists. Now just over three years old, our son is sweet, sensitive and incredibly stubborn. "I want to wear a dress!" Perhaps we've made too big a deal about the dress.

"You're a ring bearer," I remind him. "You get to wear a white shirt and some really handsome suspenders and . . ."

"No!" he shouts. "I'm a flower girl!"

Sutton does not help our case. "I think you'd make a beauuuuuutiful flower girl, Bennett!" she coos.

It's not that Drew's brother Peter or his fiancé Ali would mind having a male flower girl at their wedding. After his initial hesitation about our plans to make a family, Peter has rallied to become our biggest champion. He dearly loves his nephew, a tough, outgoing boy who loves to play with both trains and dress up clothes. One thing my son excels at is his ability to defy people's expectations of him. If that's a result of him having two dads, it's one I fully embrace.

This wedding is one of the reasons we moved back to the East Coast. After nearly two decades in Los Angeles, Drew and I packed up everything and relocated to the suburbs of New York so we could be closer to our families, so we'd be here for all the weddings, births, and happy moments. Just as everyone had warned us, having kids upended our priorities in ways we never expected.

When we arrive at the hotel, we're greeted like celebrities. All of Peter's friends and Ali's family are eager to meet us. Peter has been sharing our story with them for months. "You guys, this is my brother Drew," he announces proudly, "and his family."

We're not the only ones to upstage the bride and groom, though. "Grace!" Sutton squeals, darting across the room, almost as excited as she was the first time she saw the flower girl dress.

Drew and I gaze over at one of the other reasons we moved back to the East Coast, a tiny, gorgeous girl with giant happy eyes who's carried into the room by Susie, her mom.

"Grace, you look so beautiful!" Sutton says.

After all of Dr. S's warnings, Susie got pregnant without even trying. She had just moved in with her boyfriend and was taking birth control. Somehow, though, Grace's need to be born was stronger than Susie's fertility issues, stronger than the pills. My sister-in-law wasn't quite prepared to be a mom, but when she learned the news, she embraced it fully. Things didn't work out with her boyfriend, and now she was living back at home with her parents.

Nothing about Susie's life has been a fairy tale, except for motherhood. She's only been a mom for six months, but already, she doesn't look complete without Grace in her arms. They dance together, laugh together. They own the room.

A moment later, Drew is hugging Susie tightly. They're both in tears, as they are nearly every time they get together. Nothing is said, yet they manage to communicate everything they need to.

It's almost too perfect a moment. Drew and Susie hugging, just a few feet from Bennett and Sutton, who are singing songs from the Broadway musical "Matilda," which they've learned by heart. Sutton is performing the role of Matilda, and Bennett is playing Miss Honey, her good-natured schoolteacher. It's taken me three years to appreciate it fully, but what Susie has given us is so much more than just a couple of eggs. It's something more special than we'd imagined, more wonderful than I'd ever realized. It's a brother and sister, tiny, perfect, and gradually forming a special bond all their own.

A moment later, Drew is hugging his brother Matt. Together, they'll be Peter's Best Men, alongside a half dozen of Peter's macho buddies as groomsmen. Privately, I joke to Matt's partner Casey that we got left out because the wedding party had filled its gay quota.

While the brothers bond, Casey and I talk about fatherhood. He and Matt are right where Drew and I were a few years earlier, trying very hard to have a baby with a surrogate. Susie offered them her eggs, of course, but Casey nixed the idea. They went with an anonymous egg donor instead.

Casey shakes his head, informing me that their third in vitro attempt just failed. They need to find a new surrogate, but the laws are trickier in New York. It's illegal there to pay someone to carry a baby for you. Virtually the only way to make an agreement is to find someone you know who'll do it purely out of love. They were lucky to find their first surrogate. How would they ever replace her?

"I'll carry the baby for you," a voice says from beside us. We don't even have to look over to see who it is.

"Susie, are you serious?" Casey asks. Susie just smiles and shrugs. We all know the answer.

The next day, Bennett marches down the aisle in suspenders and a white shirt, soaking up the compliments about how spiffy he looks. Behind him, Sutton spreads rose petals for her new aunt to walk on. Drew and Matt stand at one side of the altar beside Peter. Susie is on the other.

Six months later, she will be pregnant again.

ACKNOWLEDGMENTS

ONE OF THE MANY VALUABLE LESSONS I learned from my peerless agent, Laurie Abkemeier, is that agents always read the acknowledgments section first. Therefore, I will not keep her waiting. Laurie, I could not ask for a more enthusiastic, tireless, encouraging advocate to introduce me to the world of publishing. If the day you sold my book was the most exciting day in my writing career, then number 2 would have to be the day you read my query and responded in record time. Thanks for everything, and thanks also to Brian DeFiore and the rest of the staff at DeFiore and Company.

To Flannery Scott, thanks for believing in this book and for all the guidance you've given me. You've made my first publishing experience everything I hoped it would be, and I couldn't be happier to be on this journey with you. Thanks also to Karie, Kalen, Sam, Rick, and the rest of the staff at Taylor Trade Publishing.

Enormous thanks also go, naturally, to Drew Tappon, for being my partner both in becoming a dad and in writing it all down. Drew, I couldn't have done either one without your love and support. Thanks for being the most awesome "Other Daddy" in the world.

To Susie Tappon, thanks for your generosity not just in creating our kids but in letting me share your story. If there's one thing I want the kids to take away from this book when they're old enough to read it, it's what an incredible woman Aunt Susie is. (As if they won't already know.)

To Tiffany Ireland, another incredible woman, thanks for letting us into your life, and thanks for saying "yes." Thanks also to Eric and Gavin for being part of our extended family.

I also have to thank everyone who allowed me to write about them, even when I wasn't portraying them in the most flattering light. To Greg Scordato, who doesn't remember telling me he couldn't be friends with someone who was gay and who feels awful about it, thanks for letting me put that in anyway. To Jessica, thanks for being a good sport and for talking us out of the wipe warmers. To Eric S., thanks for giving me the last word—until you write your book, at least. To Dr. S—you know who you are— thanks for being just the guy we needed to get us through all of this, and thanks to your entire staff for their professionalism and friendship. Thanks to Katye and Jenn for being such amazing people.

To my family—Mom, Mary, Kathy, Larry, Kiernan, Megan, Bridget, Mr. & Mrs. T, Mrs. Shoe, Matt & Casey, Peter & Ali, Grace, Lillian, and those yet to come, thanks for all the support you've given me throughout this journey. The love you've all shown me is what made me so eager to start a family of my own. And to my dad, Jerry Sr., who loved kids and who loved to read more than anyone I've ever known, thanks for passing on your love of both to me. I hope you get to read this somewhere. I wish you could've been here to witness it all firsthand.

Thanks to my fellow Barracudas—Dave Boerger, James Dutcher, Julie Singer, Victoria Strouse, Adam Tobin, and Janice "Sassymama" Bech for making me a better writer.

Thanks to the friends who might as well be family—Tia Lauren, Janice & C.B. Browne, Drew Greenberg, Michael Messer, Robin Sindler, Chuck & Meredith Stephenson, Alex Cobo, Tom

Kenney & Dimitry Grushko, Matthew Allan, and Michael Markowitz. To anyone who's looking at this list and saying, "Aw, man! Why didn't that jerk mention me, too?," the answer is because I know you're too humble to be called out directly. But thank you most of all.

Thanks to Daniel Jones and the Modern Love column for convincing me there was a story here worth telling. Thanks to Richard Suckle for being one of the good guys. Thanks to Melissa Kagan for making me a "mom."

I wouldn't feel right if I didn't also acknowledge everyone who's read, shared, followed, linked, reblogged, aggregated, upvoted, stumbled upon, commented on, or in any other way supported my blog. Thanks to Jill Smokler, Karen Alpert, Sandra Parsons, Paula Turner, Charly Walker, Kelly Suellentrop, Lovely Lici, the Good Men Project, Lifetime Moms, everyone at *Raising America with Kyra Phillips*, and everyone else who's been nice to me one way or another. And OK, thanks to @fender_splendor, who tweeted that he wanted in on the acknowledgments action. There you go.